"WHERE TO NEXT?"

HARRY'S AVIATION WORLD

1933-2000

Best wishes
Harry Folkard

by
HARRY W. FOLKARD
(Retired)

CIRRUS ASSOCIATES

PUBLISHED BY:
Cirrus Associates (S.W.)
Kington Magna
GILLINGHAM
Dorset
SP8 5EW UK

ISBN 1902807 17 0

PRINTED IN ENGLAND BY:
Bath Press Ltd.
Lower Bristol Road
BATH
BA2 3BL

PHOTO SCANNING BY:
International Graphics Services Ltd.
24-31 Fourth Avenue
Westfield Trading Estate
Radstock
BATH
BA3 4XE

DISTRIBUTORS:
Cirrus Associates (S.W.)
Kington Magna
GILLINGHAM
Dorset
SP8 5EW

COVER PHOTOS: TOP: The Fokker F.VIIA G-EBTS flown in by the author in 1933. BOTTOM: Concorde at Heathrow (2000). Photos: by courtesy of the AJJ Collection.

FOREWORD

by HARRY FOLKARD

I must thank my many workmates for suggesting I should attempt to write about the events within my aviation career that they have found so amusing when told over a meal or drink on our many social evenings. Whether I have been able to reproduce these interesting, and sometimes funny, events graphically enough to make an interesting and amusing read, I will just have to wait and see. Let it be said that I have enjoyed putting all my efforts into attempting this feat in the hopes of being successful.

There are some of these friends and family that I must positively mention. To start with my family, they have given me every encouragement throughout my career, and because of this my life has been so full and interesting. Then there were Cecil Rhodes and Dennis Bustard who, as BOAC Operations and General Traffic Managers respectively, became my mentors whilst I served overseas for BOAC. But there are others mentioned within this book that were directly associated with me during my career and therefore became very important in my life; to name a few I must list: Rex Crisp, John Webb, Steve Sale, Mark Balabolin and Vitali Sereda. Others with whom I am pleased to be associated include Jeremy Spake of TV fame (especially the BBC programme *Airport)*, along with Kasia, Gabi and Patricia who were part of my team at Terminal 2, Heathrow Airport; they were all involved with Jeremy although it was he who consequently became a popular TV personality.

Of course, over the years the many people I met were my inspirations and unwittingly they became the making of these incidents on which I have written. I trust they will also see the funny side of the events and not take umbrage at my comments, none of which are intended to cause any offence whatsoever.

INTRODUCTION

by JEREMY SPAKE
Author and broadcaster

For many people, including yours truly, aviation is like a narcotic: the more you get of it, the more you want. Harry Folkard is no exception to this rule, having dedicated his entire adult life to commercial aviation. The story of that life unfolds through these pages, charting much of the first 100 years of powered flight through the eyes of one of its greatest ambassadors.

It was my profound pleasure to work with Harry in his last years in the industry at Aeroflot (Russian Airlines). There wasn't a day that went by without Harry grabbing our attention with a tale or two about the good old days, when aviation wasn't so much about cheap seats and no frills but was pure swashbuckling adventure. Only the brave, foolish and wealthy would venture near to the tented terminal of Heathrow Airport to sample the delights of the Wright Brothers' dream, mapping the way for the 'Mongol hordes' to follow. Today we think nothing of joining the queues at airports clutching our electronic ticket confirmations, but how many of us give a second thought to how it all started?

If you've ever wondered, now's your chance to find out. Take your window seat, fasten your belt and make yourself comfortable as we take off with Harry on a voyage of discovery.

I wish you all a happy journey and Safe Landings!

JEREMY SPAKE

CONTENTS

CHAPTER 1	**VINTAGE FLYING MACHINES**	7
CHAPTER 2	**WARTIME TRAINING**	17
CHAPTER 3	**SOUTH AFRICA AND FLIGHT TRAINING**	23
CHAPTER 4	**RETURN TO UK AND DEMOB**	30
CHAPTER 5	**'BETTER ON A CAMEL' (B.O.A.C. 1947-1953)**	32
CHAPTER 6	**CAIRO**	45
CHAPTER 7	**ROME**	57
CHAPTER 8	**NORTH AMERICA**	68
CHAPTER 9	**SOCIAL LIFE IN GANDER**	77
CHAPTER 10	**DEVELOPMENTS IN CIVIL AIRCRAFT DURING THE FIFTIES**	84
CHAPTER 11	**THE QUEEN'S VISIT**	91
CHAPTER 12	**A SHORT STINT IN LOS ANGELES**	105
CHAPTER 13	**MONTREAL & BALTIMORE**	112
CHAPTER 14	**BEIRUT**	117
CHAPTER 15	**BAGHDAD**	139
CHAPTER 16	**FRANKFURT**	144
CHAPTER 17	**RETURN TO THE UK**	155
CHAPTER 18	**KENYA**	160
CHAPTER 19	**DESERT DILEMMA – OMAN AIR 1975–1983**	164
CHAPTER 20	**RETIREMENT TO GATWICK**	186
CHAPTER 21	**AEROFLOT (THE DOUBLE-HEADED EAGLE)**	192
CHAPTER 22	**PERMANENT RETIREMENT**	218

CHAPTER 1

VINTAGE FLYING MACHINES

This is where I, Harry Folkard, an ageing man, not only reminisce about my first powered flight, but also record my reflections of over sixty years of the subsequent and rapid development of aviation. It will introduce you to people who will both amuse and annoy you as you join me on this journey into the exploration of aviation history.

I am known only as 'Harry' to many people working in the commercial civil aviation field within the United Kingdom and in numerous places abroad. My father, another Harry, who was a very industrious Contract Construction Engineer (Electrical), unfortunately died at the early age of 40 in 1938, leaving Gertrude (my mother), my older sister Aileen (nicknamed Lana by my Dad) and myself.

Just after I was born my father found himself unemployed in the world employment crisis of 1928/1929. His funds were down to his last shilling, and he was uncertain whether it was worth going out again to look for work. He decided to toss a coin to resolve this point and said to Gertrude: "If I guess right, I'll go out and look for work." Luckily for us all, he 'called correctly' and went out on another day of searching. That day he was lucky: he found a job and held it for the rest of his short life. With this company he made steady progress, reaching Works Manager of the whole company within six years.

Landmarks in his career were impressive to me. He was in charge of all the electrical improvements made to Shell Mex House in Cairo in 1929/30. When I went to Cairo 23 years later, it housed the Head Office of my company, BOAC in Egypt. Later in 1935/36 he was once again in charge of the electrical installations within Shell Mex House in the Strand, London. In fact I watched the King George V 25th Jubilee procession along the Embankment from the balcony of that building. Whilst there my father took me on to the roof, held me seated on top of a flag pole and said: "Son, you are now sitting on the highest point in London." He had no fear of heights, whereas I was petrified at the time.

In 1937 he took over the electrical improvements of the Old Bailey High Courts in London and finally then went on to do the same at the New Westminster General Hospital. Unfortunately he died before completion of this work, otherwise he would have been presented to King George VI.

He was a wonderful Dad and I would have loved his guidance in my teenage years. However, although we had only a few years together, he showed me how to persevere to achieve my aims while also considering all those around me. Mind you, he could not be deviated from what he felt was right for us all, a fact I have adhered to throughout my career. Hence on a sunny summer Sunday afternoon we had to walk to Heston Airport, and did not take the car as Lana and I wanted. Most people didn't have a car and those who did normally went out for a drive on Sundays, showing it off to all their neighbours. But Dad decided to leave our very serviceable car in its garage and go walking. Lana and I were most disappointed; we hadn't been in the car that often.

My mother, who was a marvellous cook and housewife, agreed with him, hereby confirming that we were going to walk that day. Mum always hovered over Lana and me whilst Dad was away working and she also ensured that we children never disrupted Dad's relaxation. Children, in those days, should be seen but not heard. We were well-nourished and healthy; my sister grew faster than me and although only 14 months different in age, she was 5 ft 9 in whilst I remained under 4 ft. Mind you, I did catch up later in life and we are now both about 5 ft 10 in.

This walk to Heston back in 1933 led to my first departure from *terra firma* at Heston Airport. At this time Heston Airport was being developed into the London Airport of the future. No one thought of runways in these days, aircraft were not heavy enough to need concrete to land on. There were no "Check-In" terminals to cause problems with building permission, like Terminal Five at Heathrow. Being just west of London (near Hounslow, Middlesex) the site was convenient for Central London and was thought to be less prone to fog than Croydon Airport.

It was at Heston that the Prime Minister, Neville Chamberlain, landed in October 1938 waving the highly-acclaimed letter and saying: "Peace in our time." This he had obtained during his meeting in Germany with Herr Hitler in a last-ditch attempt to avert the second World War.

Yes, weather, and in particular fog, was one of the main problems affecting aviation in these early days. Of course, it still does give problems from time to time, although aircraft development, flying aids on the aeroplane and on the ground, intensive pilot tuition and seventy years of aviation knowledge have helped to almost eliminate this weather handicap to commercial flying.

The memories of this unforgettable day in 1933 flow back quite easily, due to the fact that it made such an enormous impression on a boy of eight-and-a-bit years. Few people of any age had had a flight in this era. Many would have refused to enter an aeroplane even if offered the chance; it was expensive, generally uncomfortable, very very risky and therefore unpredictable when it came to giving satisfaction or pleasure.

I was lucky, it was a Sunday, not cloudless, but still a lovely summer's day, the sort of day that makes you want to get out of the house and to do things in the open air. This was certainly my father's thought; after all he had spent the past week in the office or car travelling to the numerous construction sites involved with his work.

We had walked to Heston Airport from home, just over three miles, a fairly good-length walk to savour the fresh air on a Sunday away from work. Mind you, both Lana and I did enjoy the walk once we had got over the initial disappointment. The route to the airport was pleasant, an amble through country lanes between the local farms. Few, if any, cars disturbed our amble and with the good weather it made things feel very pleasant. These roads have subsequently been widened and the farmland mainly made into housing estates or the extension of the Army Barracks, (completed during the war). The main Barracks had been established for many years and was directly opposite our house. There is now only one farm left in that area around Heston Airport.

At Heston Airport that day I had my first glimpse of an aircraft on the ground. At this time you rarely saw one in the air, let alone on the ground, so it was a really special occasion. Dangerous-looking contraptions they were too, but most intriguing to a boy of my age.

There were a number of aeroplanes there, many quite small and – let's face it – even the large ones were very small in comparison to those we are used to today. Much to my surprise Dad said: "What about taking a trip in one of these planes?"

I couldn't believe my ears. Mum said: "Don't be foolish. It's too expensive and on top of that too dangerous, why take such a risk?"

Luckily for me Dad said: "It will be good for the boy, he needs to know what the future is going to be like."

I then found out that he did not include Lana in this flying experience, and naturally she complained bitterly to Mum, saying: "Why am I being left out?"

Dad immediately said, "No, sorry dear, you know you are always car-sick, so flying is out of the question."

Dad had ascertained that they were giving 'pleasure trips' at 4/6d a time (four shillings and sixpence each, a vast amount in that era, yet now only equivalent to £0.22). Mum said it was too expensive, but Dad was adamant we should have the trip, irrespective of the cost. So he said to me: "Are you ready, son?" and with that we walked towards the aircraft.

I was over the moon in having this chance and getting one over on my sister, who was left with my mother.

The aeroplane we were to go up in was well-known in aviation circles at this time. It was *The Spider*, a Fokker F.VIIA built in 1925 and used by KLM on passenger services until it was purchased by the Duchess of Bedford in 1930 and registered as G-EBTS in the UK. Its owner the Duchess, with pilot Captain Barnard and a navigator, had just completed setting the record for flying from England to South Africa (Cape Town) and back. This had never been achieved prior to this flight, although Amy Johnson had managed Cape Town to London in a single-seat Moth (later models of which, the Tiger Moth, were extensively used for pilot training during World War II.)

The Spider was a much larger aircraft than the Tiger Moth, and could seat up to eight (8) passengers, hence the interest generally at such a large aircraft achieving this long-distance flight with only a single engine.

The fuel to the engine, a 480 hp Bristol Jupiter, was supplied from a central fuel tank just behind the motor and any extra fuel had to be stored in the wings, necessitating it being pumped by hand (manually) during flight into this central tank. The Duchess of Bedford took on this task during the trip to and from South Africa, and it was a great credit to her to take on this task on such a long and dangerous voyage. Considering she was 64 years of age at that time, she would have needed all her enthusiasm in aviation to undertake this responsibility; this she gained when being taught to fly when 61 years old, and it made her prepared to invest large sums of money into the development of aviation and extending the achievements of pilots such as Captain Barnard.

Aircraft of this type, with its single engine, had the pilot sitting just behind the engine and completely out in the open. He had a small windshield for protection but he needed to wear a leather flying helmet which covered his head, ears and part of his face, as well as goggles to protect his eyes. The 'comic' pilot character of the time, Biggles, was always dressed in this manner. In the cabin, which was completely enclosed, it was much warmer and drier, although I don't think there were any heating facilities. There were two rows of seats and a total of eight passengers could be carried. I look back now and wonder how they could cram so many people in such a small space. Mind you, are they not doing much the same these days on some of these holiday charter flights?

It was easy to climb into the plane as its main undercarriage was forward with a small tailwheel at the back (the tricycle-type undercarriage used in today's planes having not as yet been developed). This meant that you had only a few steps to climb to reach the cabin floor level, but once inside the cabin you had a pretty sharp climb up to your seats. When we were inside the plane my dad made sure I had a window seat, giving me maximum opportunity to get a true idea of just what flying was like. Quite honestly I cannot remember whether we had seat belts, but I feel sure we did; otherwise it would have been too dangerous, wouldn't it?

However, some safety aspects were considered in those days, so I am told! In fact I have subsequently learnt that they made a 'hatch' in the cabin roof so that, if the aircraft landed on water, at least you could climb out onto the roof. Funnily enough, no life jackets were carried – or life rafts for that matter.

When the engine started I became quite frightened, as the whole aeroplane shook and vibrated. Looking back now it would remind you of an old lawn mower engine that spent more time being repaired than being used. With so little sound-proofing in the cabin the noise level was deafening. Still, at least we were warm, not like the poor pilot outside in the open air. I can remember pitying him out there in all climatic conditions. Can you imagine sitting out there all the way to Cape Town and back?!

There were no stewards or stewardesses to make sure we remained seated with our belts on (assuming there were any in the first place) or that we didn't stand up or expect a drink. Mind you, it was such an exciting experience for everyone in the cabin that I'm sure none of us would have dared to try standing up or moving around in case we caused the plane to crash.

Luckily, having a window seat did ensure I had the best view of the earth beneath us. I watched closely as the ground fell away from us as we took off and I felt the aircraft rise and fall as the air currents took their grip on its movement. It was brilliant. The trip itself took only fifteen minutes; it was a circular trip from Heston out over Cranford, Hounslow West, Whitton, part of Brentford, Boston Manor Park, Osterley Park and along the north side of what is now the Great West Road (not yet built at that time) and then back to Heston Airport.

Although I was a little over eight, the excitement filled my whole body, hence my first experience of flying remains a permanent memory to this day. Scenes experienced during this flight are so alive in my mind that, whenever I come home after a trip abroad and land at Heathrow Airport, I find myself trying to identify the places I flew over back in 1933.

Surprisingly, many landmarks are the same today as they were sixty odd years ago. One scene in particular involves the Iron Bridges just outside Boston Manor tube station, where the tube crosses the Grand Union Canal. To this day I vividly remember the double-arched steel girder structure which supports the rail track. It was over this landmark that *The Spider* dropped its port wing as we turned back towards Heston during my memorable flight. I was seated on the port side, so got the full effect of the banking manoeuvre necessary to turn the aircraft in flight; it was a fairly steep bank and made you feel you were suddenly descending, rather than turning, and this put my father and other passengers high above me within the cabin – a real positive memory.

Copies of *Flight* magazines issued in the 1930s confirm that this Fokker aircraft (*The Spider*) made joyrides from 134 different airfields within the United Kingdom at that time. I felt I was lucky enough to have had one of them and have cherished that event all my life.

Subsequently I have read that this particular aircraft flew to India and back in around 1932 with the same pilot and crew and was eventually sold to a titled person in Bombay in late 1934. Its life ended in 1937 when it was broken up in Bombay.

Although I have only mentioned this particular aircraft at Heston, rest assured there were other planes giving joyrides, however, they were two-seater types, one passenger and the pilot. I was too young to be allowed up in one of those and I'm pretty certain I was not yet ready for such a daring experience. As it was, my mother thought my dad mad for taking the risk of us both going on this flight! How glad I am that she did not get her way on this occasion!

A year or so later I saw the RAF display team of three aircraft, all Bulldog fighter planes, being flown in formation with their wings tied together with thick white ribbon. This ribbon was thick enough to be seen from the ground, making everyone appreciate just how good they were at flying. This was performed at Hendon every year between 1934 and 1938. Little did I realise that 20 years later I would be working with one of the marvellous men who were flying the planes in that RAF team.

'Hobby' Hobson came to Gander in 1958 to work with me there; he had been one of the RAF prewar display team, and rose to become a Wing Commander in Fighter Command during the war. His flying record during the war was quite exceptional, and he was a Spitfire pilot throughout the Battle of Britain. I don't know how many victories he had, but I know he was shot down five times without being badly hurt. He looked the perfect fighter pilot with his wavy blond hair and handlebar moustache. In his BOAC uniform you could easily see him as the fighter pilot he had been in those so important wartime years.

Towards the end of the war, 'Hobby' was sent to Istanbul, Turkey, to train pilots for the Turkish Air Force. He must have done a good job because he was treated like royalty whenever he went back to Istanbul. Turkish airports are operated by the Air Force and the men he trained became the Commanders at all Turkish airports.

Of course, 'Hobby' had joined BOAC on release from the RAF and served in many overseas stations prior to coming to Gander. In fact, during the Suez Canal crisis in the 1950s, BOAC flights were diverted from Cairo to Istanbul for refuelling. Extra staff were needed and 'Hobby' was one sent to help out. When the Airport Commander heard he was coming he arranged a Guard of Honour for his arrival. It was lined up next to the aircraft and 'Hobby' was invited to inspect the Guard in full military fashion.

He became a real asset to the Station for BOAC; he could get extra fuel when required by asking the Station Commander, they wouldn't give it unless 'Hobby' asked them. He became an embarrassment to the BOAC Country Manager because of his links with the Turkish Air Force and so he was soon moved off-station. What a waste!

My Father (also Harry). Photo: author's collection.

TOP: My sister and I.
BOTTOM: My Mother. Photos: author's collection.

The author whilst in the RAF. Photo: author's collection.

My wife Madge and I in Lisbon. Photo: author's collection.

CHAPTER 2

WARTIME TRAINING

With the advent of war in 1939, a year after my father's death, the advancement of aviation was given priority by the British Government. Boys like myself also realised that aviation was going to play a major part in the battle ahead against Nazi Germany. It was with this in mind that I joined the Air Training Corps (ATC) to ensure I would get the right initial training and be able to enter the Royal Air Force (RAF) when old enough.

The ghastly event of war did bring with it a concerted effort to enhance one's prospects against the foe. Money was no longer an obstacle against development plans. This in turn led to massive improvements in all units and machines used in war and to flying in particular. The aeroplane, the most junior and underdeveloped method of attacking the enemy, suddenly received maximum attention and therefore achieved the maximum advancements.

That minimal introduction to flying that I had had at Heston Airport produced in me a positive craving to fly in the RAF. The ATC gave me the chance to put my aspirations into order, and offered me the opportunity for further flights; this encouraged me to endeavour to achieve my aims prior to my actual entry into the RAF.

The next time I became airborne was once again from Heston Airport, but by now it was wartime and the airfield had obtained its own squadron of fighter aircraft, based there to protect the west side of London. These were Fairey Battles at this time, not the most successful of fighters in service during the war. Naturally, I didn't get a flight on one of those; no, but I was lucky enough to go up in a de Havilland Rapide, a twin-engined biplane with a cabin holding about eight passengers which had already entered commercial service within the UK. Our ATC group based at Ealing, West London had organized this particular flight, for which I was most grateful.

We had a Canadian pilot, quite a young man in his early twenties, and he made sure we got the thrill of a lifetime out of the flight. He, the pilot, was not sitting outside the cabin as on my previous flight; he was sat up in the nose of the aircraft, with a small door separating him from the main cabin. This door had been left open, making him fully visible to us cadets; if he had had this door closed, we would not have been able to see directly ahead, so this forward vision meant we could see exactly where we were going. What he did was to make this simple flight into an exciting event for all us 16-year-old boys. Through this open door we all strained to see out at what lay ahead.

To begin with, we were sternly told to remain in our seats throughout the flight, and this we did. We then made the short powered taxi into position for take-off. The pilot then positively thrust the throttles forward and we gathered speed quite rapidly. The engines were greatly improved from the one in the Spider aircraft in which I had first flown; they no longer sounded like a mowing machine, but more like car engines. The tailwheel lifted off the ground as we sped across the airfield but, to our surprise, not the main wheels. Afterwards we realised that the pilot was purposely keeping the plane's main wheels firmly on the ground as we raced across the field. We could see the boundary fence approaching fast and, just when we were about to close our eyes in anticipation of the crash, he pulled the control column back and the nose of the plane shot skywards: we had missed the perimeter hedge by a mere few feet. We were also thrown backwards into our seats and an involuntary gasp of relief was heard from us all. The excitement had really got to us young cadets in the cabin, and we were excitingly chattering away amongst ourselves. The atmosphere seemed electrified and we inhaled this excitement which made us all long for the day when we too could be pilots and control a aircraft in this manner. The rest of the flight was uneventful in comparison to the take-off we had had, which in itself had been enough excitement for one day.

I flew again in 1942 but it wasn't as exciting a flight as that one from Heston. At the time I was still in the Air Training Cadets and we were invited to stay at an RAF training camp in Oxfordshire. It was RAF Kidlington, where qualified pilots were being converted to twin- or multi-engined aircraft. They were mainly doing circuits and bumps (touch-and-go landings) in twin engined Oxfords, an aircraft much used for training in those days. The Oxford was a low-wing monoplane and could carry four or five passengers; some examples had been fitted out to train wireless (radio) operators.

On this occasion just one cadet joined each training plane, sitting just behind the trainee pilot and his instructor. We got a pretty good view from this position in daylight, but at night there was little to see at all, so it did become very boring. A training spell lasted about two hours and included night flying, something I had never done before. You had absolutely nothing to do. All lights within the houses and on the streets were covered or shaded, and it was just black outside. Mind you, with a young mind you could always imagine that a Nazi plane might appear and attack, and that made you feel a bit more excited and anxious!

The airport had just the minimum of lights, enough to let the pilots know they were landing on an airfield and not on the surrounding farmland. During a flight of about two hours you did about ten touch-and-goes in all. The trainee pilots didn't seem to have much difficulty making their landings but to me, a novice at flying, trying to read the instruments in the dark was truly an eye-strain, to say the least. In some ways I was pleased when my flight was over; it was around midnight, after all.

I did not fly again until after I'd been accepted into the RAF in 1943. Even then I had to wait until after I had done all my 'square bashing' at St. John's Wood, London and Scarborough, Yorkshire. So it was months before I had a first glimpse at my first trainer aircraft, the Tiger Moth. This aircraft, which was used extensively in Britain at the time, was a single-engined biplane, seating two in tandem; it had been developed from the pre-war Moth, the type used by Amy Johnson, the famous lady aviator, when she flew from Cape Town to London in the early 1930s. What a delightful little plane it was, extremely sensitive to the controls and very responsive to the pupil pilot's actions on the stick (control column).

Still, that is jumping ahead; first of all I had to have my attestation at RAF Cardington to see if I was suitable for aircrew training. Cardington is famous as the place where British prewar airships were made. The massive hangars, like skyscrapers on their side, were originally built for this purpose and are still in use today for developing new uses for airships.

I was then just seventeen, and I had never been away from home before. It was November, very cold and very foggy. We stayed for three days in wooden single-storey huts, about thirty men to a hut. There was no hot water and I found it terrible shaving in cold water. Still I wanted to get into the war and to have some of the excitement it was supposed to generate, at least that was how we youngsters looked on it. Luckily the elders were aware of my age and, after I completed the various tests, they did agree I was suitable for aircrew training. They said I would be called up when I was over eighteen, and not before.

So it was a year later that I actually joined the Royal Air Force, on the 13th September 1943, and started my initial training at St. John's Wood, London. The barracks there were commandeered apartment blocks near to Regents Park and the London Zoo. We used the Zoo's restaurant for meals and Regents Park roads to practise marching etc. Some said we were being fed like the animals in the Zoo, but actually the food was quite good – although we still thought we should automatically complain!

Once we were kitted out and given all our injections, we were moved to Scarborough ITW (Initial Training Wing) to learn the fundamental arts of Air Navigation, Map Reading and the Principles of Flight, as well as brushing up on our general maths. Naturally this did not excuse us from more military-type marching practice with plenty of 'spit & polish.' In fact you might be surprised how brightly your boots can be made to shine with spit and polish, the true armed forces' requirements. I found I could supplement my income by cleaning other cadets' boots at a price, and this enabled me to buy extra food in the cafés and also get extra cigarettes.

After this ordeal, and having reached the acquired standard in the tests, I went to a small airfield called Brough, which was near to Hull on the east coast of England. The airfield was alongside a large river, the Humber, and being late winter/early spring, the airport remained fogged in for the first four weeks of my stay. We saw the Tiger Moths daily, but never got in one for a flight. Life was boring and the Commanders were trying to keep us out of trouble by making us spring-clean our billet every day.

Naturally, we went out at night to have a few drinks and get up to as many outside activities we could find. We were a mixed group of lads of varying ages and from all over the British Isles. Some were well into their thirties, having been in restricted professions but then released for aircrew training only. One had been a coal miner in Durham, and was he glad to be above ground?!

On one of our many boozy nights out, we all had a bit too much to drink, but when we got back to our billet, this lad from Durham was going on about "what they did down in the pits." He was on about the hardness of the work and how tough and strong they all were. This aroused quite a bit of anguish amongst some of us and we decided that we couldn't really understand or visualize what he was on about unless he could show us what he meant within our Air Force billet.

In the billet, a long wooden hut, was a coal-burning stove and a very large coal bin full of coal; this was turned on its side, emptying its contents all over our highly polished floor. He was then told to show us how they shovelled coal back in the mines, which he did by shovelling all the coal into the bin.

Once this had been done someone said: "Hey, in the pits you aren't able to stand up. You're on your knees." So the bin was emptied again and he was made to shovel the coal back into the bin from a kneeling position. This still didn't satisfy the drunken group, and they decided he must do it again but more realistically, by being on his stomach. So again the bin was emptied and he stripped down to his waist. He was getting really hot and covered with sweat and coal dust, and also showing signs of wear; still he did manage to shovel the coal back into the bin.

Luckily for all concerned, someone said: "That's enough, we have to get some sleep and clean this place up before morning inspection". So the evening's fun ended at that point.

Eventually the day came when we could start flying. It wasn't ideal weather, but the Flight Commander decided that we, the cadets, could fly as passengers whilst the pilots, our future instructors, would show us what real flying was actually like. When it is the first time you have been in such a small open cockpit-type plane, it can be quite nerve racking, at least it was to me. Our future flying instructors, who like us had been twiddling their thumbs for the last month, took great delight at the opportunity to show off. I'm not certain that the Flight Commander expected us to experience the sort of display we were given, but luckily the Tiger Moth is highly suited to that sort of flying, although it was truly surprising that so few of us were violently airsick. I wasn't one of them, thank goodness.

My pilot instructor was a large Canadian who had completed his second tour of ops as a fighter pilot. He had spent the same month on the ground, as we had, twiddling his thumbs and thinking of the excitement he was missing back on his squadron. Naturally he was supposed to be resting, and training us greenhorns was not meant to be the punishment it actually was. So he really made up for lost time once we were airborne. Another of the instructors, also a Canadian, was likewise inspired with his freedom in the air, so the two of them decided that some close formation flying would be the answer. With the wings of one plane slotted in between the wing and tail-plane of the other, we flew around, bobbing up and down in a somewhat irrational manner as the winds and air currents caught us. As I said earlier, the weather was not ideal for light aircraft flying, being very bumpy with thermal currents, so you can easily imagine how the relative movements of the two aircraft varied as we flew so close together. In fact, if you were daring enough, you could have walked along the wings of one aircraft and boarded the other, we were that close.

During the following few weeks we got our initial flying training done. I wasn't brilliant, in fact I was too nervous initially and therefore never managed to go solo. I was a bit unnerved by my instructor's daring; however, my luck was in and he returned to his fighter squadron for another tour of ops. My new instructor was a local businessman, a civilian who had loaned his private Tiger Moth to the flying school. He had been an instructor pre-war and gave lessons as a hobby without payment although I understood that the Station Commander was fiddling him a little petrol for his private car. I can even remember the instructor's name, Mr Richardson; his experience in instructing and experience in flying Tiger Moths was very useful to me. I lost my nervousness in the cockpit and very nearly became proficient enough to go solo, but it was not considered a disgrace not to achieve this aim; in fact only one person out of my group of students achieved this honour.

During one of my training flights my Canadian instructor took over control during the lesson when he noticed a Mustang, a newly introduced fighter plane that was being built in America. Somehow or other he attracted the attention of the pilot (we had no radio), and for the next 30 minutes we had a mock dogfight. The Mustang had the speed but he could not match our manoeuvrability. We made a good showing, and ended up with the Mustang trying to fly alongside us. He had his wheels down and flaps extended, trying to fly as slow as possible, whilst we were doing our maximum speed in an effort to stay alongside. Eventually he waggled his wings, gave us a wave and was off. Towards thc cnd of the war the Mustang became a really proficient fighter-bomber, but that was after modifications had been introduced in the UK. Still, you can realise that we did have some fun at flying school and were sorry when it came to an end.

At Brough airport two of the new fighter and fighter-bomber aeroplanes were being manufactured, the Fury and the Seacat. The latter was being designed for use on aircraft carriers in the Royal Navy. The way the test pilots put these aircraft through their paces was a wonder to see; their experience in flying was truly apparent to us learners and we longed and hoped that we would accrue the same type of knowledge and ability.

By May 1944 I was at Eaton Park, Manchester, which had been taken over as a transit camp for trainee aircrew waiting to go overseas for further flying training; very little, if any, advanced flight training could be done in the UK because of enemy aircraft being always so near. Whilst at Eaton Park, I was one of nearly 2,000 awaiting assignments; furthermore, this was the selection point where previous efforts were assessed and your final training aim assigned. Of the nearly 2,000 of us, all of whom were hopeful of getting flying assignments, few would proceed any further due to the very reduced needs for aircrew at this stage of the war. In fact only one was chosen to become a pilot, with a further 200 going to Canada for training as navigators. However 400, including myself, were to be sent to South Africa as navigators/bomb-aimers; the remainder were offered air gunner training in the UK.

When you are young you are prepared to take risks. Having been given my sailing orders for South Africa, I decided I should visit my sister, who was in the army down in Derby. All leave had been cancelled, so to pay her a visit meant going AWOL (absent without leave). All railway stations and bus depots were being monitored by the Military Police, so to get away meant my climbing the perimeter fence and hitchhiking on lorries going south. I was not too good at hitchhiking, but eventually, after a whole night's effort, found myself walking along a country road in brilliant summer sunshine just a few miles outside Derby. To this day I can see the beautiful green fields and rolling hills of Derbyshire.

Lana was pleased to see me and as far as I can remember we had a small meal together before I set off back to Manchester. Surprisingly I have no recollection of how I got back to Manchester, but I did, and without being caught on this occasion!

CHAPTER 3

SOUTH AFRICA AND FLIGHT TRAINING

Now we were on our voyage to South Africa in the *Andes*, a 26,000-ton vessel completed just before war started and whose maiden voyage to Argentina had had to be cancelled. It was meant to earn its living sailing to and from the UK to the River Plate in Argentina, and had been built with a fairly flat bottom to allow it to enter the River Plate. It therefore tended to roll quite a bit. It had been subsequently fitted out to carry about 5,000 troops, but on this occasion there were only about 400 of us on board.

The route taken was from Liverpool up towards Iceland, then down the Eastern Seaboard of America until just before the equator, then eastwards to Freetown in West Africa. We were sailing unprotected (no naval escort) and using our high speed to avoid the submarines (U-boats). The *Andes* could do about 28 knots, quite fast for a ship that size.

The first night at sea was rough. I was put on watch on one of the upper decks, and I first leant against the side railings, but as we got moving the ship began to roll; then the angle of roll seemed to become greater and greater until I decided I was likely to be thrown overboard on the next roll. So for the rest of my duty on deck I clung to the inner rail, making sure I didn't go missing.

At breakfast-time the next morning the effects of the night's roughness resulted in very few of us appearing for breakfast. The ship's catering staff hadn't realised how the roughness would affect its passengers, and had cooked over 600 boiled eggs, which they had displayed along the tables in readiness for us all. Actually only four of us came to the feast, including myself. As the eggs were all hard-boiled, I expect we got what was left over from this breakfast for the next few days until they were all gone.

Surprisingly I enjoyed having breakfast, and in particular the white bread, something I hadn't seen since the war began. When the war started the British government made a decision to stop making white bread, and surprisingly I hadn't really missed it until there it was on the table before me.

The *Andes* was what they called a 'dry' ship, i.e. no booze during the whole trip. However, I had acquired a pal amongst the cadets, Stan Bird, who was going for flying training like myself, and somehow we got friendly with members of the ship's crew. When we reached Freetown Harbour it turned out to be the Captain's birthday, and as a treat he decided to give his crew two bottles of beer each; this special treat for them was one in which we also shared, as crew friends gave us a bottle each, half their ration. No one was allowed ashore, not even the ship's crew.

We took on fuel and maybe some provisions during our one night's stopover, then it was back out across the South Atlantic in our circular route to Cape Town. From now on we were able to watch the dolphins and flying fish leaping from the water just ahead of the ship's bow. The wings of the flying fish were really colourful and bright, and fascinating to watch, especially as there was so little else to do on board. What with its 4-inch gun on the bow and another on the stern, it didn't exactly look like a 'fun-loving ship' or 'cruise liner.'

Stan and I managed to get caught oversleeping one morning: we were still in our bunks when we should have been on deck duty. Later that morning saw us before the senior RAF Officer, a Wing Commander and a short plump little man. My duty was on the main deck, just where the senior officers met each morning to discuss their duties for the day. To me it was very interesting as in the somewhat cramped area I could not help overhearing what they were saying. They were discussing the charges against Stan and myself. Of course as each officer arrived in this area I had to salute him and say "Good morning," which I naturally did to the Wing Commander. When Stan and I were marched in before the Wing Commander, he was flabbergasted at seeing me, as he had had no idea that I was the airman up on the charge, Charge Sheet 242 as it was known in the RAF. Throughout the procedures he stared at me, not once looking towards Stan, even though he was on the same charge. In the end we got three extra duties, but Stan was a real cheeky chap well versed in everyday street life and he somehow managed to ensure we got away without doing any of these extra duties.

On our arrival outside Cape Town harbour, after 21 days at sea since leaving Liverpool, there was a storm blowing and the seas were so rough that we could not dock for another 24 hours. Having good sea legs, I used the time to try and find the best place to get the full effect of the roll and pitch of the ship. This I found was either in the Foc's'le or in the deck crew quarters; otherwise just behind the Bridge (amidships) where you could watch the bow rise above the waves and then pitch downward into the next large wave.

Once in Cape Town we were boarded onto a train and were taken to the dispersal camp, 'Retreat,' a few miles north-west of the city. On the train we were given a small sack of oranges each (about 30 to a sack). With fruit in the UK limited to children only, this was a wonderful occasion, to be able to taste real fresh fruit for the first time since before the war. Throughout my stay in South Africa I was to enjoy the plentifulness of the oranges, peaches, melons and grapes in the Cape provinces.

The first few days at the 'Retreat' camp were spent learning a bit about what was expected of us whilst in South Africa. I'm not sure if the

Royal Air Force was liked in South Africa, as we were known locally as "the blue plague." We were certainly warned about the places to avoid whilst in Cape Town. However, we still went into town sightseeing and generally finding out what was on offer. One thing I do remember is the luxury of the 'afternoon tea cinemas' with their armchair-type seating and the afternoon tea and cream cakes served during the intervals.

Our navigator ground training was at East London, a few hundred miles up the east coast. The troop train was very slow, and we were on board for two days travelling from Cape Town. We were at East London for three months and did everything towards becoming navigators except actually flying.

I worked hard at this navigation school and soon proved my ability to master the navigation circular calculator. Actually I was the fastest of my group on the calculator and this came in useful when taking my final navigation exam at the end of the course. In the exam I misread a position to find which the exercise was planned, which meant I had taken the wrong directions within the flight plan papers. I realised this error halfway through the exam, so then had to recalculate the whole plan in half the normal allowed time. If I failed this exam I would be sent home, something I did not want to happen.

My course instructor was invigilating us cadets during the exam, saw that I was frantic with worry and came over to ask what my problem was. I told him what I had done and he said: "OK, then start again, you are fast enough to do it in the time you have left." Surprisingly I believed him and set about seeing how much I could actually achieve. In the end I didn't quite finish the whole exercise, but at least I did enough to get a reasonable pass mark and go on to the flying school with the other pupils.

We were then moved to Oudtshorn in the Little Karroo Desert for airborne navigation exercises. It was an interesting place, very dry and hot and surrounded by ostrich farms. Whenever we had scrambled eggs for breakfast, we were certain they were giving us ostrich eggs – one used for every twenty men! However, the camp was well provided with every sports facility we needed: swimming pool, tennis courts, table tennis, and squash courts as well. I had never played squash before, although I had played fives at school, but I found it most enjoyable and played many times whilst I was there.

We were flying in the old-type Ansons, twin-engine aircraft built in England and getting near the end of their serviceable life span. They were similar in size to the Oxford aircraft used in the UK for advanced pilot training. Of course, they were adequate for our training needs and none ever seemed to crash – thank goodness!

Many of the pilots had finished one or two tours of ops up in the Middle East war zone and had been on their way home via Durban when they found themselves offloaded from their ships to do a year or so flying us students around for training purposes. They were not the happiest group, so did not endear themselves to us – or indeed the local ostrich farmers; they did what was called "shooting-up the ostriches," which meant flying very low over the farms on the way back from low-level bomber training flights. But the planes had no guns, so no actual shooting took place. How low did they fly? Well some of the planes had small twigs from trees and bushes caught up in the wing roots, so you can see: very, very low.

If the truth were known, the training took longer than was really necessary, but this was with a purpose. The Prime Minister of South Africa, General Smuts, had entered the war against the objections of the Afrikaner/Boers. Hence when the South African troops joined the fighting in Egypt, the Boers threatened to take over the country. It therefore became necessary to bring in another way of policing the country. Under the cover of providing flying training, the RAF staff could provide a good police force for the whole area and stopped a Boer uprising whilst the South African Army was fighting in Egypt and Europe.

Our flying training was in the middle of their summer. The high temperatures meant that turbulence was extreme. In fact we only flew in the mornings, commencing at 04.30 and finishing not later than 14.00. Even so, some of the air pockets could make the aircraft rise and fall 1,000–1,500 feet at a time. Have you ever tried writing a 'log' whilst the table is either trying to hit you in the face or has fallen away to around your ankles? Such an experience certainly made it apparent whether you were prone to airsickness or not.

Of course navigation, and in particular map reading, was somewhat different in South Africa. There were fewer landmarks to be found, so a small group of houses would be shown on the navigation map as a big town. On the topographical map it would be more realistically shown; however, places were so small you could miss them, whereas in the UK you had so much extra information below you that it would be easy to mistake one place for another. Still the lessons were programmed to ensure we learnt exactly how accurate we were at finding our way around in the air.

The airport and camp included what was originally the local racetrack, although no races occurred during the time I was there. My main problem was trying not to get sunburnt. I eventually gave up on swimming as my shoulders skinned and skinned from all the burns. But we did have the highest recorded rainfall for the last twenty-five years whilst I was there, 0.8 in, and that was from one storm which managed to get over the 10,000-ft hills to the west of the camp. The thunderstorms that hit the hills could be seen from the camp and the forks of lightning were remarkable. Many a late evening was spent on our beds (which for coolness we had moved out onto the veranda) watching the thunderstorms pounding along the whole mountain range. West of the mountains they had plenty of rain, but not in Oudtshoun.

It was after one of these very heavy thunderstorms that we were taken by bus out into the *feldt*-land to fight bush fires that had been set off by the lightning, another experience not usual to someone from London. Still, after three months of this sort of training I got my 'Wings' (well, Half Wing as I wasn't actually a pilot); at Oudtshoun I became Sergeant Harry Folkard, Navigator/Bomb aimer, (Observer) RAF.

My flight planning calculation speed had been excellent throughout the course and, instead of coming back home, I was recommended for Coastal Command training, and this meant going on to the coastal town of George, a few miles nearer the coast from Oudtshoun. George was the Coastal Command Training Unit and there is where I received my final navigation training, specialising in 'Sea (Naval) style' navigation. This delayed my return home to the UK.

George was a beautiful lush green place about 5 miles in from the coastline on a very fertile plain. It was only about 40 miles from Oudtshoun, and took under 20 minutes to fly (as the crow flew). However, by train it took over six hours, as the train had to climb up and down a mountain range to get there, going from the Desert of Oudtshoun to the green pastures of George. The climb was around 4,000 feet and at the top you saw the dividing line between the watered and unwatered lands: totally dry parched land with a little dried shrub and a land of very green trees, a unique sight when seen from the mountain top. As well as this, as the train had to follow such a winding track to climb the mountain, it was possible to see both ends of the train alongside each other when you were sitting in the middle carriage and looking backwards. The train became U shaped with the front directly alongside the rear, although of course one part was higher than the other.

At George all the flying was done out over the sea. It was also a different kind of navigation; we now used the naval method of navigation, which needed very precise DR (Dead Reckoning) as there are few, if any, landmarks in the ocean. We did all flying at 1,500 ft and soon learnt how to read the wind direction from the sea-lanes, which are produced by the wind. The actual wind speed can be estimated by counting the number of white horses (breaking wave crests) visible from the air.

Once out at sea you could also find the wind direction and speed by flying in different directions for short periods of time, dropping flares on each leg flown, then reading the angle of drift of the flare on each leg. Putting all these drift readings together it was possible to calculate the wind-speed and direction. It became quite a simple practice; the main thing was to improve your speed of calculation.

On one exercise we flew from George to Port Elizabeth further up the coast. Whilst refuelling on the ground at Port Elizabeth we were briefed about a ship that was heading towards the local port but had disappeared from the radar screens. There were five Ansons at Port Elizabeth that day and we were formed into a 'flight wing,' each aircraft being allocated a line of search ten miles apart going south along the coast. We were instructed to plan a 'relative square search' along the track we were given and to remain on patrol as long as our fuel would last. This meant flying up to a maximum of 5 miles either side of that track and moving the centre of the square along that given track. The coastal commanders knew the known direction being sailed by the missing ship and had planned our search of the seas backwards along that track.

As we were all trainee navigators you can imagine the excitement we felt as we made our pre-flight plans and then submitted the details to the ATC (Air Traffic Controllers). We didn't take off in formation, but we were certainly not far apart. It was hard work keeping up with the navigation work and ensuring we gave the pilots the regular course change directions to keep us within the search area we had been allocated.

None of my group found the ship, but the longer-ranged aircraft from the main fully-fledged coastal squadrons who were able to search further out to sea did find survivors in a lifeboat. It transpired that the ship had been torpedoed and sunk by a Japanese submarine, which left only a few survivors. Until then I never thought that the Japanese navy had submarines or that they would travel so far away from their homeland. This particular exercise showed us what we could expect in the future once trained and on squadron.

On completion of this course at George we were ready to return home for assignment to a squadron and active service. However, on return to the 'Retreat' camp at Cape Town to await a ship, we were invited to visit the largest naval ship being refitted in dry dock in Cape Town; this was the cruiser *London* that had a displacement of over 10,000 tons. The idea was to make us feel united with the Navy with whom we would be closely associated in Coastal Command.

Whilst on this ship's tour the announcement was made that the European war had ceased. Surprisingly, the Naval Gunnery Commander of the *London* still insisted on taking us all over his gun turrets, which had four 10-inch guns. Within the turrets you had many metal stepladders to negotiate, both up and down, and the floors within the turrets were quite oily. On one of the descents within the turret, I was directly above the Gunnery Officer and unfortunately I got a little too close to him; he was wearing his naval peaked hat with its snow-white cover and, when he stopped and I didn't, I placed a beautiful oily footprint on the top of his hat. He wasn't pleased, to say the least.

Whether it was because of this incident or not, my group were taken off the ship and sent back to the 'Retreat' camp, where we then celebrated the end of the German war.

CHAPTER 4

RETURN TO UK AND DEMOB

With all my training over, I returned to England just after the European war ended. In the UK I had one more flight in a Tiger Moth up in Cambridgeshire and then I was grounded, no longer required as aircrew. I was naturally very deflated at being grounded but, needless to say, glad the war with Germany and Italy was over.

Looking back now on this last year or so away in South Africa, I had missed the dangerous times suffered in the UK, particularly in London. Before I left to join the RAF I had seen the start of the "Doodlebug" raids; seeing one flying towards the house with its motor still burning bright and then suddenly the light going out before your very eyes, wondering if it was going to fall straight down out of the sky to land near you, or whether it would glide and land a mile or two away on someone else? From then on those at home had to suffer the V1 (Doodlebug) and V2, both of which did so much damage in London.

All I had to look forward to now was demob and home once again, but to my surprise demob and home was to take about two years. The first thing that happened was that I was sent to Kirkham in Lancashire for what they called "re-mustering into a equipment clerk." What a difference this was to flying training! Boring in so many ways, but it had to be done and so I buckled down to learn whatever was necessary. I couldn't get out of the Air Force until my demob date was fixed and that, I found out, was a year or more away.

After the training I was fortunate to be posted to Uxbridge, the RAF main base near London. Then they seconded me to the Demobilisation Unit at Wembley, very near my home in Ealing. To make matters even better, I could 'live out' at home with all the ration cards provided. What more could I ask for? Home cooking, down to the local pub every evening and all my old friends around me – at least those who still survived.

Wembley became hard work, but with it came much play. I took over the administration duties, taking the morning parade and assigning duties. Then, being in charge of sports for the group, I spent much time playing table tennis and taking groups of twenty men to learn ice-skating at the Wembley Ice Rink. Yes, I went to see the management and they granted twice weekly sessions *free*. Then of course we had our football team, which was good enough to beat the Uxbridge station team on one occasion. So all in all this period of waiting for demob was not too bad.

However, prior to my release the Wembley Demob Centre closed and I was sent up to Lancashire to a camp called Padgate. This was the postwar recruitment centre where all the conscripts were kitted out and given their “square bashing” training, as I had been four years earlier at St. John’s Wood. On this camp were a large number of German prisoners-of-war, who were strictly monitored and mainly used to do the labouring work around the camp. I was once again living on camp and in charge of a barrack block housing about fifty recruits. I had a separate room at one end of the unit with my own coal fire, washbasin, shower, etc. Along with this privilege came a German batman who kept the room spotless. It felt wrong to walk on the floor in your shoes (aircrew and ex-aircrew had shoes, not boots) after he had polished it to a mirror finish.

I now also had my own equipment warehouse to manage. It had not had a trained equipment clerk in it for the whole of the war, and so the records were in a total mess. I set about trying to get things in order and spent many hours trying to find where everything had gone. This proved an impossible task, but at least I was able to resolve some problems and then arrange to write off many of the items.

This warehouse was also responsible for arranging the laundry run to Liverpool with the airmen’s washing; this took a three-ton truck, four German prisoners and a Redcap (RAF policeman) in addition to an airman driver and myself. This trip was made regularly once every week, so we were expected and the girls at the laundry would always greet us rowdily; in fact, some of their language was so strong it surpassed anything I had ever heard in the barrack rooms in the RAF.

Fortunately, my demob date soon came up and after collecting all my entitlement of civilian clothes (and having made sure I had got the best makes provided at these demob units), I then returned once more to Ealing, my home and my friends.

Now the war was definitely over, as far as I was concerned.

CHAPTER 5

'BETTER ON A CAMEL' – (B.O.A.C. 1947-1953)

The return to civilian life took me totally by surprise; it was not as easy as life in the RAF! The facts were as follows:

1. In the RAF you knew your money would be there every week.
2. You had plenty of time for sport.
3. There was plenty of time for relaxing and drinking.

Now this was suddenly changed. As a civilian you had first to get a job before you could expect regular payment. Yes, the government said that you could go back to your old firm and get the same job back, but I was older now and the prospects of being a machinist in a small concern didn't appeal at all.

Now I had had experience in flying I wanted to be in civil aviation. A family acquaintance had said prior to my demob: "Harry, when you are home I will get you into British South American Airlines (BSAA) in their Flight Operations department." This would have been ideal for me, but unfortunately this was all talk and no action; I waited around for a few weeks but nothing happened, so then I decided I had better make my own effort to get work in the airlines.

At this time a young man who had come down from the north looking for work was staying at my mother's guest-house, and he made the suggestion that we could go to the airport together and see what exactly was on offer. As I was still quite a shy nervous type of person, even after four years or so in the RAF, I was really pleased to have his company when we went to the BOAC Recruitment offices at Heathrow airport. These offices were alongside the Bath Road (A4) and were only temporary Nissen Huts with small generators providing the electric power. The aircraft parking ramp was also alongside the A4, so you could see aircraft being prepared for international flight.

I went in and stated the sort of job I wanted, but they were not interested in my suggestions and simply asked me to sit down and complete the application forms. Then, after a short wait, I was called in for interview and was asked what sort of job I expected and what experience I had. According to them, my RAF experience in the operational sphere was inadequate for the type of job I was looking for; however, they were interested in the fact that I had had training in equipment stores. Feeling very dejected about my prospects of being reduced to 'storekeeper,' and then being told the miserable salary scale on offer, I almost laughed into their faces before walking out in disgust. My ideas on salary and working practice had been rudely shaken; civilian life was going to be much much harder than I had ever expected.

TOP: BOAC seven-a-side football team (Sir Whitney Straight 2nd from R., author 4th from L.).
BOTTOM LEFT: The author in Cairo, 1953.
BOTTOM RIGHT: The author in Gander, 1954. All photos: author's collection.

TOP: A BOAC Comet 1, in service during the early fifties. Photo: from BOAC archives.
BOTTOM: Hotels in Gander (Jupiter on L, Saturn on R.). Photo: the author.

Outside I met the other young man again. He said he had accepted the cargo clerk situation and then over a small lunch he persuaded me to do the same. Sensibly he said: "As it is such a large concern (BOAC), they will have notice boards with vacancy notices, and once you are employed by the company you can ask for transfer to better things." So I returned to the interview room 'cap-in-hand' and said (very red-facedly) that I had reconsidered their offer and would like to accept the cargo clerk vacancy. Looking back I must say my luck was in as I was accepted without more ado. So the following Monday at 07.00, 30th June 1947, I reported for duty at the Export Cargo Warehouse at Meadow Bank, Cranford. My civil aviation career had begun and was to occupy my next 52½ years.

****

On that Monday morning now so long ago there were a number of new recruits apart from myself, and one had also been a navigator in the RAF. This encouraged me, as I had felt I had taken a job far below my aspirations, and it was some consolation to know that other men were similarly disposed. Because of my RAF training in warehousing and equipment I was made a clerk in the Export Cargo Warehouse. Yes, the Warehouse was 'off airport' in those days as no buildings were available on the airport. Fifty years later the same situation was prevalent, however now because of the huge volume of cargo going by air and the airport area being already fully occupied and, of course, more expensive to rent.

Being four miles away from the airport had its problems. Firstly, Air Cargo was considered 'fill-up' revenue only. Passengers and Post Office mail had priority for prestige and revenue value respectively; some cargo did get confirmed bookings but even then it was always the first to be offloaded if weight or capacity limits would be exceeded. Secondly, cargo didn't answer back, or make immediate noises when offloaded: so different to passengers. Thirdly, cargo by air was a novelty, something only feasible under special circumstances where costs were considered irrelevant.

You must remember that the aircraft of this era, although thought to be large, were in fact actually really quite small. This can be fully appreciated when you consider the difference between the 1950 freighters, such as the Avro Lancastrian (a civil conversion of the Lancaster bomber) and York, and those of today, the Boeing 747F and DC-10F. The maximum payload in 1947 was around 12,000 kg (12 tonnes), while today it is 90,000 kg (90 tonnes). On today's aircraft one single pallet is sometimes equivalent to a full aircraft load in the past. But I digress; let's get back to 1947!

With the aircraft being so small and the passengers and mail having highest priority, cargo became the least valued commodity and the cargo staff had to pressurise the flight crews and Load Control officers into offering maximum space on each flight. Mind you, if the Load Control officer did not fill every sector of the flight with top-up cargo, a massive enquiry took place after the flight's departure to apportion blame for this error.

The Load Controller (dispatcher in today's terms) would firstly make sure all passengers and Post Office mail were accommodated and then see what space & weight could still be carried over the various sectors of the flight. Some flights to the Far East could have 10 or 12 sectors and every one had to be filled to capacity, based on the known sector loads booked or available. This is where the cargo section came into play: we would locate all the cargo we had for each destination on each flight. It could be hundreds of kilos per sector or just a few kilos, but Load Control needed to know so that they could use this in their sector weight calculations. Then they would pass down their decisions by telephone, a very precious link between the airport and Load Control which could be so often broken, sometimes even deliberately by one individual staff member (I will not name him), especially when he was given cargo figures that did not accommodate his available load.

We would then have to 'prioritise' the cargo and load the lorries & vans for dispatch to the airport. Some of the cargo, although available, was not included in the approved weight figures, but had to be loaded for despatch to the airport as 'fill-up' load. This would be loaded at the last minute in the event of a passenger failing to turn up, making 95 kg of extra weight available (adult 75 kg plus 20 kg baggage).

To manage all this last-minute stuff, a cargo clerk had to be at the airport with the standby load. His job was to onload or offload the cargo whenever these various last-minute adjustments were necessary. This occurred on most flights with the inevitable panic ensuing. Not only had the cargo clerk to sort out the actual cargo, he had to find the appropriate cargo documents for each shipment, manifest them or delete them from the manifest and get all the corrected documents to the Customs Control Room for inclusion with the 'Ship's Papers,' which in those days the Captain himself had to sign. The time allowed for these actions was about 20 minutes and this included ordering the cargo to be loaded on the aircraft (at aircraft-side), a dash across the tarmac to Customs, and making the paperwork changes etc., no mean feat in all types of weather, day or night.

Naturally, Flight Operations would also want their 'pennyworth' in the controlling of the flight. Adverse winds or weather meant that the Captain could ask for increased reserves on certain sectors and then even the booked load, passengers or mail would be offloaded along with cargo. So you can see what a 'tear around' the cargo clerks had prior to each flight's departure.

In these early days, shipments by air meant that every item being sent as cargo had to have it's own Airway Bill (AWB), and each AWB had 12 or more copies, irrespective of the weight of the actual shipment, which meant that sometimes the AWB weighed more that the cargo itself! In such cases, when you had a freighter leaving with its massive (in those days) 12,000 kg there could be a 10-20 page manifest listing these hundreds of small pieces. You could get 50 AWBs to a page and the total weight then shown maybe as little as 100 kg.

In the warehouse we had to locate all these small items in accordance with the manifests and ensure they had received Customs clearance for shipment. At that time Customs insisted on seeing almost every item prior to its departure from the warehouse, and even if they didn't want to actually see the item, they still required the customs entry form to be raised and approved by the Customs Long Room which was based on the airport. This meant that BOAC had to have clerks raising these Customs Entry forms, taking them to the airport, getting them approved by Customs and then bringing them back to Meadow Bank for attachment to the cargo documents. Imagine the hassle when this had to be done for shipments as small as 0.5 kg! Anyway, this is the environment I was thrown into when I joined Export Cargo in June 1947.

Naturally, we had a 24-hour roster to cover, including the night shifts, which were nearly always the busiest time as they were given over to preparing the loads for flights leaving before 1000 hours each day. As the airline was developing so rapidly and the demands for shipment by air cargo overseas were increasing equally rapidly, it soon meant I was promoted and taking charge of my own shift, due to the additional staff having been recruited. In fact, the demands on the facilities every Saturday night were then so great that it was decided that the two senior supervisors, of which I was now one, would act as controllers of the warehouse on alternate weekends. These Saturday night duties would start at about 2000 hrs (8 pm) and you would be lucky to finish by 1100 hrs (11 am) Sunday morning. It was an extremely long shift with many problems to resolve. Part of the night would be spent ensuring the smooth handling of cargo within the warehouse and making sure the manifesting section was preparing the manifests quickly, and then I could proceed to the airport to discuss and resolve problems over the various flights which were leaving that Sunday morning. Then it was back to the warehouse to ensure the vans had been loaded in the correct order, each destination clearly separated on the vans and, of course, that the standby cargo had been loaded first on all the vans.

But it didn't end there: it was then back to the airport to monitor the loading of the freighters. The Lancastrian and Avro York had many limitations, which had to be overcome if you were to get the maximum weight on the flight; for instance, the nose of the Lancastrian had to have at least 1,500 kg loaded in it to enable maximum weight to be loaded in the central cabin. In the central cabin each section would take about 600 kg each; however, when you had consignments of nylon stockings for Sydney, you found you could fill the section but only have about 200 kg loaded in the completely full section; this meant sorting through the joining load and making sure you loaded smaller heavier items in with the stockings to make up the weight. Naturally, the loaders felt this was a waste of time and they wanted to take the easy way out and load whatever came first to hand. So as the cargo controller you had to demand the correct loading or end up with half the load left behind. The loading team certainly did not like you.

I stayed in cargo for about four years; the section did move on to the airport around 1950 when we took over the old import cargo warehouse when import was moved into a specially-built new building.

The old import warehouse had obtained quite a reputation in 1949. One of the staff members had became involved with a very heavy criminal gang who planned to make a major robbery. Fortunately, he went to the police, risking his own life, and he was instructed just how to play along with the gang and enable a trap to be set to capture them. On the night in question, many police (a very specially selected group of strong men) were hidden in the warehouse in the wicker basket-type dollies used inside the warehouse for moving the smaller parcels around. At night the import warehouse was closed 'land-side' as no collections were possible at night. At around 2300 hrs the gang came to the door and were let in by the import clerk, who was pretending to be with them on the raid. Once the gang – who were heavily armed with baseball clubs and the like – were inside, the police (who had similar weapons) showed themselves and quite a battle took place. All the gang were apprehended and many were the worse for wear after being manhandled by the police. Still, it saved a massive robbery occurring in which millions of poundsworth of goods, including gold and diamonds, would have been taken, so an extremely successful night as far as the police were concerned.

This reminds me of another occasion when the police were not so good; it was in the export warehouse at Meadow Bank, where the robber got away, although empty-handed. On this occasion it was found that the so-called 'strong room' (safe) was not so strong. The walls were made of bricks and the door was of steel, however the roof was only asbestos corrugated sheeting and loosely fitted. On this occasion I suspected that the robber was from inside the cargo unit, but dared not say so in case I incriminated an innocent colleague.

What happened was as follows: one morning the strong room was being cleaned when it started to rain. Surprisingly the rain came in. On inspection it was found that you could move the corrugated sheets and then it was noticed that the nuts and bolts, which normally held it in place, had been removed. The police were informed and a trap set. All the valuable items were removed secretly and the BOAC warehouse security manager was told how to contact the police urgently; however they failed to tell the night shift staff, of which I was the supervisor. It was only when one of the loaders within the warehouse said he could hear someone on the roof that we were told what was expected. Then we tried to call the police (who were supposed to be patrolling just outside) to tell them that the robber had arrived. Plans are plans but sometimes they do not take account of normal procedures. It was 2250 hours and the police shifts changed at 2300 hours. Naturally the shift going off had to return to the station and hand over to the new shift. The robber knew this and so the time when he made his attempt to raid the strong room was whilst the police were changing shifts at the police station. By the time the new shift arrived the robber had got away. Mind you, he was lucky not to be apprehended by one or two of the warehouse staff, who were extremely determined in their pursuit. The robber, whoever he was, certainly knew his way around Meadow Bank with its small lake and gardens, hence my feeling that he was someone within the cargo section. In retrospect, nothing was stolen and so nothing lost, but there were a few red faces around the next day.

Shortly after this incident I found myself being asked questions about a box of Swiss watches. These packages were always packed in well-made soft wooden boxes and had labels highlighted with the 'RED CROSS OF SWITZERLAND.' It appears that one of these boxes had arrived in our warehouse and was found to contain rocks instead of watches. The square white label was still intact but on close scrutiny it was found that the four edges had been raised from the wood and a square block cut out of the box. This had been a professional job and certainly not done in the UK in our warehouse. Eventually, it was found that it had been done at the Swiss factory, as the stone rocks inside were similar to those around the factory. We were lucky it turned out this way.

It was shortly after this event that we moved onto the airport and into the old import warehouse. Here we had much more space and all the offices were contained within the same building. No more running out into the rain or snow to get manifests or clear documents with the Customs entry clerks. Furthermore, cargo loads were increasing daily with the more modern aircraft arriving such as Constellations (049s originally), Hermes, Argonauts and Boeing Stratocruisers, all of which had greater capacity. The Argonauts were basically DC-4 Skymasters but with Rolls Royce engines and cabin pressurisation.

Many changes were taking place due to Government intervention, and we no longer carried so many small shipments. It had been agreed that these very small items could go as parcel post to overseas destinations. So you got a new type of mail shipment, parcel post, in addition to the letter post of the past. Furthermore, it was now possible to obtain clearance from Customs after the goods had departed, provided you knew that they were not a restricted commodity. Mind you, the documents were supposed to be presented to Customs within 48 hours of its departure. BOAC fell foul of this regulation at the Victoria Terminal in London, and were given just a few months to clear the backlog of documents or face extremely heavy fines, so a team of five airport staff were assigned to Victoria to clear up the mess, with me one of the five; I spent three months working in Victoria making customs entries for goods that had left the country months before. It was good experience for me, for although I had been in cargo over three years I had never had to prepare a customs entry form. I had to learn fast and, much to my surprise, Customs Long Room staff praised me at the end of three months for not having submitted one incorrect customs form despite having completed hundreds of customs entries. The only complaint they could find was that I sometimes forgot to sign the form.

During these early years with BOAC I prepared cargo loads for a number of different aircraft types. In 1947 to 1949 BOAC operated a daily flight to Cairo with the DC-3 (Dakota), an aircraft type designed and produced in America during the war; it was flight M32, which departed at 10.00 am every day carrying about 20 passengers and a small amount of cargo and mail. BOAC also operated passenger versions of the four-engined Avro York, a high-wing monoplane with a tailwheel, a noisy aircraft to fly in although more comfortable than the passenger version of the Lancastrian. The York could carry about twenty passengers, whereas the Lancastrian could take only eight or nine.

BOAC also operated the Handley Page Halton, a civilianised version of the wartime Halifax bomber similar in size to the Lancastrian but with a much shorter range. While the York and the Lancastrian flew all the way down to Australia, the Halton's range limited it to West Africa.

Around 1950 it was decided by the British government that Northolt Airport should really be for military use only and that the airlines using it should be moved to Heathrow. The foreign airlines were the first to be moved, with BEA having to wait until enough Terminal space was available at Heathrow. Because of this move, BOAC Cargo section had to handle the cargo for these flights. To do so meant setting up a separate section within the Cargo unit and I was one of those assigned to this section. We had to deal with Alitalia, Air France, Sabena and Swissair, and each had different types of aircraft with varying load limitations.

The Italian Airline was still operating the tri-motor Savoia-Marchetti, an Italian-built aircraft from well before the war; this had the two pilots sitting out in the open air, the same as the *Spider* aircraft I had first flown in, and had a metal-framed body with a fabric covering. There were five or six small doors along each side of the lower fuselage into which you could load baggage and cargo, so this considerably limited what could be loaded and strict limits were set on what baggage or cargo could be accepted, a real major problem at that time.

Sabena (**S**uch **A** **B**loody **E**xperience **N**ever **A**gain) had the American twin-engined Convairs, quite a modern aircraft for this time. They had fairly good payload capacity and caused competition between us staff in the cargo unit: who could get the maximum load on board? I annoyed the Sabena manager one day as I filled every vacant seat on the aircraft with cargo as well as all the hold space. Really red in the face, he said: "This is not a bloody freighter, it's my prime passenger flight of the day." In fact there were only three passengers booked and I had left four seats for their use.

The Sabena engineer caused an incident one morning. His job was to check the engines each day before declaring the night-stopping aircraft fit for service. The first service each morning left at 07.30 and the aircraft stayed overnight at Heathrow airport; this meant an early start for the engineer and quite often he was a little late on duty. The checks he had to do involved starting the engines, then warming them up and checking for 'power ratios.' Each magneto on the engines had to be checked individually by switching one off at a time. As with all propeller-driven aircraft, guardrails were placed in front of the aircraft to ensure that ground staff didn't walk too near the propellers in case someone started the engines without warning. Prior to doing his engine-run, the engineer always ensured that the aircraft had chocks on each wheel to prevent the aircraft running forward unintentionally. These were in position on this particular day, so all looked well, but on this occasion the engineer was in a hurry because he had been late arriving at the aircraft, so, having warmed the engines up, he then applied the power to both engines at the same time, instead of one at a time. Maybe on nine times out of ten this would have made no difference, but on this occasion he must have added more power than normal because the whole aircraft jumped forward over the chocks and the propellers hit the guardrails. The guardrails were made of softish metal and were cut to pieces by the propeller blades; pieces of metal were thrown all over the whole ramp area, and some were found alongside the passenger terminal. Others cut through the metal skin of the aircraft and damaged instruments inside, so the engineer was lucky not to be hit by any of these flying pieces of metal.

Naturally, a full enquiry had to be held and that morning's flight was cancelled due lack of a serviceable aircraft. As a result, this engineer was posted back to his home base in Brussels and may have lost his job. His replacement at Heathrow never powered up the two engines together, so all learnt a safety lesson.

Air France, not to be outdone, brought in their Languedoc 161. It had four engines and a double deck of passengers, 140 in all, by far the largest commercial load at that time. Air France had over thirty of these aircraft, but they didn't last too long as the Americans were by now producing the Constellations, DC-4 Loadmasters and Stratocruisers. The Languedoc was a very flat-sided aircraft which, because of its height, appeared to have a very thin fuselage; it didn't have much space for cargo, even if it could carry all those passengers.

Swissair were operating similar aircraft to that of Sabena, so once again we cargo staff had a similar competition as to who could load the most on any one flight

In 1951 I decided to have a holiday in Portugal – Lisbon to be precise. My wife and I managed to get the last two seats on the Constellation flight to Lisbon and checked in to the Europa hotel, which was where our crews stayed. But we soon realised that this was a bad move: firstly, it was too expensive and above our requirements and secondly, it was much too far away from the beach. So we managed to find the Atlantico Hotel at Monte Esteril, a recently-built hotel with marvellous food and accommodation.

We were struggling on our £25-each-a-year overseas currency allowance and finding it hard to exist, but then we met a couple from Manchester at the same hotel who had many businesses in Manchester and somehow had no problem in getting extra cash out of the country. They took pity on us (the only other English couple staying at the hotel) and took us with them to Petra Castle and other beauty spots in the area. It transpired that they had taken a cruise from Southampton on the yacht belonging to Barbara Hutton, the Woolworth heiress, all along the French and Portuguese coasts down as far as Lisbon, but the wife had been seasick all the way and refused to go back on the yacht for the return journey. On the other hand, the husband was adamant that he would never fly. Can you guess who won in the end? The wife, of course, and I was asked to arrange for them to travel with us on the same aircraft. This I did and we were all on the Argonaut for a daytime flight to Heathrow. On the day of departure I took the husband into the bar at the airport and he downed a few large brandies. With my steadying hand to lean on, he walked out and onto the plane; as luck would have it the flight was perfectly smooth in continuous blue skies all the way and all his fears of flying melted away.

Going back a few days into our holiday, I must relate an incident on the beach near the hotel. On this particular morning we were sunbathing on the beach (the Atlantic ocean around Lisbon is far too cold to swim in) when a couple sat down a few yards away. Surprisingly I had seen the man at Heathrow Airport on numerous occasions and he recognised me as well. Naturally we spoke and introduced our wives but that was that;

they were staying at another hotel and we did not see them again in Lisbon. But on my return home and going back to work I found that while I was away they had had a work study group in to see how the cargo section worked, and the results of this study indicated that there were far too many supervisors and not enough male workers. To resolve the situation it was agreed that all the supervisors would be listed with the personnel department and, if any other department was short of a supervisor, then that department's head could choose one of the cargo supervisors rather than upgrade any of the staff within that section. As it happened, the man who had been sitting next to me on the beach in Lisbon was the Flight Information Manager; he needed an extra supervisor and was trying to upgrade one of his present staff, but this upgrade was refused and he was told to choose one from the list of cargo supervisors needing redeployment. From the list he was shown, the only name he knew was mine, and hence I was transferred to Flight Information.

The move could not have come at a better moment for me. I had had four years in cargo and felt I needed a change if I were to better myself within BOAC. The Flight Information section was adjacent to the Duty Room and at the hub of activities on the airport. Every section had to report to the Duty Room controller and, when he was at lunch or absent, the information supervisor manned the control unit. We also kept records of every flight operated by BOAC worldwide and prepared the Chairman's daily report, quoting worldwide delay reasons with full details. Of course, today you would call the Duty Room a Call Centre, but that terminology did not exist in 1952.

With so many days of fog at Heathrow, the telephones never stopped ringing. When the fog lasted three to four days, with every flight delayed or operating from other airports in the UK, the passengers and their friends never gave us a minute's peace. Additionally, just in case the weather should improve, you had to ensure that you could call passengers at any time and tell them when to come to the airport. Passengers got irate and took it out on the staff, many of whom could not take the abuse and would have to be excused or replaced. During very bad weather times, staff from passenger handling or the ticket counter were sent temporarily to help man the phones – we had no automatic answering facilities at this time.

Throughout my time in cargo I played for the export cargo football team. We played in the local league and did fairly well, so when I moved to Flight Information I continued to play for export cargo and also joined the London Victoria team. Eventually I became a member of the BOAC team and played in international games between the airlines. The Sabena team from Brussels was one I played against, and during the game I stopped their centre forward from scoring; however, I was lucky not to have given a penalty away in doing so. At the other end of the pitch I missed a golden opportunity to score, so it ended up a drawn game. Let it be said that I enjoyed all the games I played, but once I went overseas to work at 29, I hung up my boots for good.

From my contacts within the London Victoria staff (due to the football games) I learnt that there were possibilities of obtaining training and work overseas in Flight Operations, the job I had originally applied for back in 1947. I therefore made an official request for information on the training courses available and was quickly advised that the courses did not exist. Suspecting that this was incorrect, I left the office, went into a public phone box, and telephoned the person I had been told was responsible for obtaining suitable staff to fill these courses. He was surprised to hear of what I had been told and then realised why he had not been given any names of people working at Heathrow who had had flying experience during the war. He told me to do nothing as he would arrange it all from BOAC HQ, and a few weeks later I received a letter from the Heathrow Airport Manager saying how pleased he was to inform me of my selection for a place on the next Operations II course starting in three weeks' time. The same person who had signed the previous letter saying "No such courses are available" signed the letter.

It was now nearly eight years since I had done any operations-type work/calculations and so I got out all the books I could find and studied late into the night in an effort to make a good showing when beginning the training. This was the beginning of a new phase in my civil aviation career, a major step up the ladder in BOAC.

CHAPTER 6

CAIRO

The Operations II course lasted for eight weeks and was of the very highest intensity. All the other people on the course were already working overseas as operations officers who were being updated on the new flight planning methods that were needed now that the Comet 1s were operational. Previously the need for extreme accuracy in flight planning was not considered necessary, so ground staff were only given a limited amount of operational know-how. With the pure jet aircraft having a very much more critical flight range, coupled with the complexities of operational flight management, it was essential that a operationally qualified officer was based at every overseas station: hence this massive retraining requirement had been introduced.

Naturally, the original overseas staff had been given limited instructions to cover until they could be brought home for intensive training. They, naturally, had an advantage over me as they knew exactly what a BOAC flight plan looked like. They had recently been using navigation computers for calculations and weather maps to decipher trends in the weather or for reading forecasts. Most of this was brand-new to me, however I needed to do plenty of revision in order to keep up with the other trainees. Fortunately, my RAF training served me well and I was soon as good as, if not better, than most of those on the course. Only one man, an ex-fully-qualified navigator for BOAC who had been grounded for health reasons, could beat me using the flight-planning computer, and he was in fact the Senior Operations Officer at Idlewild Airport, New York (now JFK – after the late President John F. Kennedy).

These eight weeks meant very hard work for me, but to be getting into what I had always felt to be my rightful employment made it really worthwhile, and proved to be the turning point in my civil aviation career. The introduction of the Comet 1 aircraft had made all this possible and my whole life was now about to change for the better; my family would reap the benefit of it too.

Prior to my introduction to this course, one other person from Heathrow airport had been selected to attempt the course. During the lectures they thought he would pass the course, as he appeared to grasp all the instruction he was given, but much to everyone's dismay, he failed the final exams. You do not get a second chance, once failed you were 'out.' An urgent replacement to take his place was needed and everyone hoped I would be that replacement

The instructors were so shocked at his results that they were always questioning me, investigating how I was doing: was I coping? Did I need more tuition? Making sure I couldn't complain about the 'tutorial' contents of the course, or their efficiency. Some felt they had let themselves down in not being efficient in their teaching and having caused the candidate to fail. All this certainly made me realise just how important this instruction was in regards to my career in BOAC. Much to everyone's relief, I passed easily and was therefore able to accept my first overseas assignment, which was to Cairo.

Thinking back, this was one of the most important times in my life. Without my ability to master this aspect of aviation, there would have been very few prospects of a worthwhile career in BOAC. The next few weeks were hectic. Egypt was going to be hot as it would be mid-summer when I arrived, so a few bits of lightweight clothing needed to be purchased. I would be travelling alone on this first assignment. Families were not allowed to go overseas until you had proved yourself capable of working independently on a overseas station. Egypt was also not a settled country at this time. King Farouk had been exiled and General Maghib was the 'puppet leader' for Colonel Nasser, who subsequently made himself known as the new revolutionary leader of the country's insurrection. Naturally, I had some apprehension about going to an Arab state which was in such a turmoil, but at this time I felt that BOAC would not have sent me if it was dangerous! Looking back, I was so naïve: in fact they would send anyone anywhere if they felt they were needed to keep the flights operating. Mind you, if there was trouble eventually then they would pull out all the stops and do everything possible to get you home in one piece.

Cairo proved to be a very good experience for a newcomer to overseas life: firstly, no one had their families with them at this time, so we all had to keep fully in touch with each other; secondly, it was a busy station with aircraft landing at all times of day and night, and thirdly, the mixture of aircraft types in use meant you were flight-planning Argonauts, Hermes, Yorks, Lancastrians and Comet 1s. BOAC only had three other types of aircraft in service, all on the trans-Atlantic routes, and they were 049 & 749 Constellations, Liberators and the newly introduced Boeing 377 Stratocruisers.

The Liberator operation needs to be mentioned specially. The aircraft was a long-range bomber previously used by Coastal Command to monitor the Atlantic convoys of ships that were trying to avoid submarine attacks. They were then used by BOAC postwar in a very pioneering way, to carry Post Office mail across the Atlantic to Montreal, Canada *non-stop*. They were operated almost on a military basis, using the newly developed in-flight refuelling techniques. Taking off from Heathrow they would rendezvous with a tanker aircraft to refuel over Northern Ireland prior to setting off to fly the Atlantic. Then they would rendezvous with another tanker aircraft over the Newfoundland or

Labrador Coast and refuel to complete the rest of the flight to Montreal. Refuelling in flight was a very new procedure, which needed much time to fully develop, real pioneering stuff being done by BOAC.

Later on, BSAA also introduced flight refuelling on their passenger services between London and Bermuda. They only had one point to refuel and that was about 600 miles north of the Azores where the tanker aircraft was based. If the two aircraft failed to rendezvous, then the passenger flight had to divert to the Azores and refuel on the ground prior to going on its way to Bermuda. This procedure was well in advance of its time; however, because it was regularly in use it meant that the military could realise the potential advantage it could give for rapid deployment of armed forces throughout the world. In the recent Gulf and Afghanistan conflicts, long-range bomber aircraft have flown many thousands of miles to reach and return from their targets by being able to refuel in flight on numerous occasions; all this can be attributed to the courageous BOAC and BSAA flight crews in the 1947–1952 period.

A fourth reason why Cairo was considered a good experience was that we worked long hours: 24 hours on duty, then 48 hours off. This was needed overseas due to the limited number of staff on each station. It may sound impossible, but we soon got used to the shift pattern and found it better than the alternative of working 12 hours every day of the week. Of course, we were considered lucky; there were three Operations Officers, whereas the passenger side only had two Passenger Duty Officers to cover every 24 hours. They worked 24 hours on and 24 hours off, a really bad roster.

My first flight on overseas duty with BOAC was in mid-June 1953 to Cairo. Take-off from Heathrow at 10.00 with arrival in Cairo at 03.30 local time the next day, a total elapsed time of 15 hours 30 minutes. We had one stop in Rome for refuelling and a crew change, which took about 90 minutes, so the flying time was a total of 13½ hours. The present-day flight time is under six hours non-stop. It was an uneventful flight, however, but the thought of going to live and work in a strange country kept my nerves on edge the whole time.

On landing in Cairo I was met by the Duty Operations Officer (John), who quickly briefed me on where my accommodation was and who was meeting me the following day – sorry, same day; to my surprise I was expected to be ready by 8 am even though I had travelled all day and half the night and still yet had to find my hotel and get to bed.

I arrived at the hotel by 04 30 and eventually got to bed by just after 5 am with my alarm clock set for 7. I began to wonder if overseas life would always be this hectic! I did get some sleep, mainly because I was totally exhausted. When I went down for breakfast I made the mistake of asking for boiled eggs. When the eggs and toast eventually arrived they were the smallest eggs I had ever seen, looking more like sparrows' eggs to me; on top of this, when I cracked the first one open the inside was uncooked and runny, and this put me off breakfast altogether that morning.

I was then met by the Senior Operations Officer, Jim, a South African, who then informed me he was going on leave that evening, hence all the rush to get me introduced to work at Cairo airport: I was taking over his shift the following day. By 9 am I was being introduced to the Cairo Airport management team. Arabic names were being thrown at me and I wondered if I was expected to memorize them all. Then I was taken to the BOAC Operations Office to meet the local staff and see where the flight planning and operations control was actioned. As the other Operations Duty Officer, Shamus, a fairly wild Irishman, was on duty, now I had met all the Ops team.

It was then I learnt that we were fully expected to climb the stairs (no lift available) to the Control Tower for every arrival and departure of a BOAC aircraft. This was the result of a recent 'boo-boo' by one of the Egyptian Air Traffic Controllers; it appeared that he had cleared one aircraft to take off from the runway already allocated to another aircraft cleared to land in the opposite direction. Fortunately, they were both BOAC flights, and the Captains realised the mistake and the departing Captain refused to accept the controller's clearance. This incident was reported, via the crews' reports, back to HQ in London, where they immediately decided that the operations officer on duty (who was on the spot) should in future monitor the Control Tower staff more rigorously. This meant being in the Control Tower and observing all the actions the Controllers were taking.

None of us agreed that this would avoid all future incidents as we arrived usually within minutes of the aircraft landing and this gave us little chance of assessing the total aircraft movements around the airport at that time. For instance, we would not have heard clearances given prior to our arrival in the tower. Secondly, yes, we *had* visited the Heathrow Air Traffic Control Centre and Control Tower, but we were not fully trained ATC operators. Still, as it seemed to appease HQ if we did this, that is what we had to do.

After about two hours at the airport, the SOO (Senior Operations Officer) remarked that he had to change money ready for his holiday in South Africa where his wife and family lived, so this meant that any further introductions or instructions at the airport had to cease. I had met up to fifty people, most of them Arabs, and seen the office layout, and that was all. My duties were to commence the following morning at 08.00 and last for the following 24 hours. To tell you the truth, I was scared stiff. Would I be able to cope? John could see I was worried; he was going to be Acting SOO during the six weeks Jim was on leave. So he told me he would join me for the first few hours the next day and then again between midnight and 2 am (the busiest time); this made me feel a little better.

With this decided we all took off for the bank and then on to the HPH (Heliopolis Palace Hotel). The HPH was a marvellous hotel with a massive bar and lounges and was frequented by most BOAC staff at sometime or other during the day or night. Some of the managers lived in the hotel and we did have a Sales Office in the building. By the time we got to the HPH it was 1 pm and I was introduced to Stella, the Egyptian beer. All bottles seemed to be a full litre every time, and a fair number went down, along with an ample supply of various salted nuts. It was here that I met a few more of the overseas contract staff and engineers, as it was one of the meeting places on days off.

Sometime around 5 pm the idea was agreed that we should eat as well as drink, and John said we could all go to his apartment for a meal. This was fully accepted by all, so off we went. John's place was a really nice large ground floor flat, beautifully furnished. John was married although, like all of us, his wife had been evacuated back to the UK, but you could see that there had been a woman around the place by the way it was decorated. He also had an Egyptian cook who quickly prepared a meal. Our group had now grown to eight, all males. Naturally, John provided more beers whilst we waited for the food, then suddenly someone said: "It's Alf's birthday today! Shouldn't we have a party?"

I learnt later that the birthday party idea was purely an excuse to start an evening's drinking session. Alf turned out to be the senior engineer on my shift throughout my stay in Cairo. Needless to say, I could see that this party was a good opportunity to meet more of the staff at Cairo, so I was quite happy to join in the fun. The party was at Alf's home, another fairly large ground floor flat with a good sized garden. From memory I would think there were about twenty of us there. What I can also remember is that I was getting very tired, having had only two hours' sleep in nearly 48 hours, so I asked John how to find my hotel and was directed which way to walk.

At this time Egypt, including Cairo, was under martial law. Soldiers were on every street corner and even outside the small hotel where I was staying. Despite this constant presence of troops on the street, life went on almost normally for us 'ex-pats.' Anyway, I was still quite nervous as I walked along these strange streets and expected to be stopped at any moment. Luckily I got to the hotel without being challenged, then just as I entered the gate to the hotel, which was not well lit up, a soldier jumped up from the dark. He must have been sleeping (2 am) and seemed as surprised as I was at our meeting. Needless to say, he just stepped aside and allowed me to enter. I had been in Egypt for 24 hours and so much had happened. Was the rest of my stay going to be so eventful?

My first day on duty went reasonably well, although it was hard work preparing the flight plans on time. Then briefing the crews took some time to get used to. Some Captains, realising you were such a 'greenhorn' at an overseas station, used to ask many questions just to test your knowledge. They were testing me because they knew that sometime in the future they would expect me to give an operational judgement concerning one of their flights. Based on how well you responded would indicate to them how much they could trust your skills & knowledge. I soon learnt that it was essential you knew, by heart, the operational details about Cairo airport: height above sea level, frequency of NDB (Navigational Direction Beacon), length of runways and runway directions, main obstacle heights near the airport. It was also essential that I could read the coded weather reports (TAFORS) etc. The Captain required a telephonic briefing prior to his pick-up from the hotel, and to do this you needed to translate TAFORS instantaneously into plain English. Otherwise you would delay the briefing, as the Meteorological Office weather folder, in which the weather reports had been decoded, was never available until 90 minutes before the departure of the flight. On the course in London we learnt how these TAFORS were written, but it was never even hinted that you should memorise the whole coding system. This in my opinion should have been emphasised within the training period.

John came in, as agreed, on this first day & night duty, and I was very grateful for his assistance whilst I tried to get to know both the staff under me and my way around the airport offices. There was no air conditioning anywhere on the airport; our office had a small window and a ceiling fan, but summer in Cairo is hot and humid, so much sweat was generated. To keep the flight plans mainly dry, I had to spread a clean handkerchief over each flight plan to catch the drips of sweat as they fell. If I hadn't done this, they would have become a soggy mess and not readable or acceptable to the crew.

John had a 'black book' in respect of captains coming through Cairo, which contained notes on what type of request they would make about flight plan reserves; there were regulation figures set out in the operations manual but some captains would always insist on increases of some of these reserves. Knowing who the captain was then gave you a chance to adjust your flight plan before he got to the airport, or to be ready to resist his demands and persuade him that the extras he was demanding were not possible and not necessary. On this point, many arguments occurred between captain, Duty Passenger Office and Duty Operations Officer. The captain would try everything to get what he considered his needs, even if it meant offloading revenue cargo, mail or even passengers. The implications of this to us on the ground would be the need for us to write reports to HQ and the Area General Manager, plus additionally having to find alternative travel arrangements for offloaded passengers, mail or cargo.

Naturally, on some occasions the captain was definitely right in his demands and we had to do whatever was necessary to keep the flight on schedule. On other occasions we would re-route the flight by making an intermediate landing and thereby reducing the flight plan sector fuel requirements. When this happened the crew were very upset, as it meant a longer operational day for them and a landing at an airport that may not have had a BOAC-trained Operations Officer and therefore meant a personal visit to the ATC and Met. offices themselves during that stopover. Back in the 1950s, the aircraft range was very limited; most airlines and flights were flying sectors that just came within their maximum range with full payload. On some flights the sector payload was restricted so as to ensure that the next point of call was within the flight's safe range.

I never made a 'black book' on the captains' idiosyncrasies and just trusted on my memory. During the length of my stay in Cairo, I gradually built up my reputation, operational skills and competence as an Overseas Operations Officer. Looking back I was lucky to get such a busy station to cut my teeth on; it meant I was able to succeed at my next assignment (Rome) and then at Gander, Newfoundland, the busiest operational station within BOAC.

But I digress; there are other incidents that occurred at Cairo, which are interesting, but unfortunately I never did keep a diary, so everything has to be from memory. Cairo had many interesting places and you needed to experience some of them to really get the feel of the atmosphere attached to the place: for instance, the *souk*. Until you have had a *souk* stall owner entertain you, you will have missed the beauty of a true salesman's art and his efforts to get you to buy his goods. John took me into the *souk* to a few of the stalls selling typical Egyptian brass and silver trinkets. He had been there on numerous occasions with his wife, before she was evacuated back to the UK. The owner recognised him immediately, and greeted me excitedly, looking on me as another customer with money to spend, and got one of his 'boys' (a grown man) to set chairs for us to sit in comfort whilst he planned his approach for the sales of his goods. The 'boy' went to bring us Arabic coffee, Coca-Cola or some similar drink. He then went into conversation with John, asking how his wife was, also keeping me in the conversation by asking if I was married etc. Not a word was spoken regarding what we wanted to buy, or what he wanted to sell. We had to be made to feel at home before any display of goods for sale. I did buy trinkets from the stall eventually; it took over an hour and, at the time, it seemed strange to me to do business in this manner, however I must say I enjoyed the whole experience and he (the stall owner) enjoyed setting his wits against ours.

He sold us things we never intended to buy, at a price that was more than likely well over the true value of the goods, but with us going away thinking we had got a bargain, and him knowing he had made a good sale. During this shopping experience, I learnt from John the art of pretending the price was exorbitantly high and threatening to get up and walk out. If the *souk* owner knew he could still go down a bit on his price, he made sure you didn't leave. In later years when I was based in Arabic countries, you could see the same principles being adopted by the Arabic shop or *souk* stall owners.

Egypt has had amazing effects on a number of English men and women over the last few centuries. I met one such lady out at the pyramids near Cairo, but unfortunately I cannot remember her name. When I met her she was about 60 years old and living in a small Arabic house near the pyramids. Alf and John took me to see her, and she had such a immense knowledge on Egyptology that it was always enlightening to spend a few hours with her whilst she informed you of some of the history of the country.

The first journey to her place was also eventful; we were in Alf's car, a 1938 Mercedes, one of the first cars to have independent four-wheel suspension. All went well until we got a puncture in a very remote Arabic area, then as soon as the car stopped fifteen to twenty poor-looking men and boys surrounded us. Alf got the car jack out and tried to lift the axle to get the punctured wheel off and the spare wheel on, but the jack went downwards into the sandy road instead of lifting the car upwards. This crowd of rough-looking Arabs, however, solved our problem; four or five of them lifted the whole side of the car into the air and held it there while Alf hurriedly changed the wheel. Naturally, we gave them some money, for which they were most grateful, and then we were on our way with smiles all round.

The lady we visited had gone to Cairo for a holiday when she was only eighteen years old, and she loved the place so much that she never returned home. She was from a fairly wealthy family, whose father owned most of the early cinemas in England. Needless to say, although she lived a somewhat simple and hard life in Egypt, she never once went back to the luxury that could have been hers. In her early years in Egypt she had managed always to be close to where they were excavating newly-found tombs. Once an entrance to a tomb had been located, she would enter the tomb with pad and pencils and record all the wall carvings and writings whilst they retained their true colour. In fact they would seal her within the tomb so as to restrict the amount of light getting onto the walls, as this would change the colours originally painted on so many thousand years earlier. We all felt she was a very brave lady and someone who was a real pleasure to meet and know.

At supper that night out by the pyramids I tasted the oldest cheese I've ever heard of. It was made from goats' milk and had been allowed to ferment for ten years before being eaten, and surprisingly it was still white in colour, quite ripe to smell and strong in taste. I still managed to eat some with cheese crackers washed down by a cold Stella beer. It was a wonderful night out that has found a permanent place in my memory.

In my fairly short stay in Egypt, I managed to go to the pyramids once more. A party was organised by the ex-pat and local BOAC staff to be at the pyramids to see the sun set and to stay and watch the sunrise the next day. A BOAC bus was laid on, the catering unit provided us with sandwiches, sausage rolls and other savoury snacks, and to this we added a considerable number of bottles of beer. In all there were about twenty of us, including a few Egyptian female airline receptionists. A record player and records were also on board the bus, so we had music to help while away the whole night.

It was on this occasion that I fully realised that Shamus was a truly wild Irishman; he had had a few beers, not many, but was then set on riding one of the horses available for hire. I had never been on a horse's back before, whereas Shamus had ridden much in Ireland and was an extremely proficient rider, and this was where the problems arose. He wanted to ride freely across the desert, whereas the horse owner wouldn't let the horse go off its lead. Shamus was an experienced rider and the horse wanted to do what he was urging it to do, but it was also fully aware that his owner was unwilling to allow this to happen. Battle raged for thirty minutes or so, until Shamus gave in and got off the horse.

While this was going on, my own attempt to ride was severely hampered; my horse could see what was happening to the other horse and reacted nervously. I was very insecure in the saddle and the erratic movements made my attempts to hold the horse between my legs almost impossible, so I was glad when the ride was over and I was back on *terra firma*. At the end of this overnight party, it was good to be able to say that you had seen the sunset and sunrise at the pyramids, but that was about all.

While talking about Shamus, I must relate two other noteworthy events in which he was involved. During my stay in Cairo a rooftop party was held at one of the local staff's apartments. We were all invited but I was on duty so could not attend. The rooftop was not all at one level; one part of the roof was a storey lower than the other and between them there was a gap of over 3 metres. Late on in the party Shamus decided to jump from one rooftop to the other over this gap. It was from the fourth floor to the third floor, so there was quite a drop to ground level in between. He did achieve it without any problem but they had a hard job preventing him trying to jump back and up a floor.

In another incident with Shamus, he was at the Club and using the swimming pool. He liked to dive off the top board (3 metres high), but on this occasion he decided he would dive off backwards. His first attempt resulted in him landing in the water flat on his back. He had not rotated enough. The second attempt he rotated too much and landed flat on his belly. Now both his back and his front were bright red from the force of his falls, still he was up on the board again trying once more. A BOAC captain standing next to me commented: "He's going to kill himself if he carries on like this." I believe you now understand the type of person Shamus was.

In my youth I had tried to learn to play the piano, I was not a real success, but I could knock out some of the modern tunes, and this came in useful whilst I was in Cairo at the Airline Club. The Airline Club mainly consisted of a small bar, a nice restaurant, large swimming pool and a few tennis courts, and they had the latest record player and hundreds of the latest records. So music was always available and was played most of the day. Having said all this, you would be surprised at the reaction when the piano was played.

Late one afternoon I was at the Club with John and a few others, and when I asked the Club Manager if I could have the keys to the piano, much to everyone's surprise he gave them to me. The piano had not been open for months and was generally thought to be 'out of bounds' to Club members' domain. Anyway, I opened the piano and played a tune I had learnt off by heart many years before; immediately the piano sounds were heard, the record player was switched off and a number of members came over to the piano. Then after my second tune, the piano was moved into the bar and I was invited to play some more. It was now 5 pm and the usual selection of club members were arriving. Some of these were TWA staff (Americans), of whom one had some tom-toms in his flat which he went to get. Alf had a mouth organ and banjo, which he collected and brought to the Club. In the meantime I kept on playing whatever tune came to my head. Some were very poorly played, but somehow this didn't seem to matter. Live music was only provided on special occasions, so the folks in the Club felt they were getting a treat for a change. Records or a radio may provide better music, but to stand and sing to someone playing on a piano is totally different: no one seemed to want to go home or leave the bar area, and I sat at the piano from 5 pm until 3 am the next morning. I did take a meal break between 11 and 12 midnight, but this particular evening was to change my whole stay in Egypt.

On my days off I would say: "I need a rest, don't come around to get me, I will be resting." But still they came. Alf and John would be there pleading: "The Club will be boring if you don't come, please don't let us down, just come for a short while." Eventually this would get me over my reluctance to go out and I would end up staying until closing time, between 1 and 2 am.

But this activity did make my stay more enjoyable and pleasing. My piano playing improved, at least the playing-by-ear aspect. Still, I was not displeased when I was told to move on to Rome in September and to expect to be there for about only one month. It would be nearer to home and I felt I would be able to have my wife there with me.

While at Cairo my knowledge of operational work was greatly enhanced. My knowledge of the routes BOAC were flying and the hazards associated with them became realistic. It made you realise just how brave the men and women had been to pioneer these desert areas, to enable flights to go as far as Hong Kong, Japan and Australia.

When flying south to Sudan there were the tropical storms to worry about. Often when flight-planning to Khartoum it was difficult to name an alternate airport where the weather would ensure a safe landing in the event of Khartoum becoming closed due to the storms. Going north to Rome, we were operating to the extreme range limit of the aircraft in use, while landing at intermediate places like Athens would add time to the flights, cost extra money and upset the schedule plan. There were not too many airports available as alternates to Rome other than Naples. Athens was nearer to Cairo than Rome. Although there were airports in the Toe of Italy, none had been developed sufficiently for BOAC to accept as suitable for our international flights.

My Cairo experiences also increased my knowledge on what could be done by the engineers when certain technical problems arose. One night I was asked: “Harry, can you order a bag of ice urgently?”

Naturally I asked: “What for?”

But you can imagine my surprise when I was told: “To help start the engine on this b***** Hermes.”

It transpired that, when trying to start up the engine, if it didn’t start first time in the heat of Cairo, then the starter motor would jam and could be freed quickly by holding a bag of ice around it for a few minutes. On some occasions the engineer would hit the cylinder block of another type of engine to free the piston inside; this is where the rubber hammer came in very useful.

The Hermes aircraft was added to the BOAC fleet around 1950/51. The passengers on the West African routes thought it wonderful. The space between seats was greater than on any other aircraft at that time. This may sound a good sales lead, but the reason why there was so much space was because of limitations on the payload weight capacity. It was no use putting extra seat rows in place if this meant that the aircraft range was shortened. So although liked by passengers the Hermes was a loss-making machine for BOAC.

Talking to captains who flew the Hermes for years, they liked the cockpit layout and, although it was underpowered, they still felt it was a good aircraft to fly. It had one or two problems; the engines (Bristol Hercules sleeve-valves) were not only short on power, they used too much oil, so much in fact that it was said to limit the range of the aircraft. People used to joke: "We have plenty of fuel to continue flying but not enough oil in the engines." Then a few years later on it was discovered that the gearing between engine and propeller could seize up, and when this happened the propeller dropped off. This happened on two occasions and the propeller cut into the aircraft side. Once it cut through the radio in front of the operator, who was seated just behind the pilot.

The Hermes had originally been designed to have a tailwheel like that on the Lancastrian and York aircraft. However, a tricycle undercarriage had been fitted to the American Constellation 049, and this ultimately made the manufacturers realise that all new aircraft should be designed and built this way. So they made a very big change to the design of the Hermes and fitted a tricycle undercarriage, which made the aircraft look more modern, but caused changes to its flight attitude; the aircraft became tail heavy, and so about 200 Kg of lead was added up front to counterbalance this tail-heavy attitude. This did the trick but at a very heavy penalty, leaving BOAC and other operators to suffer the commercial consequences. It also resulted in the aircraft maintaining a very nose-up flight attitude: so much so that in bad weather the underside of the aircraft iced up along the whole length of its fuselage.

Earlier on, when I was still at Heathrow in the Flight Information section. One of the Hermes aircraft went missing on a flight down to Kano in Nigeria, West Africa; it was located by tribesmen 24 hours later, some 150 miles west of where it should have been. All the passengers were saved by the subsequent actions taken by the crew, in particular the First Officer. Unfortunately it was he who subsequently died, possibly because of his efforts to save the rest. The aircraft was off course due to the incorrect settings being placed on the radio compass on departure from Tripoli, Libya. Full details of this incident have already been published, so I will say no more.

Naturally, when it came time for me to leave Cairo, we had a party at the Club and I said my farewells to all my other musicians and friends. Then it was off to Rome and whatever other experiences might lay ahead.

CHAPTER 7

ROME

My flight to Rome was on an Argonaut, the same type of aircraft I had flown on coming to Cairo. I would have loved to be on the Comet 1, but they were oversold so there was no chance of staff getting a seat from Cairo. I cannot remember anything special about my flight, I only know it was an overnight trip and that I was told on my arrival at Rome that the Senior Operations Officer would see me later on in the day.

On this occasion the Hotel Europa was arranged for me, and it was much more pleasant than the one I had been given in Cairo; all the cabin crew of BEA and BOAC were billeted there as well.

Being classed as a 'European Station' meant that Rome was a BEA (British European Airlines) airport and BOAC had to accept and suffer the arrangements BEA made. BEA ground handling of passengers, cargo and mail was quite different to that normally provided by BOAC, however we had to make do with their services for commercial and economic reasons. BEA did not have trained Operations Officers as ground staff, hence the need for the likes of me to carry out the BOAC operational functions.

There were four contracted Operations Officers, which included the Senior Operations Officer, plus three locally-employed operations clerks/assistants. We had a separate office to that of BEA, which was on the opposite side of the airport and runway, but this was not because we hated each other! The Weather Office, Control Tower and ATC were on the "American" side of the airport, whereas we British had occupied the other side of the airport when hostilities ceased in 1945, so BEA and BOAC aircraft had to use the British side of the airport. This was not ideal; it meant that our flight crews had to come to our Operations Office on the east side for their briefing and flight plan, which resulted in a need for separate transport to take the cabin crew to the west side where the aircraft was parked and being loaded. This separating of functions added time to the airport arrangements for the crew, thus extending the official 'Duty Day hours' of them all. The Flight Time Limitations (FTL) of crews could be critical on occasions, sometimes forcing a unscheduled change of crew and, as a result, a flight delay. Of course, cabin crew went straight to the aircraft and did their best to ensure the aircraft was being readied correctly.

This arrangement also caused us in BOAC Ops some problems. We relied on BEA traffic keeping us up-to-date on load changes, which would ultimately give us our fuel-available figures for the flight. With the limitations which the aircraft of the day had, it was only when we knew the final fuel figure available that we could confirm we had enough to make the normal flight plan routing. It was so critical that we had to divide by 2.2046 to translate pounds weight to kilos – if you used 2.2 you could put too much fuel on board and make the aircraft overweight.

The load figures were passed by telephone between BEA traffic office and our office. There were only single-line telephones, which often were in hectic use, so it could easily cause a delay if the telephone line had problems. The multi-line telephone units had not been invented at this time, and every line had to have a separate Hand Set (Unit). How many lines were available in each office was also a problem, especially at this time in Rome. This station was busy for both BOAC and BEA and the telephones were in use constantly, hence messages were delayed quite regularly. Flight delays could subsequently occur from the lack of data being transferred between the BEA (Traffic) and BOAC (Ops) departments. Who was to blame? Very hard to ascertain and much argument occurred between the two management teams as a result.

Ciampino Airport had, for the staff like myself, the attraction of being on the outskirts of Rome, which meant we could live in Rome and enjoy the beauty and history of this wonderful city. As soon as I arrived in Rome I began to make plans to bring my wife Madge (Margaret really, but I have known her as Madge ever since I met her during the war) for a visit. What better present could you give a Catholic than a chance to visit the Holy Vatican City and St. Peter's Cathedral? Luckily the SOO, Tiny Cooling (the tallest and brainiest man I have ever met) fully appreciated my wish to see my wife after an absence of around three months, and coupled with this were my needs to discuss at HQ any future overseas assignments that they had planned – after all, my stay in Rome had been indicated as one month only.

So a long weekend in the UK was quickly organised, and this actually gave me my first flight in a Comet 1. The flight crew (which I had flight-planned and briefed) were pleased to welcome me on board as I joined them for the flight to Heathrow, London. This flight on a Comet 1 was a flight of a lifetime for me and was most exciting and memorable. This was before the Comet crashes at Elba and Naples had occurred, and the Comet 1 was at the time considered very safe, although the type had already had one crash near Calcutta; this had been explained as due to severe weather conditions, although the Indian Accident Inspector found evidence of the aircraft having broken up in flight, but his theory was not accepted, so the Comet 1 continued in service. But in retrospect his theory was proved right after the next two crashes. Should I have been so excited about this first flight on a Comet 1? In retrospect I think not!

The Comet 1 was a little underpowered, and at take-off special procedures had to be followed. The aircraft would be positioned (lined up) at the end of the runway with brakes firmly engaged, and then the engine power would be increased to take-off power whilst the brakes were still firmly holding the plane stationary. This resulted in the aircraft acting like a horse pulling at its bit, and when seated inside the plane you could feel the battle between brakes and engines until the Captain finally released the brakes, when the aircraft would shoot forward, pushing you firmly back into your seat. In my particular case, it threw me forwards as I was seated in one of the four rear-facing seats. This take-off technique ensured that full jet thrust power was available for the whole of the take-off run.

This take-off technique had been established after one Comet crashed on take-off from Rome in October 1952. The Captain of this particular flight was Capt. Foote who found that, although he had full engine power on, the aircraft was not inclined to leave the ground. He therefore made the decision – which was against the normal take-off procedures – to cut power, apply full brakes and abort the take-off, even though he was beyond the normal CP (critical point) as stated in the flight manuals. In going against the rules at that time, he definitely saved the lives of all on board; however, it did not save his reputation at the time and he was subsequently grounded. The aircraft went off the end of the runway, slicing its way through the approach lights and small trees. The wings came off the aircraft but fortunately no fire occurred. The fuselage remained intact and all on board were evacuated safely, although some had very minor injuries (cuts and bruises).

How right Capt. Foote had been in cutting power and applying brakes was proven a few months later in Karachi. Canadian Pacific Airlines took delivery of their first Comet 1 and were flying it around the world on its delivery flight to Canada. At Karachi the same – or a similar – situation arose on take-off and the Captain took the manual's stated action and applied absolute full power to the engines; but this was to no avail, as the aircraft remained firmly on the ground and crashed into a ditch at the end of the runway, blowing up and killing all on board.

Some years later Capt. Foote managed to clear his name and was granted his Pilot's Licence once again; he became a Flight Captain for BOAC on Avro Yorks and then later on Britannias; I met him often when he was flying Yorks through Cairo.

Returning to my flight out of Rome, once we were airborne the usual meal was served, but this time it was after we had reached an altitude of 33,000 feet, the highest I had ever been so far. On this occasion, the crossing of the Alps was in some ways less impressive. When in a conventional propeller-driven plane you were only 500-1,000 feet above the Alps and you could fully appreciate the majestic size of the mountains, but from much higher they all looked similar in height and not quite so impressive.

As I mentioned earlier, the flight crew knew I was on board because I had briefed them previously and, as expected, they invited me into the cockpit during the flight. This was my wish come true, and what a really great pleasure! The cockpit was a very compact area with little extra space for a visitor, but I was invited to occupy the Supernumerary Crew seat and was given a headset so that I could hear the ATC-to-crew conversations. This was good experience for an Operations Officer, to hear how exactly the crew used the flight plan details I had calculated for them prior to the departure from Rome.

During my spell in the cockpit a very unusual thing occurred. We were nearing Paris at 35,500 feet when two jet fighters suddenly appeared and formated alongside us, one on each side. The Captain was furious: how could military aircraft be allowed so near a civilian passenger plane in flight? Of course, he was right: it is acceptable for military planes to practise formation flying under wartime circumstances, but the risk of an accident was not acceptable in respect to civilian flights. The Captain gave French ATC a piece of his mind and the two military jets were ordered to leave us alone immediately. This they did with a wave of their wings in true military style.

For the final part of the flight into Heathrow Airport I had to return to my passenger seat. The weather in London was not good, low cloud and the dreaded fog, so the flight crew didn't really want anyone extra in the cockpit whilst they struggled with the elements outside. On the final approach all the passengers were straining to get the first glimpse of the land and then to know they were safely down. The approach seemed really long-drawn-out and the ground never became visible until almost immediately before we landed. The passengers were greatly relieved emotionally and started to clap and exchange comments on how wonderful the crew were to achieve such a perfect landing in such horrible weather. I must say I was impressed as well, on top of which it meant I would be home on time, without suffering any delay that a diversion would have caused.

During this visit home I learnt that after finishing at Rome I was expected to go to Buenos Aires for three months, another 'single assignment' (without my family) which I refused to accept. So I was then threatened with demotion, but after I had said "OK" to this I was then offered Rio de Janeiro for one month. This was not ideal, but I felt that Madge should be able to join me while I was there and we would then see one of the Wonders of the World. Once that was settled I requested that Madge be ticketed to join me in Rome and this was agreed.

My return to Rome was by conventional-type aircraft, the good old Argonaut once again, but even this was not without incident. As I was boarding the flight the Heathrow Duty Officer (who knew me well) approached me, saying: "Harry, I'm sorry but I have to ask you to change your seat; we want you to sit next to a very drunk sea captain (a Scot) who has been causing problems."

As the only staff passenger on the flight I had no option but to agree. It was then that I learnt what had upset the ship's captain so much and also why he had had too much to drink. His story was as follows: he had begun his journey from Prestwick Airport with a flight leaving at 05.45 to ensure he would be in London for the 08.00 departure of his flight to Singapore. Having made such a early start to his journey at the end of his home vacation, you can imagine his disgust when told that the travel agent in Scotland had mixed up his departure time from London; 08.00 *am* should have been 8.00 *pm*, and this meant that, not only had he to cut short his final night at home with his family, he now had to spend over twelve hours at Heathrow airport awaiting his evening departure. In retrospect the check-in agent at Heathrow should have offered him hotel accommodation, but for some reason or other he had felt it was his agent's fault, so why should BOAC accept the costs? Naturally, being a Scot, the captain wasn't prepared to pay for a hotel and decided to spend the day seated at the bar in the departure lounge. Twelve hours of drinking would make anyone tipsy.

We managed to get this passenger seated and I sat down beside him. At this time he didn't know I was 'staff,' so he was not rude or abusive to me, but now he was on the aircraft I found out why he was still moaning; it was the fact that he was *not* seated in the front row of seats (as a captain he was always at the front and not somewhere towards the rear). On this flight he had been given what was generally considered the "best seat" on this aircraft type for the long journey to Singapore, and the best seats on piston-engine passenger aircraft are always those *behind* the engines, whereas on pure jet aircraft the best are *in front of* the engines. This he could not either understand or accept: he felt the staff were mistreating him in the same way as the agent had in Glasgow.

By the time the doors were closed I felt I was in for a rough ride to Frankfurt, our first point of call. I tried hard to keep him talking about his fleet of ships in Singapore, but it was hard going until the engines were started; however their purr in his ears and the feel of the aircraft moving seemed to settle him completely, as if he was on one of his ships and 'under way'; he went sound asleep and even slept through the whole transit time at Frankfurt. When I got up to disembark at Rome some eight hours after leaving Heathrow, he did stir enough to consider getting off to stretch his legs before flying on to Cairo and eventually Singapore, so my return to Rome didn't turn out to be anywhere as bad as I had originally anticipated.

It was now back to the grindstone, coping with the multitude of flights operating to the north and south of the airport. Negotiations with the Europa Hotel ensured that when Madge joined me, the room cost would not go up (I already had a double room, so no real problem for the hotel). When Madge arrived we soon settled in; the hotel was near the 'Wedding Cake,' as it was affectionately known (the Victor Emanuel Memorial) and just down from the 'Spanish Steps' with its wonderful display of flowers for sale, which meant she could easily wander around the central part of Rome whilst I was at work.

Not long after her arrival, a message from HQ asked if I would mind staying another six to nine months in Rome; this I gladly accepted, as they knew Madge was with me, so although it showed as a single assignment, I was in fact accompanied, although without the married status additional expenses for BOAC. Nevertheless, under these circumstances both parties were satisfied.

With this news I then negotiated with the personnel department in London to obtain a flat for us and to pay for it instead of for my room at the hotel. Eventually they agreed and the search for an apartment was on, but in the meantime I found another better hotel near to the Via Venito, the posh end of town close to the American Embassy. The Hotel Denison was Danish-owned and run and had a good daily menu. Alongside the hotel was the massive wall to the "Hyde Park of Rome," the Villa Bolgiashy, and it was near the Portal Pincarny (Gateway to the Park).

Staying at this hotel was an American couple, and subsequently we found out that the husband was the new US Consul to Rome. They were looking for an apartment like us, but whereas we couldn't pay more than 50,000 lira per month, their limit was 250,000 lira. With this price differential, it was not surprising that they were the quicker to find a suitable apartment, and before long we were invited around for dinner. They certainly had a marvellous place, and it came complete with grand piano and Italian butler. Dinner was done to perfection, with a candle-lit table and one side of the table for each of us, with no chance of rubbing elbows whilst eating. The conversation was warm and friendly, but we realised that it was unlikely we would ever invite them to dinner at our house (or rather flat) that we hoped to find.

A few weeks latter we did find a very small well-furnished apartment near the Piazza Bologna, one of the suburbs of Rome. Here we did our daily shopping in the morning market. Mussolini had devised a system whereby the farmers brought their produce into town, and set up stalls each morning to sell direct to the public. The market would then close at 1 pm and by 2 pm you would never have known the market had ever been there. It meant the goods were cheaper and fresher, and everyone was happy with the arrangement. Madge found much more contentment being able to do her own shopping and preparing of our meals each day. It meant we were now living a normal married life in a foreign country, our first attempt at living a true 'overseas life', no longer the tourists, but foreign residents.

We had no car in Italy – in fact I still didn't hold a driver's licence – so we travelled around on the local buses and trolleybuses. We also did a lot of walking within the city and around the Vatican and St. Peter's Basilica. Needless to say, not being a tourist and knowing we were due to stay in Rome for more than six months, we didn't feel the need to rush to see all the historic sites and eventually end up not seeing some of the ones most tourists go to. However, we did grow to feel a part of the community of Rome and to accept the local conditions as normal. For example, young ladies have to expect their bottoms to be pinched whilst standing like sardines on the buses, something I found most distasteful but could do nothing about.

The rest of our time in Rome was enjoyable and, from the work side, a great experience. During this time we did see the end of the Comet 1 era. Firstly we had the Elba crash with its total loss of life of all on board, following which the Comets were grounded for many months whilst investigations took place. The flight crews of the Comet fleet were so confident that the aircraft was completely safe that the authorities eventually agreed and Comet 1 flights resumed, and subsequently I therefore became involved in another enquiry concerning the Naples crash.

In the time after the Elba crash and the return of the Comet into service, a number of test flights were carried out, particularly in the Khartoum area of Sudan, for high-temperature and tropical high-altitude tests. At the end of these tests and just before the Comet 1 came back into service, Captain Peter Kane, the Fleet senior captain, took charge of the flight home to London. This became a very momentous achievement, as it broke the record for the fastest flight from Khartoum to London. It was also the longest flight on record for a pure-jet aircraft; it was flight-planned to land at Rome *en route*, but as it approached Rome at 40,000 feet the crew requested clearance to London (Heathrow) with Gatwick as alternate. The Italian ATC rang me to ask if it was possible for the aircraft to fly that far, as according to his flight plan the fuel would run out 20 minutes prior to his arrival at London. I explained to them that as he had not reduced altitude and that he would continue to climb on his way to London, his hourly consumption of fuel would be reducing, thereby increasing his endurance accordingly. In the event they made it to Heathrow with no problems and Peter Kane told me later that on arrival at Heathrow he actually had enough fuel left to divert to Prestwick in Scotland if he had needed to. It was only after the fatal crash of the Comet 1 at Naples that the Comet crews fully realised that the aircraft had a technical problem.

The last of the Comet 1 crashes occurred late one evening. It was a BOAC Aircraft but on 'dry lease' to South African Airways (SAA) with South African crews on board. This lease arrangement had been going on for almost a year and I had got to know the flight crews whilst I was in Cairo. The crew operated the two sectors London/Rome and Rome/Cairo. This meant the operations briefing took place on the West side of the Airport. Instead of the crew coming to our office, I had to go and meet them in the passenger terminal and bring all the weather information and flight plan with me. This I did, and as it was near the end of my shift I spoke on the phone to the Night Operations Officer, who went direct to the office, and I then took the staff bus home. As it happens, the aircraft had crashed before I reached home, a most upsetting occurrence for us all.

Within BOAC we had a very well known and sometimes looked-down-upon Captain who always seemed to be in the right place at the right time and, on top of that, always made the right decision, whatever the circumstances. On the night of this Comet 1 crash he happened to be on his way to Rome in an Argonaut, and not far from Naples. Hearing all the ATC Calls going out for the SAA flight he had all his crews looking out for a possible sighting of the missing aircraft. Somehow or other he thought he saw something in the sea and descended down to about 2,000 feet to investigate. From this altitude he felt certain it was parts of an aircraft and informed the ATC authorities. Subsequently, local fishing boats did find parts of the Comet, thanks to the Captain's information.

It was, as always, Captain "Wonder Boy" Gibson's natural ability to do things like this that kept his reputation throughout his flying career. Not only was he gifted in this way, he was also a very fine pilot. Many a passenger, on departing the aircraft, would ask the First Officer: "Who landed the plane, it was so smooth?" It seemed that it was always Captain Gibson who had made the perfect landing, never the First Officer, and it made so many First Officers angry as they never achieved the smoothness of his landings or got questioned and praised by the passengers.

Back in the UK, the scientists and aircraft investigators made continuous tests on a fuselage of the Comet aircraft. They had the one that had crashed on take-off at Rome in 1952 to do the tests on. By using this fuselage they proved exactly how the aircraft broke apart due to metal fatigue around the windows. They even worked out exactly which window broke first and in what order the passengers and crew were sucked out of the aircraft due to depressurisation. From this detailed information the worlds airliner manufacturers could calculate the strength of construction needed to ensure future aircraft types would not suffer similar fates.

Now, fifty years on, many revelations are being published in the British press concerning the Comet 1 era. Would I have been so pleased to get a flight on the Comet 1 if these facts had been known in 1953? Would the crew have been so positive in their belief in the safety of the plane? I doubt it. Looking back in hindsight one has to think of the engineering and management Directors who ignored the known facts and took so little notice of the risks they were accepting, in the belief that the 'Jet Age' advantage BOAC had gained would have been lost to Britain if they had delayed the introduction until after the necessary checks had been carried out. History has proved that Britain would still have been the leaders if caution had in fact been taken. As George Brown, the Chancellor in Tony Blair's government would say: "A more prudent approach should have been taken."

During our time in Rome we did give one special dinner party, but it was only for four guests and ourselves – the dining room wouldn't hold any more people! Still, as our first attempt to entertain colleagues and their wives, it was a big event to us. What I do remember clearly is the amount of washing-up I had to do after they had all gone. The beauty of our little apartment was the fact that we had a massive amount of chinaware and glasses. Hence, after each course we just stacked the used dishes in the kitchen and served the next course on fresh clean plates etc, With a starter, soup, main course, dessert and then cheese & biscuits plus coffee it's surprising just how many items are by then in need of washing up.

Still it was a highly successful evening in which Madge exceeded all expectations in the quality of the meal provided. We were fortunate to find in the market the first of the wild strawberries for sale. They were fairly expensive but for the occasion could not have been better; they were soaked in sugar to which was added a decent helping of red wine, and they really tasted marvellous.

My mother also took the opportunity to visit us in Rome, having her first-ever flight. Much to our surprise she took the event very calmly, and even had a nap on the way. Whilst she was with us we took a bus trip down to Naples and hoped to visit Capri, but unfortunately the weather was terrible with rain and high winds all day, so after having a cup of coffee in Naples we got on the same bus back to Rome. Not the most successful day out!

Few other events remain in my memory about Rome, with the exception of the marvellous days spent at the Vatican viewing the treasures and reading some of the history of the whole area. Still the posting had to come to an end. One morning 'Tiny' Cooling (SOO) said he had a message from London HQ requesting my return to London for a permanent overseas assignment. Naturally, my first reply was: "Where to?" When Tiny said they wouldn't say, this made my mind go into overdrive: it had to be one of the worst possible stations such as Bahrain, Basra, Khartoum, etc., and so I returned to the UK dreading to hear where we would be living next.

The journey home only had one event of note. During our stay in Rome we bought ourselves a very large metal alloy trunk, about 5 ft 6 in long, 2 ft 6 in wide and the same in height, and when it was weighed it registered 82 kg. Our baggage allowance was officially 90 kgs and we had 6 more suitcases as well as the trunk. It would have been a problem if we were travelling by Comet 1, but they no longer operated; the Argonaut was much more forgiving and in the event it was not a full flight. When we arrived at Heathrow we had to present all baggage to Customs and they had special benches on which to display your cases. Our baggage filled one of these benches and when the Customs officer came to us he asked: "Is this all *yours*?"

Madge and I were standing together with me holding a rolled umbrella. In Rome you do what the Romans do and they always had rolled umbrellas because of the frequent showers. In the UK it was somewhat frowned upon to carry an umbrella in this way unless you were working in the City and were a top businessman.

My reply was a casual "Yes."

He then asked how long we had been aboard. When I told him we had been living in Rome for 10 months, he cleared all cases without opening even one, so off we went to get a taxi to go home to my mother's house.

The size of the trunk caused some amusement. It was around this time that there was a general search out for Ben Barka, a notorious terrorist whom they expected to be found dead. One of the airport porters said: "What have you got there, mate? Ben Barka?", and the people around roared with laughter. It's a good job we have London-style taxis, my baggage would have been difficult to fit into any other form of vehicle.

After a few days leave I reported to HQ to ascertain where I was going, and I was then sent to see a different Personnel Manager. Being a novice to overseas assignments, I didn't realise that this next posting was to be to a different part of the world from Africa or Europe, hence the change of Personnel Managers. Anyway my first question soon enlightened me of the reason for the change.

I asked: "Why the change of Personnel Managers?" to which the immediate response was: "Don't you know where you are going?" When I said: "No," I was quickly informed that I was going to Gander, Newfoundland. I had never thought it possible that I might be posted to North America. Mind you, as to what Gander would be like, I knew it would be a somewhat isolated place with much cold bad weather; still, it was not Khartoum, Bahrain or Basra – it must be better than any of those places. Madge had never heard of the place either, so it took me some time to explain just where it was and the type of weather there.

Anyway they made sure that I had all the leave I was due and we spent the time at home gathering what we thought we would need in Gander. We also sold our house; I felt we might find it hard to settle down in Gander if we still had a house in the UK, and it's so easy to become dissatisfied with a assignment like this to a strange country. As it happened, the assignment was suddenly cancelled a few weeks later as accommodation suitable for a married couple was not yet available.

So back I went to see Personnel and was once again passed over to another Personnel Manager. It was then that I heard we were now going to go to Rangoon, Burma. This didn't sound as good as Gander and it meant that all the cold-weather clothes we had bought would be useless; we would now have to shop for light-weight waterproof clothing. This revised posting didn't make us happy and, as luck would have it, it too was subsequently cancelled, so it was once again back up to HQ; here I was passed back to the Personnel Manager for North America and told that the Manager (Maritimes) – Gander, Goose Bay, Stephenville, Moncton and Sydney, Nova Scotia were the Maritime Stations – George Watson, had arrived in the UK and was assuring everyone that brand-new accommodation (houses) would be ready for Madge and myself within ten days or so of our arrival. Based on this information they were happy to send us to Gander for a full contract assignment.

It was our lucky day, the next seven years would direct our lives for the rest of our days, and so in hindsight we are extremely lucky and happy. "Gander, here we come!": we were fully ready for the adventure!

CHAPTER 8

NORTH AMERICA

Prior to going to this Atlantic Station I had to get training on how to flight-plan the different kinds of aircraft operating on these routes. They included the 1049 Super Constellation (and smaller 049), the 749 Constellation and Boeing 377 Stratocruiser. These aircraft had a longer range than the Argonaut, Hermes and York, therefore were more suitable to fly over the large amount of ocean with no near navigational aids or emergency airports to land at along the way. Routeing decisions were naturally far more critical to select than when flying over land.

These were the first American-designed and manufactured aircraft that I had had to deal with operationally. The flight planning was slightly different and had to be got used to. On some occasions you would use "Pressure Pattern Flying," employed when you calculated a set course to fly by using the knowledge of the winds around the pressure patterns *en route*. The actual track the aircraft followed was controlled by the winds but resulted in an eventual arrival over its final destination. It didn't always work, but some flights leaving Nantucket (just outside New York) would set a course of, say, 075 degrees magnetic and stay on that course right across the Atlantic to find themselves over Shannon, Ireland, their next destination. Much depended on how well the weather maps reflected the actual conditions experienced.

Over the Atlantic the ATC was called "Oceanic Control" and the main stations were Prestwick in Scotland and Gander in Newfoundland. There were no defined Airways Routes; aircraft could be flight-planned in any direction or altitude subject to the winds and provided they were acceptable to Oceanic Control. Hence, depending upon where the flight originated, a trans-Atlantic flight would be handed over between Prestwick and Gander Oceanic Controls somewhere along Longitude 30 degrees west according to the many different places that the aircraft had been planned to cross.

"Pressure pattern flying" was soon changed to "Best Time Track" flight plans, which entailed using the weather charts provided by the Meteorology Office in a different way and calculating the quickest flight route using the wind components indicated by the isobars on the charts. This method was quite accurate; it was surprising how much time and fuel could sometimes be saved, and it was used right up until the time that the amount of traffic over the Atlantic was so great, and the aircraft range had so improved, that Oceanic Control would define a number of specific routes that aircraft could select to follow. In other words, we now have produced specific Routes that aircraft must follow, and this is still what happens today.

Having had a quick bit of training it was now time to go to Gander. Nowadays it would be quite simple to go to whichever airport you were assigned, but in the mid-1950s the weather could still have a major effect on air travel. We boarded our flight to Gander one day in early June 1954, thinking that the next morning we would be in Gander and starting our duties in Newfoundland, but the weather immediately intervened; on take-off we were informed we would be landing at Shannon in the Irish Republic to refuel, and whilst on the ground there we were served a very nice meal (dinner), resulting in our spending five hours' travel prior to actually commencing our first flight across the Atlantic Ocean. We still had twelve or more hours of flying before arriving in Gander, but little did we realise, at this time, that Gander was not necessarily our next point of call.

The sector Shannon-Gander was spent mainly attempting to get some sleep, not easy when your mind was racing around with the prospects this new assignment would bring. However, we hadn't anticipated being told (ten hours into the flight) that the weather at Gander was so poor (this was in June) that we would have to overfly and go on to Montreal (the final destination of this particular service). In Montreal, Immigration and Customs (all French-speaking) gave us a hard time. Every suitcase and box of our belongings was opened. Why were we coming to Canada without obtaining visas? Who were our sponsors? Were we immigrating to Canada? Eventually I managed to get hold of a BOAC representative who soon cleared our problem, a problem that would never have existed if we had landed in Gander. In Gander Immigration and Customs were very pro-British with no language problems or racial reactions. However, in spite of the French connection, we were landed OK and sent to central Montreal, where we were given hotel accommodation.

The next three days were spent sight-seeing, but with our minds far from tranquil as we had to stay in touch with the BOAC Town Office in case there was a flight to Gander at short notice. While held up in Montreal we did manage to climb the 360 steps up to see the midday gun being fired, an occurrence that has gone on for years, if not centuries. The hotel was good and we were introduced to grilled salmon cutlets, something neither of us had previously eaten. Truthfully, we had not really changed our eating habits from those under wartime rationing in the UK; only once had we had an extra two sausages above our normal rations from the butcher at home; our short time in Rome had not adjusted our eating habits to take advantage of the abundance of foods available in Canada and the western world.

Our forced sojourn in Montreal eventually came to an abrupt end. A BOAC flight had landed in Gander and clipped the wing of another aircraft whilst taxying to the stand. The wingtip needed replacing and so the passengers were stranded in Gander until another aircraft could be sent to Gander to pick up these delayed passengers. The nearest aircraft was in Montreal, and we were out looking around Montreal and not contactable at the time, although fortunately we went back to the hotel for our lunch, where we were immediately grabbed and sent to the airport (Dorval) to position to Gander and commence my duties. It was a real rush around getting ourselves repacked and on the flight, but we were pleased to be eventually going to Gander and whatever was in store for us.

Our first glimpse of Gander was unimpressive. The cloud base was only just over 200 feet and everything looked grey and misty. Considering it was mid-summer, we were not impressed. A continuous light drizzle was falling and, although the grass was green, the wooded landscape and lakes did not seem attractive or encouraging, especially after seeing the facilities at Montreal. Still, this was where we were supposed to settle and work, and we had resolved within our minds that this is what we intended doing.

Our first few days in Gander were quite strange. There were no signs of new houses being built (although we had not yet been shown where the new town site for Gander was), and we were taken to an 'H' block ex-military-type hut arrangement and shown what was expected to be our apartment for the time being. As we entered, Fonze Holloway (the station handyman) said: "You are *lucky*, you have a carpet!" This took us so much by surprise that we didn't notice that we had no furniture in what was supposed to be our furnished lounge. In fact, when we had come to our senses, we realised just how much was missing from the apartment. For one thing the beds were disgusting: two army hospital cots that were stained from head to toe. This was the last straw, and I demanded to see the Manager (Maritimes), George Watson, and demanded replacement of the beds. George Watson, true to his word, went with us to buy the best double bed available in Gander, and it was delivered the next morning.

It was then that we learned that the move into our new houses had been delayed and that we could expect to be in our so-called apartment for at least 6 months. We also learned who were our real friends amongst the contract staff. All contract staff were living at the same camp site and in similar-type accommodation. However, they had raided each apartment as it was vacated, removing any furniture that they considered desirable, so we, the last arrivals, were left with the bare minimum. Of course, George Watson should have monitored what was going on but, being the trustworthy type, accepted whatever he was told by Fonze Holloway and assumed everything was in order. Anyway Francis de Salvo

Hall, one of our flight operations assistants from London, helped me raid the Caribou Club for easy chairs and a table and, while this meant we were still not very well furnished, at least we could relax together.

The BOAC camp site was at the western end of the runway, the opposite end to the office and terminal buildings; there were no shops there and so you relied on using the Duty Land Rover, although we only had one on station, which was used to cover all shift changes and then, if possible, for staff shopping trips. Most flights landed between 22.00 and 06.00 daily, however we did have to cover the office 24 hours per day to ensure that there were always staff at the office in the event of a diversion or a delayed flight. Normally, the day-shift staff member would come home for his lunch and this made the Land Rover available for the wives to be taken shopping. The squabbles over who had the Land Rover were many and often; it could hold only six people at a time and often eight or ten were waiting its arrival during the lunch-hour staff break. This made us realise that the quicker we had our own car the better, so we saved every bit of money we could and in the October we felt we had enough to venture down to St John's (the capital of Newfoundland) to chance our arm and buy a car.

During these first few months in Gander we made a great friendship with one of the local Operations Assistants, Johnnie Power. He had been born in St. John's and knew someone in one of the biggest garages there who would help us select a reliable motor; this was most reassuring, as the second-hand cars available in Gander were all well past their sell-by date. So with free tickets on TCA (Trans Canada Airlines) we took the morning flight to St. John's. Johnnie Power's friend met us at the airport and took us to the garage, where he handed us over to the Sales Manager to show us around. This friend was a mechanic, so dared not try to openly influence us against the Sales Manager, but by staying nearby, he would nod his approval or otherwise.

It was here that my Madge showed her bargaining prowess, once we had selected the car we felt suited our needs. It was then that we needed to get the price down to what our budget would stand. Initially we were trying to get a small English-style car, as having just arrived in Canada we were not used to the idea of having one of the large American cars; however we soon found out that the small English cars did not withstand the Canadian climate and were rarely worth buying if over a year old. The salesman showed us a two-door Pontiac and suggested we take it on a test drive, then we would see the advantage of buying a Canadian-model car. He was certainly right; the car was marvellous to drive, everything worked, it was spacious and it would withstand the winter weather and the rough roads around Gander. Our main problem now was to get it for a price we could afford.

Fortunately, the salesman had Irish ancestors and, although he had never been to Ireland, had a broad Irish accent. Madge, being from Ireland, felt at home and pressurised him into lowering the price of the car, and eventually she succeeded in bringing it down to our maximum limit and we signed the deal. Madge had really enjoyed herself and we both ended up very pleased with our day's work. The car was now ours but we still had to get it back to Gander.

It was then that we learnt that the last train of the year left Clarenville the following day at 11 am. It was vital that we caught it as there was no road between Clarenville and Gander and cars had to be ferried by train over this part of the route. This meant a very early start (5 am), as there were nearly 100 miles over unknown roads to drive, so we asked where to get a good meal, had our dinner and booked into a small guesthouse for the night; we got to bed as early as we could, although it was still after 10 pm.

The next day, 29th October 1954, it was still dark when we started up the car and began to find our way out of St. John's. We had had no breakfast but had been told where we would find a good café just at the end of the paved roads, about 30 miles outside St. John's. The car was behaving perfectly, we were making good time and I was getting used to driving the Pontiac, when suddenly we found that the road had turned and we were racing directly at a massive clump of rocks fifty or more feet high. Instinctively I swung the steering wheel over to the right in an effort to remain on the road. The car made a 90-degree turn and when I released the wheel fortunately it automatically centralised the steering and we were now travelling along the same road once again, but on the wrong side. Also Madge was sitting on my lap as the sharpness of the turn had bodily lifted her off her seat and onto me. Neither of us talked for a few moments whilst we got over the shock of the occurrence, and it made us realise that we were in for some journey getting to Clarenville.

Not long after this we found that we had a puncture. I stopped and got the car jack out along with the spare wheel. It was the American-type jack that hooked onto the bumper bar, something not heard of these days, and unfortunately, while it would lift the body weight of the car, it would start to slip once it felt the full weight. As luck would have it, a car full of 'Newfys' came along on their way to work, so I waved them down and in true 'Newfys' fashion they set to to change the wheel for me. They must have been late for work but you have never seen a wheel changed so quickly; we tried to thank them but in a second they were in their car and on their way.

But we were again on our way as well, and we soon came to the end of the tarmac road. Knowing we had a punctured tyre and a car jack that wouldn't lift the car, we decided that we must get the tyre and also the jack fixed. The one and only garage agreed to fix both but only in their spare time; cars requiring petrol had first priority. This put paid to us getting any breakfast prior to completing our journey.

Thankful to be on our way at 09.15 with 75 miles still to drive and all on gravel surfaces, off we went; at times we were doing over 75 miles per hour with the dust flying out behind us. Much to my surprise Madge was often urging me to overtake lorries when it was impossible to see through the dust they were making whether any vehicle was coming in the opposite direction. On one occasion we heard what we thought was a train whistle coming from the trees alongside. We failed to understand that this whistle was directed at us until the road suddenly turned and we shot across the rail track. Our faces turned white at the shock of seeing a train approaching the crossing no more than 50 yards away.

The rest of the journey into Clarenville was uneventful, and as we approached the town the speed limit was reduced to 20 mph, but we had to ignore it as we still had to get to the train. Clarenville is not a large place, just a few hundred dwellings, a couple of shops and the railway station, but it was important locally as it was the end of the roads into the centre of Newfoundland. Everything had to go by train from here on if it was needed anywhere to the west or north.

I soon spotted the train engine and its driver as the flat-topped railcars were positioned onto the passenger coaches. Using the car horn I indicated that we wanted to board the train with our car and the driver pointed to where we must go to get our tickets; this we did in all haste and then found where I had to take the car for loading. The driver was very helpful; he went and collected another flat-topped railcar especially for our car and I managed to back the car up an extremely steep slope on to it. Once this was done we looked around for somewhere to buy some food, but soon realised that our only choice was the small shop on the station, where they only had sweets; so we grabbed a few bars of chocolate and rushed to get a seat on the train.

Seated in the old-fashioned carriage, we reflected on our journey so far and felt thankful that we had achieved our goal without any accident. Now we could relax and eat our chocolate because we were starving, so we opened a bar and were about to eat it when we noticed that it was green with mould. We opened the next, and the next, only to find that they were all in the same state – uneatable. We were furious, but still happy – at least we were on the train and heading for Gander.

The ride from Clarenville to Gander took nearly four hours, although it was just a little more than forty miles. The 'Newfy Bullet,' as the cross-Newfoundland train from St. John's to Stephenville was known, was certainly not known for its speed and the Clarenville-to-Gander section was the slowest. In fact it was nearly 4 pm when we were allowed to disembark at Gander.

Being the last flat-topped railcar to be loaded at Clarenville meant that we were the last off in Gander; there were twelve flat-topped railcars each containing two cars ahead of ours, so we had quite a wait before being permitted to drive off. I ought to mention the primitive way the cars were secured to the flat railcars: 4 in x 2 in blocks of wood each two feet long were nailed to the flat-bed in front of and behind the wheels of each car. There were no chains or ropes to secure the vehicles, so it was in fact just as well that the train went so slow. It was the nails used to secure the cars that lengthened this saga of our journey back to Gander. To drive off the train meant carefully driving over strips of metal placed in the gaps between the flat-bed; these strips were not that wide and one of the railway staff had to ensure they were correctly aligned before allowing you to proceed over each gap. What they also could have ensured was that the nails used in securing the cars had definitely been removed, but unfortunately this was not the case, and as a result we ripped two of our tyres in the process of disembarking and they were completely flat and ruined by the time I had driven to the nearest and only garage in Gander.

Getting home to our apartment under our own steam was eventually achieved only after we had had to buy two new tyres and await their fitting, the usual problem being that refuelling of cars had priority over all other functions. After the enforced wait we were really starving and thirsty by this time and extremely tired, so when we finally got home we decided for quickness to open a tin of soup and boil the kettle for a cup of tea. Once we had had that, it was to bed (7 pm) for a well-earned rest.

The next morning, fully rested, we proudly displayed our purchase from St. John's. For some weeks we had great pleasure in relating the experiences of our journey from St. John's and I expect many heard it time and time again. For Madge and myself it will always be a gripping memory and was the turning point in our stay at Gander. By the way, we sold that Pontiac seven years later when we were posted to London at the end of our contract in Gander, and it was still in very sound condition. Years later I heard that it was still in use by the person I sold it to, so we had really had a good bargain in St John's.

TOP: Our house and Pontiac car in Gander during the mid-fifties.
BOTTOM: The Pontiac has been dug out on a typical snowy morning, but Jeannie seems willing to offer some help! Photos: the author.

Our band, the *Solidaires*, in Gander. The author is on piano at extreme L.,

CHAPTER 9

SOCIAL LIFE IN GANDER

From the 30th October 1954 Madge and I began to enjoy life more in Gander. We could now go for a ride to the shops or drive to the new town site and see how the construction of the new houses was progressing; it also helped us select which one we wanted etc. Also we could go to bingo nights or the cinema if I was off duty; we didn't have to wait for a lift with someone else. The car gave us the freedom we needed if we were going to settle down and enjoy this isolated posting.

Around this time Paddy Dunne arrived on a temporary assignment for a few months to cover someone's leave. He had a vast amount of experience at numerous stations overseas with BOAC, and was married, but his wife did not like overseas life and preferred to stay in the UK and send their children to school locally. But Paddy enjoyed overseas life and they both enjoyed the extra money it brought to the family. Staff on temporary duties were always accommodated in the local hotel, and in Gander's case, this was in wartime barrack blocks adjacent to the terminal building, aptly named Saturn and Jupiter. The rooms were very small and all meals had to be taken in the terminal building restaurant, which meant walking 100 yards across the road, no matter how bad the weather was; it certainly didn't compare with the comfort we had had in Rome with its luxury hotels.

Paddy was a real character; he could tell a joke better than most people and could see the funny side of many otherwise unpleasant circumstances. Madge needed cheering up and I felt that Paddy and his humour would do us both good, so I arranged to bring him home with me after finishing my day duty. We reached home around 5 pm and I introduced Madge to Paddy and the three of us hit it off straight away; he could see the funny side of being stuck in a terrible hotel and he also appreciated our disgust at the accommodation we were enduring. Once the formalities were over we had a drink and discussed anything and everything that came to mind.

We were crowded into the kitchen that also acted as a dining room. As the dining room table was only 3 ft by 2 ft 6 in there was nowhere to layout our best china etc. The meal started around 7 pm and we remained seated around the table for the rest of the evening and half the night, as Paddy had so many incidents to relate from when he was at Foynes in Ireland (the Shannon flying boat base) to Tripoli in Libya. Naturally the drink was flowing freely and, although Madge doesn't drink, she was still fully involved with the conversation and the amusing events recalled by Paddy. Paddy, being a true Irishman, always had his little man with him, his leprechaun, whom you would find seated either on your right or left dependent on where Paddy decided he was. It was one of the happiest and funniest evenings Madge and I have ever had, and it broke the ice for us at Gander; from now on life in Gander was associated with laughter and happiness, as Paddy became a part of our activities and enjoyment.

To give you an idea on what was making us laugh so much, I had better relate one of Paddy Dunne's tales. The funniest one I can recall concerned his posting in Tripoli. The incident occurred in the late 1940s, probably 1949 or 1950. BOAC had York freighters whose flights started in Calcutta and, after numerous stops *en route*, eventually arrived in Tripoli prior to continuing to London Heathrow.

The York was a high-winged aircraft with the fuselage near the ground and a small tailwheel, which meant that the rear of the aircraft was just off the ground. Because of this low stance, the engineer was able to go to the small rear door, open it, put his head inside and call up to the crew: "Any snags?", whereupon the crew would normally reply: "No snags." On one particular York flight, a parrot was loaded in Calcutta destined for London. It endured all the many stops and got quite familiar with the happenings that re-occurred at each station. This was the case all along the flight and the parrot, being such a 'copycat,' soon joined in the fun. When the Station Engineer opened the rear door on arrival at Tripoli, he made the normal comment: "Any snags?' and the parrot, quick as a flash, replied: "No snags." The aircraft stayed overnight at Tripoli and this incident caused so much amusement that one or other of the ground staff would go up to the aircraft, open the door and shout: "Any snags?" and the parrot would promptly reply: "No snags." To make everything sound even funnier, Paddy Dunne would imitate the parrot's reply by talking out of the side of his mouth. It certainly made us laugh and still does to this day.

The next day our neighbours asked: "What were you up to last night? All we could hear was laughter coming from your place." They just couldn't imagine how only three of us could have such fun, the likes of which had never been heard of in Gander before.

I feel now that I had better make you aware of the sort of place Gander was. We had our first signs of snow during September, although it never fully settled until late November. The last falls of snow were at the beginning of May, and it was known to be up to 10 feet deep on the ground at this time. The period between June and August could be a mixture of sunshine and showers. I always said: "We have 9 months winter and 3 months bad weather." With this as a basis to what life was like in Gander, it is easy to realise what a hardship posting it really was, in particular for the wives. We men had our work, which was intensive and demanding. BOAC had as many as 500 flights per month crossing the Atlantic Ocean and they all went through the airspace controlled (operationally) by Gander Operations. Every flight was flight-planned from Gander, or re-flight-planned or re-directed to one of the other airports under our responsibility, which were: Goose Bay (Labrador), Stephenville (Newfoundland), Moncton (New Brunswick), Sydney and Halifax (Nova Scotia) and finally St. John's (also in Newfoundland).

Although our main work was Operations, we still had to deal with Passenger, Cargo and Mail aspects at the airport. The passenger side was only a real problem when a delay occurred. There was so little you could offer the passengers during the delay, but it still didn't stop them giving us as rough a time as they could. Mind you, we did have the Caribou Club, which had been formed when Imperial Airways operated flying boats to Botwood near Grand Falls, the next town to Gander but fifty miles to the west.

In those early days there were up to 200 staff and aircrew based in Newfoundland, and the Club was used to give some sort of recreational facilities on base. In those days the manager and his wife ran the whole camp like a hotel. Most of the staff were single and meals were served in the mess in a formal manner, with the manager seated at the head of the table and everyone in semi-formal dress. Waiters served all meals and the manager's wife was responsible for hiring and firing the cooks and waiters as well as deciding what food would be served. Fortunately, by the time we were in Gander that formal type of prewar life was over. Madge and I would not have liked to have had to eat with all the other staff; we much preferred to prepare our own meals, even though we had such primitive facilities.

The crews certainly didn't like the 'crew slip' (stop-over) at Gander and many a crew would try to divert to Goose Bay or Stephenville if the Gander weather was problematic. In this way the Captain could then extend the duty hours, refuel the aircraft and fly on to New York, Boston or Montreal, whichever was the flight's final destination. This meant that the crew waiting at Gander would be left stranded waiting for a flight, any flight, to land.

It is said that on one occasion, when the weather at Gander was particularly bad, one crew had to wait *seventeen* days for a flight to land. One Captain suffering this way was annoyed beyond the limit when the staff asked the CBC (Canadian Broadcasting Company) to play a special request for him (by this time he had been waiting about ten days); it came on the radio (which was always blaring away at the Caribou Club), just as he entered the club for his evening drink. The request was for *'Stormy Weather, There's no Sun up in the Sky, Stormy Weather,'* and when the announcer dedicated it to the particular Captain he was so upset that he just turned round and walked out.

It was because of incidents similar to this that the crews got together and all agreed that they would extend their Duty Day up to 24 hours, or beyond (at Captain's discretion) and with approval of all the crew. This meant that they could fly London to New York, Boston or Montreal without a slip, something they could not be forced to do by the Company. Therefore, no crew slips were needed by the time I reached Gander: what a relief! With the removal of the crew slips the station staff were reduced to just nine for BOAC.

At this time Allied Aviation (a ground handling company) was formed and contracted to handle all flights landing at Gander. They did all the passenger check-in and cargo acceptance work as well as providing all the ground-handling equipment necessary to service the flights using Gander airport. The Managers of TWA, PANAM, BOAC, Air France and SAS controlled this company, and they governed the number of staff they (Allied Aviation) could employ and the amount of equipment they could purchase based on the predictions advised by the Manager of Allied Aviation.

Allied Aviation handled every flight landing at Gander and the airlines not included in this partnership were charged at a different and higher rate, which helped reduce the final sum paid by the five partners. The Allied Company were paid 10 per cent of the total cost of running the station; they were happy and so were the five airlines involved. Prior to this innovation, each of the five airlines employed up to 200 staff each on site, but the numbers needed could be greatly reduced when operating as a single unit.

By the time I arrived, the only thing left over from the period prior to Allied Aviation's arrival at Gander was the Caribou Clubhouse, which gave us somewhere nice to meet and have a drink at the bar and, on occasions, dance to live music or records. The premises were also used sometimes to entertain delayed passengers, provided the Mounties (police) gave their permission. I remember one such occasion when we had passengers at the Club; it was New Year's Eve and the flight from New York to Prestwick suffered a technical delay. We had around 100 passengers stranded, mostly Scots wanting to get home for Hogmanay in their Old Country. I must say that although they were truly upset at not getting home in time for New Year's Eve, the food, drink and music we provided made them much happier. One particular Scotsman grabbed my arm as I helped him off the bus at the airport after the party and said: "You remind me of my brother in Scotland whom I haven't seen for forty years." It was in fact his first attempt to go home since having immigrated to America.

In Newfoundland you could buy alcohol at bars, clubs and hotels but you had to have a permit to have a drink in your own home. In Gander, once we had obtained our alcohol permit, we were then permitted to order our requirements from St. John's. The train to Gander shipped it and we collected it from the station when it had eventually arrived.

Surprisingly, we always seemed to have enough to cover our needs! Mind you, we could always think of some special need to entertain so-called "business clients" to get extra allowances. The Club was limited as well, so an evening entertaining delayed passengers always meant we could get an extra supply agreed at St. John's.

As previously mentioned, the car gave us the freedom to visit places out of Gander. One of our first trips was to Grand Falls, which meant a 50-mile drive over rough gravel roads and across the river near to the actual falls. The river crossing was on a really primitive ferry, a type of raft with a small boat tied to its side and linked to a cable stretched across the river. The water coming over the fall meant that the current was quite strong and it was a wonder the raft didn't get carried downstream with its load, which was a maximum of two cars per trip. I must say that on our first trip over we were quite worried; still, you soon accept this sort of thing as normal once you have accepted life in Newfoundland.

Once over the river you came onto a stretch of paved roads that ran from Grand Falls to Botwood and the old flying boat slipway. Of course no flying boats operated now, but you could see where those planes were docked and repaired. They had been using this base during the war and until around 1949, the end of the flying boat era. Many people regretted the end. My neighbour in Gander was a wireless operator in Oceanic Control and he had records of every message sent and received between one of the flights from Foynes and Botwood in 1934. The flight had taken over 24 hours in those early days, so when you came on duty after a night's rest, the same aircraft and crew would be contacting you. They were really long flights at that time, not just three and a half hours as done by Concorde.

This neighbour had another interesting tale to relate. Prior to being part of Oceanic Control at Gander, he had been a railway signalman near St. John's. On one foggy day he suddenly heard a noise above him and, looking up, he saw a German airship hovering above, from which a crew member was calling to him asking which way to St. John's. Aviation was quite primitive in those days! Naturally he pointed the way, and off went the airship with the quick comment: "Thanks!"

Grand Falls was quite a large town with some good shops to browse around. The main industry was well established by the British Company Bowaters and they processed the logs floated continuously down Gander Lake to the mill in Grand Falls. The town was established purely because of the mill and the work on offer attracted the population to the area. The Gander area was uninhabited until the airport construction started in the late 1930s, and with the war starting its demand for people grew rapidly. For this reason it was a very young town with the main age group being in their early twenties and thirties. When we arrived the population had risen to about 5,000, of which 3,000 were children: the long cold winter nights ensured a steady increase of local inhabitants! The location of Gander was the result of a survey completed in the 1930s, and to this day it is questionable as to whether the right spot was chosen; it didn't have the best of weather records in respect to aviation.

The next most important airport for Atlantic flights after Gander was Goose Bay, Labrador. Fortunately, when Gander was closed because of weather, Goose Bay was normally open and was therefore used as the main alternate. Because of its importance BOAC decided that they should have a representative based there. This posting was more isolated than Gander and a lot further north, and I learnt later that they had tried to arrange for Madge and myself to go there, but as only a hotel room and not a house would be the only family accommodation available, they had decided to send a single man there instead.

The man selected, Richard, was in his mid-twenties and was well known by Paddy Dunne. He was sent to Gander to 'learn the ropes' about the area and to be briefed by Manager (Maritimes), George Watson. He turned out to be the nephew of the BOAC Chief Pilot Johnnie Woodman, and he was ragged about this by Paddy Dunne. He was one of the original trainees, joining at the age of 18 years, and had been sent overseas as a junior assistant, but he felt he was being exploited and underpaid and under-promoted in respect to the job he was doing. Eventually, they brought him home to the UK and gave him the senior Operations and Traffic courses and he was made up to Station Officer (Overseas). On his interview by the General Manager Traffic prior to coming to Goose Bay, he was asked why he was still single, and his answer was quite sharp: "Well, look at the places you have posted me to!" The General Traffic Manager looked up his records and found he had been to Dacca (Bangladesh), Tripoli (Libya), Khartoum (Sudan) and a few similar places. Anyway, not to be stumped, the Manager said: "Maybe you will be luckier at your next posting. Where is it?" When told it was Goose Bay they both burst out laughing.

We welcomed Richard at Gander and took him around to the bingo and cinema along with Paddy Dunne. After these sorts of nights out, we usually ended up at the Caribou Club for a drink. As the bar closed at 11 pm we always asked for a few beers to be left out for us at the bar. We did this the night we took Richard out with us but didn't realise that he never drank alcohol. The bingo hall had been very hot, and when we arrived back at the Club we all grabbed a beer, including Richard; like us he downed it in almost one gulp and as he took the bottle from his mouth he started to sing, he was already drunk and unable to stand steady on his feet. Paddy Dunne was extremely good; he understood the situation perfectly and looked after Richard for the remainder of the evening. The poor fellow was quite ill during the night and was nursed by Paddy until he went to sleep. Eventually Richard did get married in Goose Bay to a young Canadian lady and he still lives in Canada somewhere.

It was now coming up to Christmas, our first in Newfoundland, and the snow was regularly falling. Luckily the houses were now ready for us, but the furniture had to be ordered and this raised one more question: what old furniture could be taken to the new houses and how much extra needed to be ordered? In our case it was decided that we needed a houseful including a new cooker and refrigerator. Those who had collared all the furniture at the camp found that they were only getting a small amount of new stuff, and this really did put the cat amongst the pigeons: why should we be the only couple to move into a completely brand-new home and be supplied with brand-new furniture? We told them we were not giving up any of this new furniture, as we had suffered because of their greediness for the last five months and we were rightfully getting compensation only now. We were also lucky in getting the first house taken by BOAC at the entrance to the new Gander Town. It meant that we could go to the shops without being spotted by anyone else in our group. This gave us a lot more freedom, something we truly cherished. It also cut out quite a bit of the gossip concerning ourselves, which is what we also wanted. It allowed our friends to come and go without the whole station knowing.

The houses were of wooden construction and consisted of three bedrooms, lounge and dining room combined with a basement the complete area of the house itself. In the basement was the oil-fired central heating system, which blew hot air into every room; all this resulted in us really looking forward to Christmas in real comfort. What a difference from the old camp site! The only thing we missed was the Caribou Club; however we did have one final party at the Club, which was great fun for all.

By the time our houses were ready to be occupied, some of the shops had opened and, although all roads were still just gravel and sometimes inches deep in mud, at least we did have shops to visit close at hand and three or more times bigger than they had been previously. Life was slowly becoming more modern and normal; we even had a new school and church being built. The old-time army barrack blocks were obsolete at last.

CHAPTER 10

DELEVOPMENTS IN CIVIL AIRCRAFT DURING THE FIFTIES

The next few years went past smoothly and with great happiness. In 1955 we got our first little girl, Jeannie, and in 1959 our second, Kathryn. On top of this I had been enlisted into the local orchestra and was playing at Clubs all over the island. The latter all happened by chance; Jack and Vivian, who were members of the Newfoundland Club (very difficult to join as the Club had a police restriction on the number of members), invited us for an evening out to dance and chat over a few drinks. Jack came from the North of England and was locally employed by BOAC as an Ops Assistant. His wife Viv was Canadian and owned the gift shop at the airport. They had been in Gander for a number of years before we came. Anyway, the group playing for dancing would do three numbers and then take a 30-minute break. This annoyed me and, after I had had a few drinks, I decided to ask them if I could play the piano while they had their drinks. It was agreed and I sat down at the piano and rattled off my party pieces (those I had learnt to play in Cairo). Much to my surprise, before I could finish the second piece I found that the entire group had returned, picked up their instruments and were playing along with me. I remained at the piano for the rest of the evening, being well supplied with drinks the whole time.

This chance evening resulted in my joining the group, trying to read music once again and earning pocket money at the same time. I was quickly given membership of the Newfoundland Club and remained a member for the next six years. The band became known as the Solidaires, and we travelled to many villages and towns like St. John's and Grand Falls to play on special occasions. We even did regular 30-minute broadcasts for the CBC (Canadian Broadcasting Corporation), which were broadcast nationwide. This all made the social side of life in Gander most pleasant, so I was happy both at work and at play.

On the work side, I gradually became accustomed to the work pressure of Atlantic flight-planning. It certainly was more exacting than flight-planning on airway routes as we had in Europe. Every flight plan went on a different route that you had to work out and measure yourself. There was only one Operations Officer on duty at a time, with one of the assistants monitoring the messages arriving from Oceanic Control.

Each of the aircraft types in use at this time had different manuals from which to calculate its speed and fuel consumption. Each aircraft type also had different weight limitations and different flight level restrictions based on its weight, so the circular hand computer was in constant use making all the calculations necessary. The Stratocruiser had the largest weight limitations, necessitating altitude restrictions; on take off at maximum weight (MTOW) it could only reach 11,000 to 13,000 ft initially and after about three hours they could rise to 15,000 to 17,000 ft. Then, after a few more hours during which it had used up a considerable amount of fuel, it could reach 19,000, 21,000 or 23,000 ft for the rest of the journey.

Flights crossing the Atlantic had 2,000 ft separation with westbound flights on even flight levels (10,000, 12,000, 14,000, 16,000, 18,000, etc.) and eastbound at odd flight levels (11,000, 13,000, 15,000, 17,000, 19,000 etc.). On westbound flights the normal winds were headwinds, so flights would remain at lower levels where the winds were not so strong. I can remember one SAS DC-6 accepting 4,000 ft as its flight level across the whole Atlantic, which was very low for a ocean crossing, even a bit on the dangerous side for a commercial flight. For eastbound flights it was better if they could get as high as possible to gain from the tailwinds that prevailed.

The Stratocruiser on eastbound trips could try to take advantage of these high-altitude winds by climbing to its maximum flight level of 25,000 ft, then setting the engines on normal cruise power and allowing the aircraft to enter what was called a power-glide until it had descended to a height it could maintain. This climb and glide procedure took about three hours to perform, resulting in the aircraft being able to then maintain about 17,000ft. If necessary, it could do the same thing again, climbing to 25,000 ft, going into power-glide and levelling off at 21,000 ft for the rest of the flight. In this way, it was always as high as possible and getting the benefit of the stronger tailwinds assisting it on its way. This sort of operation was not liked by Oceanic Control as the aircraft was going through so many altitude levels, risking interfering with other aircraft going in both directions, and this meant that it was rarely approved; aircraft had to struggle along at lower levels until they were light enough to climb higher later in the flight.

I feel I should make a comment about the weather ships positioned at precise locations in the Atlantic Ocean, and used by both ships and aircraft as navigation aids. You knew their exact position, so could take magnetic bearings from their radio beams and calculate your own position accurately. These ships stayed on station all the time, with crew changes made every three months or so, and at that time the opportunity was taken to replenish the ship's stores and fuel. It would always be an all-male crew, the same as remote lighthouses.

Naturally, having these long weeks and months in male company, the crews always cherished the sound of a female voice. I have heard from some of my pilot friends that, whenever they contacted one of the weather ships they were asked: "Can we talk to one of your stewardesses please?" This could usually be arranged and some hilarious conversations would take place; the ship's crew and the flight crews always enjoyed these occasions.

At this time BOAC employed some of the pioneers of aviation and among these were the captains flying the Atlantic. One such person was Capt. Bernard Frost, the most acknowledged aviator in respect to 'jet streams.' He realised that certain pressure patterns shown on the weather charts would indicate just where you were likely to find the jet stream and even how strong the winds were likely to be. This information could be used to great advantage if flights were routed correctly, although we Operations Officers in Gander did not always appreciate his intervention. We would have prepared his flight plan from Gander to Shannon, Prestwick or London, when he would send us a message saying: "Flight plan via 55N 40W, weather ship Juliet to final destination." We knew this was not the fastest track that night, but he was the Captain making the demand and so we had to re-flight-plan his trip as requested; it meant that he had seen the possibility of finding a jet stream and he wanted to prove he was right. His request meant that we would have to get out the maps, draw the track and measure the distances before making the new time and fuel calculations for the flight plan.

He was known to go looking for jet streams even on his westbound flights. He would request Oceanic Control to clear him to 24,000 ft whilst on his way to Gander, and then on reaching this altitude he would measure the wind and then immediately request descent to his original flight level. He always sent a message quoting what wind speed and direction he had found, so that the Met Office could add this information on their charts to verify the situation over the Atlantic. Of course, the passengers never knew that he had done this, or that it might have caused a extra fifteen or twenty minutes' flying.

BOAC realised that it was Captains of this era who were helping to develop aviation knowledge, so although they kept a close watch on their actions they never actually stopped them proving their points. Without this sort of action by these venturous men, aviation would have never developed to the present-day extent. The width of the Atlantic being a minimum of 2,000 miles meant that a very large area was unknown and could not be monitored closely for weather changes. Weather information is so important to aviators even today, but fifty years ago it could result in flights losing their way and even lives being lost.

Of course, as aircraft improvements were achieved, the limitations on flight-planning were reduced as aircraft could fly further and higher. In the late 1957/8 the DC-7C came in to service and could fly direct from London to New York, cutting out all intermediate stops such as Shannon, Keflavik in Iceland, Gander or Goose Bay. Then by the 1960s the aircraft range had risen to allow flights to go from Los Angeles to London non-stop, a truly remarkable feat at the time.

Before this came about however, we had the Comet 4 aircraft come into operation. Initially a Comet 4 was based at Gander doing daily proving flights to New York and Montreal in readiness for the introduction of pure jet passenger flights across the Atlantic. On this score, BOAC and Britain were in a race with PANAM and the Americans with their Boeing 707s. Who would be the first to cross the 'pond,' as the Atlantic was known? We got to know the flight crews staying with us in Gander quite well; some were pilots from the Comet 1 days and were very keen to get the Comet 4 opening up the Atlantic to this fast means of travel.

The Comet 4 was a very safe aircraft, and was over-powered in comparison to the Comet 1. One particular captain loved to show off just how good a take-off performance it had; he, Reggie Lantry, had flown the Comet 1, and by using the same take-off procedures when flying the Comet 4, the aircraft took off more like a fighter aircraft than a passenger jet. At Gander he would line up on the end of the runway, firmly engage the brakes and then rev the engines up to take-off power before releasing the brakes. The effect of this was to have the plane 'heaving at the bit,' like a stallion threatening a mad gallop but being controlled by its rider. The whole Comet 4 would feel as if it was trying to hover prior to the brakes being released, then with brakes off it would surge forward pressing everyone on board very firmly into the back of their seats.

The immediate gain in speed was tremendous and before you knew it the nose of the aircraft was facing the heavens in an almost vertical climb. Whenever, he did this the captain would proudly report to the Tower: "End of runway, altitude 1,800 feet, turning on course to ----." The usual departure pattern from Gander was to remain on the runway course heading until reaching 1,800 ft, this being normally achieved about five miles from the airport, but with Capt. Lantry's take-off this was achieved whilst still over the airport.

I was once on board a flight from Gander with Reggie when he made this sensational sort of take-off, and it was indeed truly sensational. The passengers seated ahead of you are seated in a straight line directly upwards with the floor of the aircraft at a 80-degree angle. Whether all passengers appreciated this exhilarating take-off I am not sure, but for me it was one of the 'wonders of flying.'

When the Comet 1 was introduced, its fairly short range limited it to the Hong Kong and South Africa routes, and it could not cope with the Atlantic. The Comet 4 with its better range was being introduced on the Atlantic, the Atlantic route being the most prestigious and commercially profitable route to fly, the 'Blue Riband' route in shipping company terms. Air Traffic Control (ATC) in New York had not previously experienced pure jet aircraft like the Comet 4 and it had to be explained to them that, once this type of aircraft descended below 20,000 ft, its range was so substantially reduced that it could not accept the landing pattern delays endured by piston-engine aircraft. A dedicated landing sequence had to be available and permission to land assured.

Jet engines work more economically at high altitude; a Comet 4 flying at 20,000 ft would have a maximum range of about 1,500 miles, whereas at its normal cruise altitude of between 33,000 and 40,000 ft its range improves to nearer 3,000 miles. This difference meant that ATC had to rethink its whole attitude towards the introduction and limitations caused by the arrival of pure jet aircraft and act accordingly. When a Comet 4 or Boeing 707 was approaching New York (or in fact any other airport), the captain had to know whether he could expect any delay in his approach to land before descending below the 20,000-foot level. If there was to be a delay, then he might have to decide to divert to his alternate airport, otherwise he could run out of fuel. It was for this reason that BOAC sent the Comet 4s to Gander for a few months, to allow New York and Washington airports time to train the ATC Controllers on how to handle this new type of pure jet aircraft. This same sort of restriction was also in force during the period when the supersonic Concorde flew the Atlantic.

Eventually that all-important day came when BOAC could initiate the first pure jet passenger flights across the Atlantic. Captain Stoney (Senior Captain, Comet Fleet) set off from New York and Captain Alabaster (Deputy Comet Fleet Captain) set off from London. The New York flight planned to fly New York-Shannon, with the chance of overflying to London direct. The London flight routed London-Gander-New York. We had beaten PANAM by a few days. The BOAC Chairman travelled on the London flight and made his press release statements during the transit in Gander. Naturally, we were all at the airport to see the flight and to meet all the dignitaries involved. Hobby Hobson requested I come in and do the flight plan from Gander-New York for him, so I was fully involved in this inaugural flight to New York.

This flight from London-Gander-New York was not without incident. On take-off from London they were unable to get full pressurization as a hold door was not properly closed. The flight engineer rushed to the rear hold of the aircraft and raised a hatch in the cabin floor, which revealed that the hold door was out of position. As hold doors on the Comet opened inwards and upwards, he placed his feet on the door and pushed in down into place, and in a few seconds the pressurization came into operation and all was well. I met Captain Alabaster as he came off the aircraft; he said: “Harry, we had a problem at Heathrow. Will you kindly ensure the hold doors are properly closed before we take off.” Naturally, I said: “Yes”. It soon became normal practice to ’wire lock’ the doors before each departure to avoid any re-occurrence of this sort of incident. If the flight engineer had not been as quick in resolving the door closing over London in flight, they would have had to jettison fuel and land, and the planned first flight prior to PANAM's would have failed. History would have had to have been re-written.

During my stay at Gander, aviation made many advances. The introduction of the Comet 4 and the Boeing 707 was only one part of it. We also saw the long ranged DC-7C from America and the famous four-engine turboprop British Britannia 312, affectionately known as the "whispering giant." This aircraft was made more famous because, although it was a technically a jet aircraft, it did not accrue the jet surcharge on fares as it had propellers and was therefore classed under the conventional aircraft rating. This saved about $70 per flight across the Atlantic, so it was a real winner as far as the Americans and everyone else were concerned. It cut about three hours off the normal prop aircraft flight times and it was so much quieter, a real boom for BOAC.

At this point I feel I should say a little more about this perhaps most famous of aircraft ever built in the UK, the Britannia. There were two versions, the Britannia 102 (short-range version) and the Britannia 312 (long-range version); although both types were used on the Atlantic, the short-range version had to make intermediate stops between New York & London and Montreal & London, whereas the long-range version could normally make New York-London non-stop. Since it was a jet engine, air pressure built up by the engine rotated the propellers, whereas a piston-engine plane had the propellers driven directly by the engine through a gearbox. The propellers of the Britannia therefore had to have brakes, otherwise they would rotate, driven by the wind - very dangerous for staff working on the airport.

I can remember talking with a Mountie who was watching Princess Margaret's flight start up on departure to London from Gander. There was a very strong wind outside and as soon as the propeller brakes were released, all four propellers started to rotate. "My, that's marvellous," he said; "I've never seen an aircraft start all four motors at once." Of course, if the wind was in the wrong direction, then the engineer on the ground would have had to hold each propeller *with his hand* until the air pressure produced by the engine took control of the propeller. When this was done, they could only release the brakes on one engine at a time. Holding the propeller does sound dangerous, but wasn't really.

The Britannia was rightly called the "whispering giant" as it was the quietest aircraft of all time. Although it could not quite keep up with the pure jet-powered aircraft it was still 100 mph faster than normal piston engine aircraft. It had one other strange peculiarity in regards to other models of aircraft at that time: because the ailerons were controlled through their aileron trim tabs, rather than the whole aileron itself, the whole aileron would hang down on both sides of the wing when the aircraft was stationary. Under normal conventional-type aircraft controls, one side would be 'up' and the other side 'down' when the aircraft was stationary. When the Britannia aircraft moved forward at a reasonable speed, the airflow over the wing would bring both ailerons up to their rightful position and they would then be fully controlled by the Captain's normal control column movements. On frosty mornings this made it hard to know if the ailerons were frozen in position and therefore needing de-icing.

Around this time there was a battle going on between the USA and Britain over what sort of land-based navigational aids should be introduced, VOR (Very long range Omni directional Radio range) or the DME (Distance Measuring Equipment) which was being financed by the USA in an effort to get its implementation worldwide. On the other side, Britain couldn't afford to financially sponsor their Decca system for short-range navigation, and DECTRA for long range, to be installed worldwide. The British system had advantages over VOR/DME in the initial set up, but the American equipment has subsequently been much improved in recent years.

The long-range DECTRA was installed in the UK with its master station near Prestwick, Scotland and the slave station in Newfoundland. The RAF was used to trial the system and the Vickers Valiant bomber was the aircraft chosen. They made a number of crossings from UK to Gander using the system for navigation, but also using their own navigator to ensure the accuracies of the navigation details. I spoke to the navigator of the last check flight on his arrival in Gander, who said: "From my navigation I calculated that we were 32 miles south of track, whereas the system said we were on line for Gander. Thinking my navigation was 'spot on,' I gave the captain a new course to cross Gander. What happened? We ended up 32 miles north of Gander – the system was right after all." Needless to say, the British Government was still unable to impress the Americans that the system was the best and as so many other countries had already installed VOR/DME, none were prepared to change. The mighty dollar had won the day.

CHAPTER 11

THE QUEEN'S VISIT

Comet 4 flights were always flight-planned from the destination backwards. You started off with the weight you needed for landing, this being weight of aircraft plus payload plus fuel to alternate and landing reserve, all added together. Knowing this final weight you could accurately calculate exactly how much fuel you required for the flight. In these early days of pure jet aircraft, Oceanic Control could easily guarantee separation over the Atlantic, so we could flight-plan on cruise climb (the most economic way) for all Comet aircraft. The initial altitude at top of climb would be 31,000 or 33,000 ft, and then the flight would cruise climb up to around 39,000 to 40,000 ft before starting its descent to land. In other words, as you used up fuel the aircraft became lighter and therefore increased its altitude, which then enabled further economy in fuel consumption. The same procedure had been used for Comet 1 aircraft in the 1950s and this technique extended its maximum range.

At the same time as these new aircraft were being introduced, we also saw aircraft like the York, Argonaut, Constellation and Stratocruiser ceasing operations with BOAC; they were not grounded but were used by charter companies instead. Aircraft like the DC-6 were downgraded to charter flights as well. Because of the increased pressure for speed, we even decided that at Gander we could cope with 30-minute transit periods, the only station to achieve this as standard on BOAC long-haul flights.

However this could only be achieved with good communications between all departments of ground handling. The Ground Control Officer would be passed the 'on blocks' time and to this he added 20 minutes. At this new time, he would automatically make the departure announcement. Engineers, operations and catering staff had to advise the Ground Operations officer if they were going to cause a delay. Surprisingly it worked very well, even when we had five or six BOAC aircraft on the ground at once. Mind you, by this time we had a brand-new passenger terminal at Gander, which the Queen had officially opened on her last visit to Newfoundland. Of course, the present-day security screening of passengers was not necessary at that time, so freedom to move passengers on and off aircraft was no problem.

Weather within the maritime states and in particular Gander was a major problem. We suffered so much fog, snow, freezing rain or drizzle that flights sometimes had to be diverted to their alternates; luckily, these always provided a safe landing place. Often when I was returning to Gander after leave, we would be diverted to Sydney (Nova Scotia) or

Moncton (New Brunswick), so different to the situation experienced today. The landing aids that we have now permit landings to be made in really severe weather, however these were not in use in the period 1954 to 1961. At Gander we did have a American radar approach team that had been formed during the war; they were extremely good in comparison to what was available elsewhere, but still not good enough to ensure all aircraft landed when the weather was extremely poor. I can remember an Air France captain coming in one night when the visibility was poor, and when he met the 'dispatcher' he asked: "What do they mean by 'up a little?'" Of course he was referring to what the radar controller had said when he was on final approach, but he had landed safely even if he was not too sure of all English phrases and instructions.

The Queen's visit in 1959 caused quite a stir throughout Newfoundland. Many Newfoundlanders, in their hearts, had never wanted to be part of Canada, and felt they were better off under UK rule. I don't agree: Newfoundland was too far away from Britain to get the full support for what it needed; it is only since it became part of Canada in 1949 that the general development of the country has advanced. Being such loyal citizens, they were trying to make sure she had no problems during her stay. The plan was for her to land at St. John's, the capital, have a day or so there, then fly up to Gander, open the new terminal, and then go on to Stephenville on the west coast. In the event of weather stopping her landing at St. John's, the flight would divert to Stephenville and the tour would be reversed.

I was sent to Stephenville to prepare for the diverted aircraft, in case that happened. The officials due to meet the Queen at Stephenville were shocked to hear about this alternative tour arrangement; their wives had fixed their hair-do appointments for the day before she was due and if she came two days early they wouldn't be ready. As happens on these occasions, they put their heads into the sand and did nothing, but prayed for the best.

On the morning of the flight, St. John's airport was fogged in, and it looked very likely that the aircraft would divert to Stephenville. We were all frantically wondering what to do, so I arranged through the Met. Office in Stephenville to make some special weather readings at St. John's every 10 minutes. Suddenly the fog lifted and the Queen's flight landed, but her aircraft was only on the ground for about 15 minutes when the fog came down again. What a miracle! Many said: "She really is a Queen to get this treatment!" We were all spared many problems, and I could pack my bag and go home to Gander in readiness for the Queen's visit there.

In the new terminal at Gander, there was piped music 24 hours a day, but the acoustics in the terminal were perfect and the music was never too loud, always at the same level wherever you stood: the engineers had done a wonderful job. Prior to completing the inside of the terminal they had a artistic competition to produce a mural some 50 feet by 12 feet along one side of the main hall. The artist who won was a Canadian from the mid-west; he made a small miniature about five feet by two feet and worked from that. It was marvellous to see him bring this mural to life from such a small example.

Continuing on with regard to the Queen and her travels, whenever she or one of her close family crossed the Atlantic on a official visit overseas, I was the one at Gander selected to cover her visit, which usually meant she would land at Goose Bay. I quite enjoyed my occasional trip to Goose Bay, which was necessary because Richard had been withdrawn from the station after a fairly short time. The local handling Company Representative, a single man in his fifties, always looked after me well. Goose Bay was a fisherman's paradise and the Representative was well known for his fishing expeditions. He had enough equipment to 'kit out' up to six anglers at a time. He would hire a local floatplane to fly them into the interior lakes to set up camp, although I was not a fisherman so never went with him. He also had access to the Base Store (the USA Air Force duty-free shop) and used it to get whatever equipment he wanted. Between my first and second visits he decided he needed to have an extensive record collection. so in a few months he had purchased hundreds of records, and had indexed them all under Composers, Titles and Artists/Orchestras. The equipment he bought to play these records was of the highest quality available at that time, and he accumulated this massive array of equipment and recordings, yet he only had a large single room at the hotel. When he turned the volume up to show how good his equipment was, the whole building vibrated. With such expensive recordings he also bought special record containers in which to store them in total safety, another high-cost item of equipment cheaper to purchase at the Base Store (BX Store). On my trips to Goose Bay, I also took advantage of the Base Store whenever I could, but that was quite rarely as I never seemed to have any cash spare.

On one of my visits to Goose Bay, George Watson decided to come with me. He felt he should greet the Queen when she transited his territory, although I could never make that contact as I was always tied up with the crew on flight plan and ATC clearance matters. Because George Watson was making the visit a duty visit for himself, we went a couple of days early to Goose Bay and it gave me the opportunity to take him to places like North West River, a Grenville Home Mission station that had been set up about seventy years earlier; this was north of Goose Bay and the furthest north I have ever been. Luckily, it was summertime and the river was no longer frozen solid. As there were no roads to it, we had to fly, my first trip on a floatplane. The plane was a Beaver, a single-engined high-winged type; within the floats were the landing wheels, so we took off from Goose Bay airport using the wheels and landed on the river using the floats. The landing on water was most impressive, with the spray coming up off the floats towards the windows. We docked at a jetty and were greeted by a young English lady doctor in a summer 'off-the-shoulder' dress. It was then that we noticed the massive mosquito bites, and began to see the little devils flying around us; they seem to be able to hibernate under the snow all winter and then hit you all summer in these northern parts; luckily they don't carry malaria.

One missionary and his wife had started this particular mission, and although he had subsequently died his wife was still living there although now in her nineties. She had raised three sons: the eldest had become a doctor, who worked at the hospital they had built; the second son was now the priest of the mission and had his own church on the opposite side of the river to the mission home and hospital buildings; and the youngest son worked at Goose Bay as a traffic clerk and only occasionally visited his mother at the mission. The mission had done well in the area in many ways; however, the Eskimos and Indians had made their camps around the church, and rarely went hunting because they found the mission would provide them with food and clothing when they had none.

Part of George Watson's visit to the area involved his visiting the hospital as a dignitary and saying a few words to whomever he met. The maternity ward was full of expectant mothers (all Indian or Eskimo) and, after walking through, George decided he should say something, so he turned round and said: "I hope you get better soon"; it was as much as I could do to keep a straight face.

The Queen was flying onwards to Vancouver in a Britannia 312, a flight of more than eight hours, so it was not a simple flight plan, but the plane came in on time and left on time as well, so my job was done. That night we had a few drinks after supper. I remember going to bed and had a good night's sleep, then the next morning on the way into breakfast I noticed the glass was broken in one of the restaurant's doors, so I asked: "How did that happen?" Imagine my surprise when I was told: "You did it last night as you left the restaurant on your hands, don't you remember?" I didn't, so I was then told how I had attempted to walk out on my hands. That was a party trick from youth, and it appears I almost made it, but kicked the door glass with my foot as I went through, hence the broken pane.

A highlight at Goose Bay was its Eskimo population. They were often high on drink more than likely, but nevertheless very happy. The American base had plenty of work for them and they paid well as far as the Eskimos were concerned. So, for people who had never had money in their pockets, they suddenly found they had money to spend on numerous things, including booze. They also bought motorbikes, small ones but nevertheless motor bikes; they were always supplied with a tank full of petrol and, when the petrol was gone, they would throw the bike into the ditch. What else could they do? Fill the tank? No one had told them about doing this. When they had enough money again, then off they would go and buy another bike.

BOAC and other airlines were always looking to shorten routes from Europe to America and there were possibilities of faster routings by going nearer the North Pole and avoiding the strong westerly winds that affected the westbound flights. For this reason, George was asked to have a look at Frobisher Bay, an island way up north and halfway across Canada, where TWA were already operating. He went there for a few days and came back saying it was fine: just like Gander but no trees. This went down like a lead brick with us in Gander; we could see George recommending we start operating that way and one of us would then be posted there, so we all said: "No thanks!"

The next time I took off in a Beaver aircraft was from Dead Man's Pond, a smallish lake near the main airport at Gander from where the local light aircraft operated. In the summer they operated on floats and in the winter wheels and skis. The Solidaires were going to play at a mining town in the north-eastern side of Newfoundland and well north of Grand Falls. It was early spring and the lakes were still frozen, but they had large cracks in the ice which you could plainly see when flying overhead. We took off OK from the frozen Dead Man's Pond and headed for this iron ore mining town; all of us were looking out at the frozen lakes and ponds below us, which all looked as if the ice was already very thin, and we felt unsettled at the prospects of making a forced landing on such a shaky-looking surface. As it happened the weather deteriorated at our destination and the pilot decided to return to Dead Man's Pond. The trip and dance was put off for a week and the next time we decided to go by car and boat.

The mining town was a town owned by the mining company. If you worked for them, you were given accommodation: house or rooms subject to your status. As a treat to their workers, they organized a dinner dance for all their staff and families. This was where we came in with the Solidaires. There were no roads beyond a certain point and it was agreed that we would be picked up by one of their boats, a 50-tonner, to sail the rest of the way. We set off just after 9 am to do the drive, having loaded the cars with a crate of beer to each car plus the instruments. We stopped at a tavern for a drink and a sandwich on the way and joined the boat at about 3 pm. On the boat trip, we had to skirt around a couple of icebergs; this was in June and the sea was not frozen but very cold with these icebergs clearly visible.

Once at the town we were given rooms at the company hotel and also dinner. By 8 pm we had to be set up ready to play for the young ones in town, which turned out to be hard work as they wanted only fast tunes for jiving to. At 10 pm we then started playing for the adults. Whilst we played, we were fed with plenty of drink but only spirits, no beer. By 4 am we decided we had played enough and finished with 'The Queen.' All of us felt hungry and we were invited to a local's house for a rabbit supper (the locals had hunted rabbits and then home-canned them). All was well until we found that the contents of one of the tins they had opened had gone off; the smell was terrible, and to make matters worse we didn't know whether they had thrown the rotten one away or put it in with the rest of the food. My stomach wouldn't allow me to eat anything they offered, preferring to stay hungry. We had about two hours' sleep and then set off back to Gander, boat trip and all. As you can imagine we were very tired, to say the least, and immediately we reached home I went straight to bed. This trip became a yearly event for the band; however, I was on leave the next time they went.

I feel I need to give a bit of detail regarding the make-up of the band. The leader, Ed Goff, was Sales Manager (Gander) for TCA (Trans Canada Airlines); he had belonged to many other small bands in the maritime states. He came from St. John's, played alto sax & clarinet, and sang. We had two other sax players: one, Howard, was a natural musician, who had taught himself how to play guitar & button accordion, and was then taught how to read music by Ed Goff and, in addition, how to play tenor sax. On top of this he had made his own Hawaiian electric guitar and played it beautifully. His main work was as a cleaner for the airport authorities.

The other saxophonist was one of the Meteorology clerks at the airport, so he didn't turn up for all dances. The double bass player, Cliff Powell, was in Oceanic Control and he eventually became a Senior Controller; he was also a self-taught musician and he and I hit it off very well. Whilst the wind instrument players took a rest to get their wind back, Cliff Powell and I would continue to play and were sometimes joined by the drummer, Jack Stamp, and this extra music was much appreciated by the dancers. Jack Stamp was a taxi driver in Gander, self-employed and always available.

The brass players came and went. One trumpeter was a Canadian Air Force officer who was based at Gander for a short while, then another was a trombonist and an engineer. On one occasion we even had a female vocalist. Ed got a bit jealous of her taking over the singing, so she didn't last that long. Mind you, she was good, though.

At Christmas (I believe 1959) we took part in a pantomime, *Cinderella*, with the local dramatic society. We collected everyone who lived in Gander who could play an instrument. In all there were fourteen players in the orchestra on this occasion. The leader of the dramatic society was an Englishman who had visited Newfoundland with a group of professional travelling actors, and he and his wife had enjoyed Newfoundland so much that they decided to stay and joined CBC in St. John's. He subsequently became Radio Gander's manager. He and his wife were very good actors and had performed in pantos in the UK; as they had the script of *Cinderella* with them, they modified it to take in some of the local scenes. We made three performances to full houses, which were considered fantastic. The producer, the Radio Station manager, became quite famous throughout Canada as the official adjudicator for amateur dramatic societies. He was good too, quite witty with his adjudications.

I must say I enjoyed playing with the band, although it was not easy, with plenty of late nights coupled with a fair amount of drinking. But it did mean that I saw a lot more of Newfoundland than the average contract worker with BOAC. It also meant that my daughter Jeannie always had plenty of music in the house. The band would come to practise new numbers at my place, as I had bought an old piano for myself. It hadn't been tuned for nearly 50 years, so I bought my own piano key and did it myself, which took time but I eventually made it. My two children could fall asleep while the band played, and with six or seven players we could make a fair amount of noise. Jeannie now often uses music in her work as a Headmistress of a junior school in Essex . . .

By the time our daughter Jeannie was five years old, a new Convent school had been built, so she had one year of schooling in Gander. The Church next door to the school was completed around the same time; it was quite modern but still very pleasant for services. The town centre had become much larger, and this gave the wives somewhere to look for clothes for themselves and the children. Some of the roads were by now paved and, in addition, so was the square in front of the shops, and this cut out all the problems of muddy boots to which we had grown accustomed. Outside the house, we even managed to grow grass and flowers in our garden. There was very little topsoil left after the house was constructed, so we had to go into the woods and collect bucketfuls to spread over the ground. But with the amount of snow and the length of time it was settled on the ground, it meant we had a very short growing season.

One of our neighbours had a dog that produced a litter of puppies and we were persuaded to have one. He was almost a dachshund but not quite; we called him Tippy because of the white end to his tail. He became a real part of our family and was a very good guard dog around the house and in the car. When we went shopping we had no need to lock the car doors, as he wouldn't let anyone in but us. He also became the guard dog to our next-door neighbours, Gordon and Violet Stanley; he stayed with them whenever we went on leave and became so much at home there that he must have felt he was in charge of both houses. When we finally left Gander I was unaware of where my next permanent posting would be, and because taking him home to England would mean him going into quarantine for six months he became Gordon and Violet's dog from then onwards. But we always got a Christmas card from him with his footprint on it!

At one time Violet became very ill and had to go into a sanatorium in Stephenville on the other side of the island. Tippy kept Gordon company whilst Violet was away, and Gordon wrote saying how wonderful it was to have Tippy around. He would take him with him whenever he visited Violet and he made such a fuss of her each time. He was with them for over twelve years, so was well over 14 years old when he died.

During our last summer in Gander, 1960, we had a real heat wave; this was after a winter of unusually heavy snowfalls. When aircraft landed, the snow either side of the runway was so deep that they disappeared between the snow banks. The snow took ages to melt even though the weather became so hot. This hot dry weather soon set fires going in the pine forests around this area. They originated on the opposite side of Gander Lake and, although the lake was about one and a half miles wide, the burning ash and twigs were being blown across to our side. Patrols along our side of the lake were arranged to fight any possible ignition of the shrubs or trees. On the far side of the lake a full-blown forest fire developed and went out of control. The town of Gander was under threat from these fires and we were all forced to be ready to evacuate at a moment's notice. Fortunately, the wind direction then changed and we were saved the evacuation problems.

I should explain that lakes in Canada have to be really large to be called a lake. To English standards, Dead Man's Pond would have been called a lake, but in Canada it was only a pond. It was about half a mile wide and one mile long, whereas Gander Lake was one and a half miles wide and 32 miles long. Gander Lake was also extremely deep, in places thousands of feet.

For wild life we had moose, caribou and black bear. The bears were seen in town occasionally as well as the moose, but I never saw any caribou, as they stayed further north than Gander. Some of the locals would obtain a licence to hunt once a year; this was normally for moose and they would bring the carcass back to town and have the local butcher cut it up and store it in cold rooms labelled in their name. Moose steaks are quite nice and tender if the animal isn't too old. Many a hunter had tales of events whilst hunting, one keen but inexperienced hunter being the BOAC Accountant in Gander and another George Perry, a Newfy.

George Perry decided he could do with having his own supply of meat to feed his ever-growing family. So he hired a local trapper, almost an Indian, as a guide and set off with rifle and food for a few days. The guide found tracks of a moose and set up camp to await the animal's arrival.

TOP: The furthest north I ever managed to get, the Grenville Home Mission, North West River, Labrador. Photo: the author.
BOTTOM: A BOAC Comet 4 on the first direct trans-Atlantic flight. Photo: author's collection.

TOP: A BOAC Britannia 102 ("the whispering giant"), in service during the late fifties. Photo: Bristol Aircraft archives.
MIDDLE: A Vickers Valiant bomber, used on this occasion for testing the Dectra long-range navigation system, which was never finally accepted worldwide. Photo: author's collection.
BOTTOM: A DH(C) Otter floatplane used by a local business and based at Dead Man's Pond, Gander. Photo: author's collection.

They had been waiting and looking around for over three days and George was beginning to think his guide was useless; he must then have got into a bit of a doze when suddenly the guide nudged him and pointed to a large moose less than twelve feet away in the trees. George hastily grabbed the gun, got it loaded and then took aim, but he wasn't properly balanced for shooting and when the gun went off it pushed him flat on his back. As you will have guessed, the moose went happily on his way unscarred. George gave up hunting from then on and came home to relate his experience.

Prior to Newfoundland coming under Canadian rule, it was officially ruled by the British government in the UK.. Being so far away from Britain did little to develop the country's roads or general prosperity for its inhabitants. When Newfoundland became part of Canada, gradual improvements were made but this did take time. Joey Smallwood was the Prime Minister for many years and although not everyone liked him, he did force radical changes into practice. The small groups of four or five families were forcibly moved into small townships which had been specially built for them. Although they had schools and shops with every development, they didn't take kindly to these forced moves at the time, but the subsequent years have enabled the children to become better educated.

The Police Force while under British Law were known as the Newfoundland Rangers, and what a hardy lot they were too. Each Ranger had to cover a huge area with isolated hamlets dotted along its coasts; many areas had no roads in or out and you only got there by boat. Fishermen's families were the inhabitants of these villages and intermarriage between these close-knit families was rife. Cousin would marry cousin and so you would find Mary Lea O'Reilly marrying Sean Patrick O'Reilly, cousins twice removed.

The Ranger under Canadian law then became the Mountie. He continued to visit these small hamlets, ensured that all arguments were settled properly and in general received details on what had happened since the last visit. Being so isolated, it usually meant him having to stay a night in one of the houses.

One Ranger (Mountie) I met told me of how they were treated on these visits. Once their official formalities were over, they were welcomed like long-lost friends, being invited into all the houses and offered dinner. They had to get used to eating whatever they were given, and as they were in fishing hamlets, it would normally be fish. He told me that once, when he looked into the boiling pot, all he could see were the eyes of the fish bobbing up and down in the pot; that would put me off the meal all together.

During the war there had been flights, almost daily, going from Goose Bay to Gander and *vice versa*. The flights positioned the ferry aircraft crews to where they were needed for the delivery of fighter planes to Shannon and on to England. On one of these shuttle planes, a Newfoundland Ranger was coming from Goose Bay back home for a few days off duty, and he left his pistol in Goose Bay, seeing no reason why he would need it on holiday. On the same plane were a number of other personnel coming to Gander, one of whom was a cockney joker. Each passenger had his own parachute, which was strapped on prior to boarding the aircraft, as it helped to form part of the seat for the journey. The DC-3 had no heating for the cabin but a special type of oil heater had been specially fitted and would be started up whenever it became too cold to bear. As the cabin became very cold in winter the crew on this occasion started up the heater once they were airborne, but in doing this smoke bellowed out and it filled the cabin. The cockney joker shouted: "Fire, fire, all jump out!" whereupon the reaction amongst the passengers was instantaneous: half of them jumped out with their parachutes before the crew could stop them. The pilot informed Gander control of what had happened and aircraft were sent to search for these missing passengers, the Ranger amongst them, but unfortunately none were found.

About one year later two very frail men walked out of the woods near Gander. One was the Ranger who originally weighed 16 stone and was now less than eight stone, and with him was a navigator who had jumped at the same time. Their tale was quite incredible. It appears they landed within a few yards of each other but the navigator had broken his leg in the drop. The Ranger fixed his broken leg as best he could and made a tent using the silk from the parachute. With the navigator unable to move the Ranger decided to stay with him and use his skills to keep them both alive. The weeks turned into months and the navigator got the use of his leg back, so they decided to walk out of the forest. Using his shoelaces the Ranger did manage to catch one rabbit. He could have got a moose if he had had his pistol with him, but no such luck. Being well into winter, the trees were clean of berries, so they both wasted away. It was late spring, almost summer, when they were found, after what can only be described as a marvellous feat of endurance and perseverance. The Ranger survived OK and built up his strength to return to his post in Goose Bay. What hardy men these Newfoundlanders are.

At Gander hospital was a Scottish trained doctor, Jim Paton, who had immigrated to Canada, arriving not long after the airport came into full swing in the late 1940s. The hospital was then more like a first aid post but it grew as the airport grew. No one had much faith in this newly qualified doctor until one day, when a worker was hit by a propeller of an aircraft. With little or nothing to work with Dr Paton patched up the injured person, setting his back and holding it in position with bandages. The worker was then airlifted to the USA for hospital treatment; on arrival at the hospital they X-rayed him and found that his back was perfectly set and therefore saw no need to remove the bandages and risk doing further damage. This news soon returned to Gander and faith in Dr Paton rose immensely. He stayed in Gander for the rest of his life and was loved by everyone.

Whilst we were in Gander an Irish dentist set up practice; he was a huge man with massive hands, but he had the lightest touch, and he and Dr Paton became great friends, finding immense pleasure in playing practical jokes on each other, some of them at quite a lot of expense. The dentist, Mike, once bought two or three goats and let them loose inside Dr Paton's house and garden. It was one way of getting back at the Doc for something he had done to Mike.

In Gander there were no private doctors' practices, the only doctors being those working at the hospital, and likewise no chemist shops. All medicines were purchased from the hospital, which was getting busier all the time, and so another doctor was recruited. If you were sick you rang the hospital and spoke to whichever of the two doctors was on duty.

To relate a funny tale and to show how full of fun Dr Paton was, one of the Immigration nurses working at the airport had severe diarrhoea and telephoned Dr Paton to ask for some medicine. He said he was coming to the airport for some other reason and would bring something with him for her. When he got to the airport, he walked into her office and, without stopping, dropped a small paper bag on her desk. He was almost out of the office by the time she had opened the bag and read his note, which said: "Try one of these for size": it was a bag of assorted corks. The air was blue as he retreated out of the office. It was his kind of humour, and especially directed at those he knew well.

From all I have said, I am sure you realise that Gander was a town with a heart, full of young folks working hard but at the same time enjoying life fully and generally. The Newfys are a very honest, faithful nation of very hardy people who were a pleasure to know.

The nature of the weather conditions in Newfoundland I have already described as 'nine months winter and three months bad weather,' which meant you needed to be positive in your thoughts, ideas and spirit if you were going to make a good effort at living here. For me, of course, I had my work that I found exacting and demanding. Aviation was still in an early development stage and the need to take great care in everything you did was essential. The limitations of the aircraft in service at this time meant that extreme care had to be taken in planning the operational aspects of Atlantic flights. This knowledge made me feel honoured to be part of this worldly experience. It also taught me how to drive on ice and in heavy snow. It also gave Madge and I muscles from digging so much snow! We lived on the main street in town and the snow ploughs made regular trips past our house to keep the road open to traffic. However, every time they went by, they managed to push a pile of snow across the entrance to our driveway. If I was away at work, Madge would go out and dig the snow away from the drive so as to allow me to drive straight in. Then at night we would have heavy snow and in the morning find the car completely covered, so before being able to go to work I had to dig the car and the driveway clear of snow, no mean task. Somehow or other the car always started, so that was one good thing. Nowadays they have small domestic electric snow blowers to remove the snow, making life so much easier.

Madge had the challenge of providing a homely environment for us both and eventually our two children. Looking back we appreciate the real experience and benefits we gained in Gander. Because of my nearly seven years in Gander, I was listed within BOAC as a operations expert, which would lead to my future assignments in Los Angeles, Montreal and Baltimore/Washington.

CHAPTER 12

A SHORT STINT IN LOS ANGELES

The memories of this era in Gander make it hard for me to move on with my story, but I must.

In the January of 1961, with the advent of more and more aircraft being able to cross the 'pond' without stopping in the Maritimes, it became necessary to close down Gander as a operations station. With communications being easier, more responsibility could be passed to London (Heathrow) and New York or Montreal operational personnel. So it was time for us to uproot and return to the UK.

Some of my colleagues took advantage of becoming "locally employed" in New York as Duty Managers, and others went to Montreal and Toronto. Sandy Millar stayed in Gander as he was married to a Canadian, and I came home to England and whatever that would bring.

After a few weeks' leave I was told that I was going to Los Angeles to prepare that station for the first ever non-stop flight to London. Once again, it was a race with PANAM, as they wanted to be able to boast over BOAC. But in the event BOAC won again and I am proud to have been partly responsible for the achievement.

PANAM were using Boeing 707s the same as we were, but their Pratt & Whitney American engines used less fuel than our Rolls Royce engines, so we had more of a restriction on payload for our flights.

My assignment was only for a temporary period, as the permanent staff in USA had to be American citizens. Still, my job was to ensure that the operational arrangements were correctly implemented and that the first two flights definitely made it non-stop. They had to match the advance publicity which was being circulated. I was sent via New York to get acquainted with the support staff based there and to meet the person – selected by Union seniority – who would eventually take over the Ops side from me. After a couple of days there I proceeded to Los Angeles via San Francisco, and being routed this way I decided to have a look at San Francisco whilst I had the chance.

I visited Fisherman's Wharf and sampled some of their marvellous seafood; I also went on a bus tour, which included Chinatown and the Twin Peaks, plus the Golden Gate Bridge. I was really lucky as I had completely clear views from Twin Peaks, while a couple next to me said they had been coming for ten years and this was the first time they hadn't been covered with fog or mist.

On arrival at Los Angeles I was met by Rex Crisp, the Station Manager, who had been interviewing and selecting staff from all over the USA for the glamour of working so near to Hollywood. The Union imposed limitations on him, and he had to choose from the staff list they provided in each grade and seniority. However, if he could prove that the Union's choice for a particular job was not the most qualified person, he might be able to get the one he had chosen, although this rarely happened. He quickly took me to my hotel, the Club Delmar situated right on the beach at Santa Monica. What more could you want? The swimming pool at the hotel was filled with seawater that came straight in from the sea.

He gave me an hour to settle in my room and then, with his wife Wyn, we went out for dinner. Over dinner he questioned me about my experience and briefed me on how far he had got in preparing the station for flights. As we were leaving to return to my hotel he gave me the Los Angeles Highway Code book and said: "Read it: you are taking your driving test tomorrow morning at 9 am."

If you have seen the highway code for that city you will know that it has 67 pages, it lists all the different coloured kerbs used, it tells you what distances you are expected to keep between cars and many other specific points that you are expected to know when taking the written test, which consists of 100 multiple-choice questions, all of which you must get 100% correct. You can imagine my shock and how I spent a few hours that night studying this book before going to bed.

I breakfasted early the next day, had another glance at the codebook and was picked up by Rex just after 8 am. At the test station I first had to complete some forms, then take the written test and finally get my eyes tested. Much to my surprise, I got the necessary 100% and my eyes were apparently all right as well. Now there was the official driving test. The car Rex had hired was the biggest Cadillac you have ever seen, an automatic with power steering, power brakes and whatever else that could be automatic. I then had to drive it for the first time on a totally strange road system, with the tester sitting next to me looking out for any errors. Somehow or other I didn't make any mistakes and got my USA Californian Driving Licence: what a relief! But they only lasted for three years and then you had to have your eyes tested again and re-sit the written test to get it renewed.

Now this first hurdle was out of the way, I could now concentrate on the job at the airport. In 1961 the airport was a series of areas designated for different types of traffic or to dedicated airlines. Domestic flights had the main part with international flights being kept separate, however the check-in facilities for both domestic and international were alongside each other, although the walking distance from check-in to departure gate was quite long and winding. Office space was difficult to obtain, especially near the check-in area, so our Operations and main offices were about a mile away from the check-in terminal; for this reason we had to have a ten-seat minibus, which became my own transport while in Los Angeles.

The thought of BOAC – called 'BO-AC' by the local people – coming into Los Angeles caused quite an interest all round. They were used to having KLM, SAS and Air France, but 'BO-AC' seemed different. They liked to hear the English accent – even though mine was nothing to write home about. Still it did mean I got every sort of cooperation from the airport authorities, Met. Office and ATC. On one visit to the ATC Area Control, I was introduced to the Controller with Licence No. 1 for the USA; he turned out to be an Englishman who had settled in the USA forty years earlier, and he made sure that all help was given to me. This I needed, as to get this flight going properly a completely new ATC route had been requested which cut off quite a few miles from the flight and took the plane over Denver on its way towards the Canadian border. This meant we were maintaining the shortest distance to London and the nearest track to a "rhumb line track" – the track flown by aircraft. (A rhumb line track crosses every meridian at the same angle, and represents the path of the aircraft or ship crossing the world.) The task of getting this new route approved was mainly up to HQ in London and the British Diplomatic Services, so all I could do was to pressurise the authorities locally. Without this new route I would have greater difficulties flight-planning for a non-stop crossing to London.

At this time the Boeing 707/436 (the model used by BOAC) didn't have the fuel range to make this journey every time without an intermediate refuelling stop, but it could do the distance on a reasonable number of occasions, weather permitting. However, within the industry it was a case of trying to improve the travel facilities, which meant trying to cut out as many stopovers as possible. The PANAM Boeing 707s had American engines developed later than the British Rolls Royce Conway engines we were using, so they were expected to have a slightly easier time making the non-stop flights from Los Angeles.

As I expected to have only three months in Los Angeles, I made arrangements for Madge and the kids to join me as soon as possible; their arrival was within two weeks of mine and meanwhile I had rented a small apartment next to the beach at Santa Monica. The owner was a Russian Jew, and both he and his wife were most helpful to Madge and myself. Jeannie was signed on for school and I took her there every morning in the BOAC minibus, a Ford Thames with the driver and one passenger seated either side of the engine and directly over the front wheel drive steering; Jeannie loved to sit beside me in the front. It took some time to get used to driving the minibus, as you had to go past the turning before you started to turn the steering wheel, otherwise the rear wheels would mount the pavement. With the family in Los Angeles I felt contented and could get on with my work happily.

As these flights had never been flight-planned before, I had to obtain the meteorological route charts every day and then calculate the best time track to see which route would have been most favourable under the prevailing winds of that day. After a few weeks, it became clear how essential this new route was going to be. I found that there were extremely strong westerly winds going across central USA, with average 'plus' wind components of over 100 mph. However it still took longer than flying by the rhumb line route over Denver and Canada with a small tail wind of 2 mph. Sometimes the best time track could take you directly north and then along an almost polar route over much uninhabited territory. Although this showed it would be the best timewise, I never found a Captain willing to accept this route and go up into the unknown northern parts of Canada. Polar route navigation had not yet been pioneered.

Whilst I was doing these daily calculations, the American staff were gradually arriving and getting settled in ready for the first flights. They were all well-experienced staff and were soon settled in their new surroundings. To many it had always been their ambition to work in Los Angeles, and preferably with BOAC, so they were very pleased to be there.

One of my jobs was to take the senior group of staff to see the alternate airport – should LA (Los Angeles) Airport be closed due weather. It was called Toronto, but it was not that place in Canada; however it was over 60 miles away and if our aircraft landed there it would have to depart from there too, which meant getting all passengers and crew by road from one airport to the other, no mean task and one to be avoided if at all possible. Still, everyone needed to be familiar with what facilities we would be granted in such an event, so the visit was essential; I drove the minibus, and it was my first attempt at driving across town on the massive numbers of highways with numerous crossovers. I wouldn't have liked doing it on a foggy night.

In Los Angeles BOAC had a marvellous Sales Manager for the Hollywood area. He was the typical Hollywood film star Englishman: he spoke perfectly, he was tall, he dressed perfectly in a 'dressed' but casual manner, and on top of that he had the perfect complement in his wife. They were truly a marvellous couple and had the film world eating out of their hands. Everyone wanted to travel on BOAC from LA and it was largely because of this couple's influence. The list of distinguished guests and film stars booked for the first two flights couldn't have been better for BOAC publicity. Mind you, many had free tickets!

Time went quickly and before I knew it the first flight was due. The Station Engineer got really worried when all his stores of spares went missing; they had left the UK on time but he just couldn't find out where they were. When eventually he did find them he was furious: the BOAC

Store man in San Francisco had them and was arranging carriage by road to Los Angeles. He had decided that it was better not to send them too early and arranged for them to be delivered 24 hours before the first flight. As there were quite a lot of spares it meant that the engineer had to work around the clock unpacking and checking every item at the last minute, instead of being able to relax in preparation for the commencement of services. Still at least he had them and that made his potential problems acceptable.

Eventually the first flight arrived; it was not intended to be non-stop London to LA, so it made the scheduled refuelling stop at Toronto, Canada. Naturally, there were a number of special guests inbound as well as those booked for the outbound flight. Because of the remoteness of the aircraft parking the BOAC minibus was used to take the technical crew, Captain, First Officer and Engineering Officer, from our operations office to the aircraft once they had accepted their flight plan, weather folder and NOTAMs (Notices to Airmen). I had the privilege of doing this whilst I was in LA and it took much concentration, as it was always at night and you had to cross many active aircraft taxiways that were 'uncontrolled' for ground vehicles; aircraft always had the right of way, so extreme care was necessary.

After dropping the crew at the aircraft I would go to the VIP lounge and check up on whether anyone had been offered a ride to the aircraft. Often they had, especially if they were female and a film star of note. I was once honoured to have Gina Lollobrigida on board, and also, on another occasion Diana Dors; they were both charming, but I preferred Gina.

One other person I must mention was the station passenger Duty Officer at LA, whom I had first met in New York, but who was now performing at LA. His announcements were absolutely fabulous; his pronunciation was perfect BBC English and his voice seemed to resound everywhere so clearly. The American staff and passengers would stop whatever they were doing just to listen to him make an announcement; he was another major asset to BOAC in LA.

With staff so qualified, my services were no longer essential and London HQ wanted me to go to Montreal urgently as they had problems between flight crews and station staff to be resolved. As it happened, Madge and the kids were leaving LA the day I learnt I should go to Montreal. As I wanted to see Madge and the family back in the UK before I went off to Montreal, I quickly settled my affairs in LA and joined them on the same flight to London.

It was Friday night when we boarded the plane. In those days we always travelled in first class, a privilege we truly cherished. Once settled down we had a fabulous evening meal with all the trimmings. Then we settled down a few hours' sleep, to be awakened for "brunch" (a newly-named meal because it was too late for breakfast and too early for lunch). We arrived in London at lunchtime on Saturday. It was a wonderful night flight and as the children slept most of the time there were no problems for us. We made it non-stop in just under 12 hours' flying and during that flight we reached the maximum permitted altitude for Boeing 707s, 42,000 feet. The Comet 1 and Comet 4 could go much higher, but that was because of design differences.

My short time in LA had been most entertaining, good experience and had enabled me to see something of the West Coast of the USA with the family. We had visited Disney Land LA, the film studios and other exhibitions. And of course we had driven down Sunset Boulevard in our own BOAC minibus, all eyes watching us as we went by with the BOAC logo and 'Speedbird' printed on both sides of the bus.

Kathryn, our younger daughter, was a bit small for her age and in Beverly Hills they stood in amazement as she walked unassisted. We had also found Murray's, a fabulous self-service restaurant in Santa Monica, where they served helpings so massive that we had enough in two meals to feed the two children as well as ourselves. Although we had lived in Canada it was not the same as living in the USA, especially in LA.

Being in Los Angeles and on the West Coast of America made you realise and appreciate just how much air travel was used in this part of the world. For instance, United Airlines provided a "First Class only" daily service with a Boeing B707, San Francisco to Los Angeles, Monday to Friday, leaving San Francisco at 08.00 with arrival 09.00 in Los Angeles and returning the same evening at 18.00 from LA with arrival San Francisco at 19.00. Every seat had its own particular passenger, who commuted daily to work in LA. The directors in the film industry and other large business concerns preferred to live in San Francisco but had to work in LA. To ensure that they always departed and arrived on time, United Airlines had a standby aircraft parked on the adjacent stand to cover any technical hitches. So that the passengers were always treated with total respect, the same cabin crew were rostered to cover these services, and they were expected to make the passengers fully at home throughout the flight. This type of service was operating way back in the 1960s, and its like has never been considered necessary anywhere else in the world to this day.

The helicopter was also in much use for people coming to the airport from their homes. Los Angeles is such a spread-out place that you rarely met or associated with other airline managers when off duty, as you would find that they lived anything up to 100 miles away from your residence. I know that the SAS Manager, who was ex-BOAC, often came to the airport by helicopter, as he lived 60 miles out from the airport.

My coming home with Madge gave me the weekend at home prior to my reporting to HQ first thing Monday morning. They were surprised to see me and said they had expected me to go direct to Montreal; still they were not too upset at what I had done, as it gave them the opportunity to brief me on what had happened to cause the problem in Montreal. The following day I was on my way to Montreal knowing what was in store.

CHAPTER 13

MONTREAL & BALTIMORE

Whilst in Montreal I was going to be on my own; Madge was going to be busy buying a house in the UK as we were also adding to the family and needed a base there.

The first person I met in Montreal was an old colleague from Gander, Johnnie Power, a Newfy who had been posted to Montreal when Gander closed down. Additionally, the new Station Manager, Steve Sale, had been at Gander as a trainee and he knew me well. He had been rushed in from San Francisco when relationships between the management at the airport and the crews were at rock bottom. One thing is certain, if you get on the wrong side of the flight crews, then you are finished; the crews will 'fix' you if you don't alter your ways.

Steve Sale had come in to try and resolve issues between crews and the station that had developed with the previous Manager. Steve was a very intelligent person, and had taken Saxon English for his degree at Oxford because he found it challenging; he was really more of a mathematician and could easily have obtained his degree in maths, but it wouldn't have been such a challenge.

I went straight to the office and talked to Steve whilst having a look around. Later that day Steve had arranged a meeting to discuss the station's problems and plan how to rectify the situation, and he asked me to come along as he valued any input I could give. The meeting went quite well, and I said I could see what the major problem was, the desk layout in the office.

The duty officers were on the front desks and became directly involved with the crew as they entered the office; now the crew always wanted attention for some minor thing or just to chat, and if you didn't respond they thought you were ignoring them. The assistants could stop the duty officers being disturbed by the crew if *they* were on the front desks instead, and this would allow the duty Operations Officer to be free to continue his more important work uninterrupted until ready to brief the crew. But somehow or other the duty officers had decided that they should be at the front with their assistants in the desks behind, and this meant that the assistant wanting to update the operations movements board had to come from behind the duty officer to make the adjustments; in doing this he disturbed the duty officer, and it was also time-wasting.

I also didn't like the general layout of the office furniture, which forced the duty officer to move all over the office to collect items he needed for his flight planning.

Steve immediately said: "Harry, fix it, whichever way you think right."

Some one else replied: "You cannot move the furniture, it has been arranged that way on the specific instructions of the Senior Stations Manager for Canada" (the man to whom Steve reported).

Steve immediately responded: "I'll sort that problem out with him, we need the station working properly."

So now I had a task on my hands, to make the changes necessary and still keep the support of all the staff in the office. But, surprisingly, I soon had the staff on my side. They had not liked the layout of the furniture as decreed by the big boss and so soon helped in moving it around. Mind you, they were more than likely expecting that Steve and I would get into trouble once the boss saw what we had done.

The assistant Ops clerks felt they were being upgraded by being moved forward and it did mean they had less walking to do to get to the movement board. Additionally, they became more involved with the crews prior to the duty officer making his briefing and explaining the flight-planned route to the Captain. One of the duty officers offered to rearrange the storage of all the flight plan printed sheets, so that all documents for one destination were filed in order within one set of cabinet drawers. Prior to my arrival this had been a time-wasting exercise because it involved going from one set of drawers to another to find all the pages belonging to one destination flight plan.

As a result the efficiency within the office improved very quickly. The crews were attended to promptly and the complaints stopped coming in. The overall manager did make comments about the rearrangement of the furniture, but Steve soon told him not to interfere as the work was being done better and the crews were happier with the station.

I stayed at Montreal until July; Johnnie Power and I rented an apartment near the airport, but it had no air conditioning and it became pretty hot; still, it meant that Johnnie and I saved money, which pleased us both – with Madge buying a house in the UK I needed all the money I could get. In fact, I telephoned Madge on one occasion and the bill came to $60, so the next weekend I decided to visit home as the fare was only $40 return. On that Friday I worked until 6 pm, briefed the crew and, having completed the flight plan, boarded the same plane. We arrived early Saturday morning, so I had all of Saturday and Sunday with the family before getting the flight back on Sunday evening to arrive at Montreal at 07.00: no chance to go to the flat, I just went straight to work. My, was I tired at the end of that shift!

Around this time BOAC Montreal were recruiting new staff as they were taking over the ground handling (passengerwise) from TCA, and I became involved in giving these new staff their initial training. Part of the training involved making sure they could drive on the aircraft ramp. The vehicles we had were not automatics and some of the staff had never driven a manual gear-change car. One young lady I was training to drive and change gears managed to go from first gear into reverse without a sound; one minute we were going forward at 10 mph, then suddenly we were going backwards: I couldn't help but laugh! But my initial training must have made an impression because, when I went back to Montreal 17 years later and went into the operation office, my name was mentioned; a staff member turned to me and said: "You left here on the 7th June 1961!" I said that I knew it was in 1961 that I left Montreal, but I could not remember the date. I asked him how he could remember the date so far back, and his reply was: "I joined on the 3rd June 1961 and you gave me my first four days of training." Mind you, he didn't say whether it had been *good* training, but it had stuck in his mind ever since.

When I left Montreal it was to go back to Gander once again to be relief for Sandy Millar's vacation. He was the only one of the contract staff to remain at Gander, and had changed from 'contract' to 'locally engaged'. George Perry the accountant was also with him in Gander as he had always been locally employed. The band in Gander soon heard I was returning and met me off the flight; it was like old times once again, and I was invited to play with them whenever I could. The workload at Gander had greatly reduced so it was a pleasant opportunity to be back with friends. Very few flights came in whilst I was there, although I did arrange for RAF Britannia flights to transit with troops going for winter training in New Brunswick.

From Gander I was then assigned to Baltimore (Friendship Airport) which was the nearest airport to Washington, the US capital; the other airport in Washington was far too small to take the long-range heavy aircraft like the VC.10 or Boeing 707. A new airport (Dallas) was under construction in the State of Virginia. In Baltimore I was to be Acting Station Manager for six weeks. It was also a new additional station for BOAC, only opened three months earlier; it had four flights per week to and from London and they all routed inbound through Boston but non-stop to London. It should have been an easy station, but as soon as I arrived, I found that they had organised at least three additional charter flights per week. This meant my easy times were a lost dream.

The BOAC VIP Lounge at Baltimore (Friendship) airport was a very pleasant large room. What I can remember specifically about the place was an extremely good wall map of the world. It was like a picture of the world taken from over the North Pole. The world had been peeled as you would an orange, into four sections or 'petals,' with the southern hemisphere spread out and separated. It meant that New Zealand was at the opposite end of the map to Australia, in this respect most odd, but for Baltimore it meant that a straight line going centrally across the map joined Washington and London, a novel way to show passengers (VIPs) their actual route to be flown to London.

Charter flights always bring problems. Sales people are so keen to get the business that usually they fail to ensure that the load will actually fit into the aircraft type for which they are booked. As an example, on one flight they had booked a full orchestra with nine massive double bass boxes, large kettle drums and even a full-sized harp. Naturally, it wouldn't all fit in and the argument was: "Who was responsible and who is going to pay for some of the instruments to be flown out as cargo on another aircraft, even on another airline?"

The harp was a definite no-go on the BOAC aircraft (a Britannia 102), as it wouldn't even go through the cabin door, let alone the hold doors. I eventually managed to get it on a PANAM Boeing 707 freighter to Brussels. The charter was going to Antwerp, so Brussels was nearer than London, and it could then go by road to Antwerp. Not only did we have this bulky load joining, but also the aircraft arrived with extra crew baggage (motorised lawn mowers) in the hold, so the head loader said to me: "I don't think we will get everything on with this extra crew baggage," to which I responded: "Well, load what you can and then let me know, I'll sort the crew out."

Naturally, space for normal baggage belonging to the joining group run out and I was asked to decide what had to be done. On speaking to the Captain I learnt that one mower was his and the other the first officer's. Naturally they were reluctant to offload their own baggage, although excessive, and I told them I was not leaving baggage behind, so they had better decide where else it could be stowed.

But when needs be, a solution can always be found: these charter flights were operated with "24-hour-duty crew," comprising three pilots (two Captains and First Officer) and a navigator. To allow the navigator to cover the extra duty hours, a bunk bed was installed just behind the cockpit, so with the agreement of the navigator the two mowers were stowed on this bunk, releasing the space for the rest of the baggage in the hold. With the last problem resolved the flight left and I could go home for a well-deserved rest.

As normal with postings of this nature, you were offered hotel accommodation with everything paid, although you were entitled to find your own accommodation and claim allowances, and this is what I did. I was lucky, as the Airport Commandant knew an elderly couple who had a very large house and let rooms for income extra to their pension. It was a lovely house in the suburbs of Baltimore, with a large room to let, and they would give breakfast and dinner if required. I opted for room and breakfast, for which they wanted $15 per week. As my allowance was over £15 per day, I said I would pay them $30 per week, so I became the honoured guest: my breakfast each day was larger than anyone else's, and on Sundays the breakfast was a special American affair with pancakes and maple syrup, and then special sausages, with as much coffee as you could drink. It suited me fine!

For my evening meal I went into Baltimore where I found a nice pub that served really tender steaks, Idaho potatoes and salad, and this became my staple diet for the next six weeks. Then towards the end of the six weeks I learnt that my next posting was to be a permanent assignment in Beirut, Lebanon. News spreads quickly amongst overseas staff and, within days of hearing this news, I got an offer from the new Manager in Detroit, who had just moved from Beirut on promotion; he would willingly swap postings with me as he didn't like Detroit and was prepared to accept a downgrading in order to go back to Beirut. I never did put the question to HQ of such a swap, but felt certain it would not be considered under any circumstances. However, it was good to know that Beirut was not a disliked station by overseas staff and that I would be going there in November, one of the nicest months for Beirut weather-wise.

So I said my farewells to North America and returned to the UK for some leave and then it was welcome to the Middle East once again.

CHAPTER 14

BEIRUT

Madge and the family, which had increased by one with the addition of a son, Michael, would not join me in Beirut until Michael was a few months older. As it happened I felt it gave me a chance to get to know the place and the type of work involved. Also I could ensure that the accommodation was suitable for young children of six years and under. It meant that Madge and I would be separated over a Christmas period for the first time since we were married, not a happy prospect to look forward to, however Madge needed time to get used to the addition within the family and, now having our own home in England, she was in good surroundings with her mother and sisters near at hand.

My flight to Beirut was via Rome, where I managed to see and talk to some of the staff who were there during my previous stay in Rome. Arrival in Beirut was late evening, with the climate lovely and warm and fine. John Webb, who had been to Gander on a number of temporary postings, kindly met me and took me to the flat prepared for my arrival. On the way from the airport into town I got my first taste of the restrictions of movements they were trying to enforce in Lebanon. Soldiers at the main road intersection out of the airport stopped us; they wanted to see our passports etc. so John said to me: "Pretend you don't understand what they are saying and leave all the talking to me." This I did, and for some time we were held there whilst they tried French (which John knew well) and Arabic – at which John insisted he didn't understand what they were after. I was quite embarrassed at the whole proceedings and wondered how staff could tolerate this sort of harassment. Anyway, the soldiers eventually became fed up and gave in, and we were allowed to proceed without more to-do.

Afterwards John told me that he knew all the time what they wanted, but he couldn't see why we should have to state our business every time we went in and out of the airport; because of this the contract staff had decided on this action and never answered any of the questions asked. John and a number of the staff had been at Beirut during the recent internal war when families had had to be evacuated, and had found out how to deal with the situation. As ex-pats, you were a special group of people whom the army had been told not to molest in case it harmed the prosperity of the country; the ex-pats knew this and took full advantage of this situation. The initial few weeks were taken up getting on terms with the various controls and restrictions that were part of the daily life in Lebanon.

The actual controls would have made life unbearable if they were enforced, but somehow, the ex-pats had been able to overcome the restrictions by simply ignoring them and the locals had not been strong enough to do anything about it. For instance, the staff member I was replacing had occupied the apartment that I took over. The apartment was not in my opinion suitable for housing young children like mine; it was on the tenth floor of a twelve-storey building, the highest at that time in Beirut. Each apartment had a balcony with a low balustrade, far too low where children are concerned, and even I felt scared when standing near the edge. Still, the lease on the apartment had another three or four months to run, so I was forced to stay there for the time being. This meant that I had to take over the payments for electricity and water, so off we went to the head offices of the companies concerned. As in all Government offices in Lebanon, whenever you entered they were full of people trying to sort out their bills, be connected or whatever. Much to my surprise my colleague showed me how the ex-pats acted on these occasions; we didn't go anywhere near the counters, but we opened the office door and walked in behind the counters, grabbing the person we knew was dealing with our account and got him to action it there and then. He changed the contract straight away, just as we requested, and we were in and out in less than ten minutes, where as under the public's normal procedures, we would have been there for hours. I now knew how to get things done in Lebanon as an ex-pat.

It was here in Beirut that I was re-introduced to the 24-hour on-duty pattern with 48 hours off as previously used in Cairo. There were three of us to cover all flights, so if we did 12-hour shifts it would mean we would be on duty every day of the week, whereas by doing 24 hours on we then had a rest day followed by a day off. It was agreed between us that if the pressure of work necessitated someone else being on duty (i.e. two people), then the man on his rest day would go in to help, but the man on his day off would not be disturbed. It was sometimes necessary for two people to be available and then it was tiring, but at least you were assured of one complete day off out of every three . . .

My 'single' status at Beirut came in useful on the first Christmas there. BOAC had quite a few local staff and families as well as the contract staff and their families, and it was arranged that a staff Christmas party would be held in the Bristol Hotel – where all the cabin crew stayed – and would be available to all. The Manager, Mr George Rice, was well known to us all; he gave a dinner party every month to contract staff and families at which he would produce some of the most exquisite food and ice cream cakes imaginable.

At the Christmas party someone had to dress up as Santa, and on this occasion I was given the opportunity because the older children would recognise any of the other fathers taking the part. Mr Rice christened me

"Papa Noel" and I was from then onwards always greeted in this manner by him. The wives helped me dress for the occasion, and apparently I made a good Santa. The elder children were kept guessing the whole afternoon as to who Santa actually was, although some had in fact met me at their homes. One young boy who didn't believe in Santa tried to grab his present from me, but quick as a flash I removed the present and gave him my hand to shake instead. This stopped him in his tracks, as he was then obliged to say "Thank you" before getting his present. I learnt afterwards from some of the parents that it was the sort of treatment he was due and they were pleased I reacted accordingly.

The New Year came and in January 1962 Madge and family joined me. I had had wire netting fixed across the balcony to safeguard the children, but at the same time I had my eye on another apartment out of town at Haddath (north of the airport and halfway up the mountain inland from the sea) which was on the ground floor and had its own garage as well as 42 steps up to the front door.

Whilst on leave between leaving Washington and going to Beirut, I had bought a brand new car in the UK tax-free! I got a good bargain, as someone else had ordered it and then cancelled the order, most likely losing their deposit. It was the same make as I wanted and, providing I was prepared to accept the colour, they took an extra 10 per cent off the list price. As the colour was a lovely blue I grabbed the opportunity with both hands, used the car for a month in the UK whilst on leave and then had shipment arranged to Beirut. A few weeks after arriving in Beirut, I was notified that my car had arrived and was ready for me to collect. Prior to making the collection, I spoke to one of the MEA (Middle East Airlines) Duty Officers whose uncle was a Senior Customs Officer at the docks, and explained that, having bought the car as a UK export, I had saved the customs duty, although if I took it back within two years I would have to pay that duty after all. If, however, I imported the vehicle into Lebanon, I should also have to pay their duty, and paying duty twice was something I wanted to avoid if at all possible. They understood my predicament and devised a way for me to delay paying the import duty for six months, which I accepted, so I was then able to collect the car without duty payment.

The agent for the manufacturer came to help get the car ready to drive and to give it its 'first service' under the purchase agreement. The mechanic asked: "Will you drive the car to our workshop, or should I?" to which I replied: "You know the way better than I do, so you drive." On the way, we were driving down a one-way street (in the right direction) when I noticed a car coming towards us on the wrong side of the road. I waited until the last second to see if my driver was going to try and miss the oncoming car, but it seemed that he wasn't; I was so flabbergasted that he was not making any attempt to miss the oncoming car that I grabbed the steering wheel and swung the car away from a direct collision. I shouted at the driver for being so stupid and he said: "But he was in the wrong, he shouldn't have been coming down this one-way street in that direction." You can guess what my reaction to this was: "To hell with who is right or wrong, it was my brand-new car that was going to be damaged, let alone the two of us injured." He then asked if I would like the car delivered once the service had been completed, so I said firmly: "No, I will collect it myself."

Because of the method in which I imported the car into Lebanon, I got a special number plate, elliptical in shape and white with black lettering and, I subsequently found out, normally given only to Diplomatic cars. It came in very useful on occasions; road blocks were continuously being made and all cars stopped, however when they saw my number plate and also noticed that the car was a right-hand drive one, I was waved through, leaving all my colleagues to wait in the queue.

I took advantage of this duty-free arrangement for a long time. When the six months was up, I presented the papers once again; they had to go to a higher Customs official for approval, and on each occasion, it was approved. However, it subsequently had to go to the highest Customs official, the Director General of Customs. This situation eventually occurred some two years after my first entry into the country with my car. This time I went to the Director General's office and was sitting in his outer office with his personal assistant when the Director General came out of his room, threw the papers on the assistant's desk and said something in Arabic.

The assistant said to me: "Did you understand what he said?"

I replied: "No!"

The assistant then said: "No, it should never have happened in the first place," and then, much to my surprise, he continued: "Do you want to start again? If you do I will show you the way."

I thanked him but said that I didn't, I would no longer have to pay tax in the UK on taking the car home and that was my main aim right from the beginning, to avoid paying double tax. So I then got normal Lebanese number plates and paid the import duty but, much to my surprise, they reduced the amount of tax because the car was now two years old, so I saved a lot in the end.

With the whole family in Beirut I was kept busy. Living out of town, although it was ideal for getting to the airport, meant that for shopping, ballet lessons for Jeannie and going into Town office, a lot of driving was necessary. Of all the contract staff, I was the only one who regularly drove into town when going to the main office. The others would drive as far as the Bristol Hotel, park their car and then get the 'Service', a type of taxi service where you shared one car with three or four other people. It was very cheap but somehow I preferred to drive in and find a parking place there.

I nearly always parked on a bit of a hill directly behind the Town office, which was in the Intra Bank building. It was one of those illegal spots that the police turned a blind eye to, that is, until five years later, just a week before I was to leave Beirut for good. On this particular day, I was in the Town office clearing up my affairs in readiness for leaving Lebanon. I was there quite a long time, much longer than usual, and when I came out my car was missing. Using the Arabic speakers from the Town office I learnt that it had been towed away and that I would have to report to the court the next day before it would be released. Knowing that you could usually get around restrictions like this I went to the local police station to speak to the officer in charge. He was a fine young man who could speak fairly good English, and for the next hour or more I tried every way I knew to get him to agree to release my car. However, in the end I had to give up and take a taxi home. Although I failed to get my car back on the road, looking back I really enjoyed making the attempt to get him to change his mind. On numerous occasions he nearly gave in and let me have the car back, but then every time suspected he would be in real trouble from his boss in the morning, so once again said no.

Most foreigners would get one of their Arabic runners to go to the court to resolve their problem, but I decided to do it myself. So the next morning, fairly early, I went to the court, which was in an old Government building. The Road Offence Court was on the top floor (the third) with no lifts, only stairs. The height between floors was over six metres and the temperature was over 30°C, but I struggled up the stairs, and on getting up to the third floor then found my way barred by a human mass of people, all Arabs. Over their heads, I could just see the top of the small door leading into the actual courtroom. Without realising what I was doing I just loudly said: "Excuse me," and much to my surprise the crowd parted and I walked straight ahead and into the courtroom. Someone closed the door behind me, but at least I was inside. I then found that I could approach the clerk of the court, give him the piece of paper the police had given me, and wait to see what would happen next. They wanted my Lebanese driver's licence, so I told them it was locked in the car. Had I another driving licence? I said "Yes" and gave them my English driving licence, but that was no good, as it didn't have a photograph on it. Then, looking through my wallet, I found my California licence, which did have a photo; it was out of date but that didn't seem to worry him. He fined me 10 Lebanese pounds (sterling £1.10s), which I paid willingly and then I was on my way to collect my car, very relieved at getting off lightly for what could have been a serious situation.

Reverting again to my period in Beirut, there are a number of incidents that stand out in my memory. During one summer holiday travel period, one of the Comet 4s had a problem causing a delay and overnight stop with a full load of passengers, a large number of whom were school children going home to their families for six to eight weeks in places like Bombay, Bangkok and Singapore. Also on board was a young man about 22 years old who was going out to work in Singapore. This young man asked for a doctor at breakfast time the next day, and the hotel staff called me to get permission to call the doctor at BOAC expense. This I agreed but at the same time went to his room to see for myself what was wrong. The doctor was there and, having taken one glance at the man, he declared: "He has chicken pox, which is contagious; he requires an isolation hospital bed and I will try to locate one." On hearing this, the hotel manager demanded that I get him out of the hotel as quickly as possible.

The doctor was good to his word and found an isolation bed for the young man, but the job then was how to transport him. None of the hospitals would let us use their ambulances because of his contagion, so in the end I had to agree to take him in my car; I needed someone to show me the way, which was no problem, but by this time the aircraft had been repaired, and the rest of the delayed passengers were taken back to the airport to board the plane and get on their way. It can take up to ten days for chicken pox to show itself and I suspect that many of the children on that flight had their holidays spoilt because of being infected by this young man.

The sick passenger was kept in hospital for just six days, and then the doctor then declared him no longer contagious and able to continue his journey. So I made the necessary arrangements for him to travel on the next flight to Singapore, collected him from the hospital in my car once again and then shook his hand as he boarded the aircraft. He was, supposedly, non-contagious by this time but, needless to say, ten days later I was covered with spots and spent the next two weeks isolated at home with the family. What happened to all the passengers on the flight he joined in Beirut? How many of them became infected like me?

Then again there was the passenger who arrived at Beirut from Jeddah (Saudi Arabia) only to be told that his flight, as shown on his ticket, operated on a Saturday and it was now Monday. I was automatically called to deal with this person, who was naturally upset, and when you hear his story on what had happened prior to his arrival in Beirut, he was fully justified. It seems his agent in Jeddah had booked him on a flight from Jeddah to Beirut and told him it left Jeddah at 09.00 on Monday morning. He queried the departure time as he thought it left at 08.00, but he was doubly reassured and given confirmation that 09.00 was the correct time. So on Monday morning he duly arrived at the airport at 08.00 hours, only to witness his flight taking off. Needless to say, he was furious, and forced the agent into getting him to Beirut by another route, as he needed to connect with his flight to London and not miss it. The agent came up with a routing via Riyadh (capital of Saudi Arabia) and so after travelling all day he had eventually arrived at Beirut only to find that he had been booked on a flight out of there five days later. He certainly had good reason to be upset, wouldn't you agree?

Anyway, I was able to pacify him considerably and booked him on another BOAC flight leaving for London with a different flight number and routing, but at least it would get him to London at approximately the same time as he originally expected. He was now feeling much more at ease and so I escorted him into the departure lounge, where he could get a drink at the bar. As it happened, on this particular night one of our engineers (Charles Savage) had taken on a challenge to fit a fifth pod to the aircraft (this was the name given to an attachment under the wing which made it possible to carry a faulty engine back to base for repair, and was always referred to as a 'fifth engine ops.' Charles wagered that the job could be completed during the 45-minute normal transit time, his boss accepted the bet and this "Beat the Clock" exercise began.

He had his team of mechanics geared up ready for this challenge and as the aircraft taxied onto the ramp, it was followed by a whole train of dollies loaded with the equipment needed to fit this engine under the wing. The activity was intense around the aircraft and although things seemed at first to go well, I felt that we were bound to have some sort of delay.

On my way back past the departure lounge, this upset passenger saw me coming and rushed to the window, asking me: "Are we leaving on time?"

My answer was: "I'm sorry to say we might have a short delay, we are putting a fifth engine on."

As quick as a flash the passenger retorted: "Ask a stupid bloody question, get a stupid bloody answer. I've never heard of an aircraft with five engines."

Many a time since, I have laughed about his remark, and fully recognised why he felt that I was pulling his leg; his previous problems had made him sceptical of accepting anything he was told about this particular trip to the UK, so he was not inclined to accept what to him was a frivolous comment.

Back at the aircraft, they were having problems lifting the engine into position as the gantry cables (lifting cables) were breaking, so the engine was lowered back into its cradle on the ground and taken back to the hangar. The delay was then caused by refitting sections of the wing that had been removed to accept the engine, so when I boarded this passenger the aircraft still showed no sign of ever getting its 'fifth engine.' So I am sure that to this day he believes that I made up my reply, just to try to pacify him frivolously.

Although this particular passenger could not believe that aircraft do fly with a fifth engine tucked under their wings, it is a fact that this was common practice in the late 1960s through to the 1980s and beyond. In fact, it became possible to carry different models of aircraft engines inside the cowling of the engine pod used on these occasions. However, it is not so often practised nowadays as there are many more freighter aircraft available that can uplift the present-day aircraft engines like those used on the very large Boeing 777 models. If you can visualise the size of a Boeing 737 fuselage, the Boeing 777 engine has the same diameter: it's that large.

On another occasion, we were missing one passenger on departure. A frantic search went on and I eventually found him in a much lubricated state. Somehow, I managed to get him moving towards the aircraft and onto the ramp bus. When we arrived at the aircraft side I considered him fit enough to board, which meant that at least we could get the flight away without delay, but as the passenger started to climb the steps to board the flight he turned and said to me in a very drunken voice: "I bet you don't know what I have in this parcel I'm carrying?"

I said "No," not thinking he could have very much as it was so small.

He then said: "I've got a live bird, a very rare breed and I am taking it home to add to the London Zoo's collection."

I was shocked. Could it be imported into the UK without a licence? Was it going to violate quarantine regulations? I decided that I would let him board and spoke to the captain about the implications. He agreed to leave the passenger on board and continue in his departure routine for London; in the meantime, I would return to the office to read the regulations and call him on the company frequency to advise him of the outcome of my studies. So I rushed back to the office, got out the "Tim" (Traffic Information Manual) and found that a bird could be imported if cooked. When I passed on this information to the Captain he replied: "Well, we'll just have to cook it."

I subsequently learnt that the purser went up to the passenger and told him what was going to happen, but when they opened the parcel the bird was actually dead, so there was no need to cook it and it was disposed of by jettisoning it from the aircraft. A very sad story, but typical of the thoughtless actions taken by some passengers and the difficult situations imposed on Duty Managers of airlines worldwide.

On yet another occasion, a flight from London arrived carrying the King of Bhutan with his Queen. Bhutan is a small country adjacent to India and is part of the Himalayan Mountains. They were both very small people, only about 5 feet tall and of very slight build, and I quickly arranged for the VIP lounge to be opened for them and escorted them there; then I arranged for refreshments to be delivered and left them alone in this enormous lounge area. Returning 30 minutes later to escort them back to the aircraft I found the lounge full to overflowing with Arabs of questionable status, and I had to force my way through the Arabs to find the King and Queen seated on throne-like chairs and completely surrounded by this Arab group. I extradited the Royals out of the lounge and onto the aircraft, giving my sincere apologies for the rude intrusion that they had experienced in the VIP lounge.

After the flight had departed, I went to the airport authorities to complain about the unruly group they had allowed to enter the VIP lounge whilst it was in use by the royal couple. In typical Arab fashion, they explained that the group were at the airport to greet the ex-president of Lebanon, his "paid supporters," there to ensure he had a noisy greeting on his return back to the country. Under these circumstances, they dare not keep them locked out of the VIP lounge. Naturally, they had only expected senior officials to welcome the President, not all the riffraff which had got into the lounge.

I must say, I was quite surprised at the ease with which the King and Queen had accepted this crowd situation; maybe they were used to the same sort of intrusions in their own country.

Beirut was a happy and busy station. Many BOAC staff had been seconded to MEA as engineers, computer managers and sales managers; this link with MEA was in part because BOAC were contracted to help to develop the airline. The families of all these contract staff had become very close since they had returned after being separated for months by the local war. With the wives sent back home the men had had to keep together while the hostilities were going on, and that way they could warn each other about developments. Once the wives and children started to return, a dinner party at that family's home always welcomed the home-comers. Everyone was invited, so only those actually on duty were absent. This dinner party idea carried on for years and so you found that you gave a party every month and were invited to between 20 and 30 others each month. Therefore, what with doing 24-hour duty shifts and rushing children to school or dancing lessons, there was little time to rest.

Les Smith (Sales Manager for MEA and an ex-Chindit from the Burma war), John Webb and I took to climbing the hills and mountains of Lebanon at weekends. I would go on duty Friday morning, finishing Saturday morning at 08.00, then I would go home, shower, change into something light and then pick up the other two, then away we would go into the foothills. We would then climb and ramble all day long, return home between five and six pm, have a few beers and a good shower, and then Madge would produce dinner for all three families. Around midnight it was off to bed for a well-earned and needed rest. At least I was fortunate; I did have the following day off to fully recuperate.

On one of these occasions, we got a permit to drive to the south of Lebanon, near Israel, to see a Crusader Castle (Beaufort Castle) that we had heard about. It was a long drive and although we went armed with cameras, they were all taken from us at the bottom of the hill below the Castle. We then had to take a soldier in the car with us to the top and into the Castle. Although we could see into Israel from the top, we couldn't see any defences for either side of the boundary. The Castle was badly damaged, and not well kept, so overall it was not a very successful visit. However, we came back via Tyre, on the coast, where Alexander the Great's sunken city can still be seen.

Balbeck was another place worth seeing, although it too was not well preserved. The best thing I can remember about Balbeck is going there one evening to see a ballet performed within the old Roman structures, with beautiful lighting effects.

My invitation to attend this performance was obtained through my next-door neighbour, Gerry Camanarda, the *Times* Middle East correspondent. He was an extremely tall individual who had travelled the world for the *Times of London*. His wife was a titled lady called Iris and she became a marvellous friend to Madge whilst I was at work. They had an enormous dog, a bloodhound that had a habit of charging down the 42 steps leading to our flat (indicating that Iris hadn't managed to grab him first) to greet us whenever we returned home. Our young son Michael was frightened to death by the dog, which was at least six inches taller than he was. Gerry and Iris Camanarda had four children in all, two away at boarding school in the UK and the other two much younger and still in Beirut. We would go on picnics together in a mountain reserve purchased by the British Government on which they intended to build a school for Arabic studies. Somehow or other the school never did get built, but we used the area for our picnics. It was here that Iris Camanarda introduced us to the Spanish *bocadillo* (sandwich). We also used to marinate steaks at home 24 hours prior to going on a picnic and then cook them on the ends of long forks I had had specially made, in the flames of a open fire which we would light. Both families loved these days out together.

As neighbours to Gerry and Iris, we were invited to some of their dinner parties with all the other newspaper correspondents in attendance. On one of these occasions Kim Filby and his wife were present; they were an interesting couple, although he always seemed to be drunk. The night after this particular party, he disappeared and was eventually found in Russia, having defected from the west. His wife eventually left on one of our BOAC flights under much secrecy; the press wanted to interview her but she had been kept out of sight since her husband had disappeared.

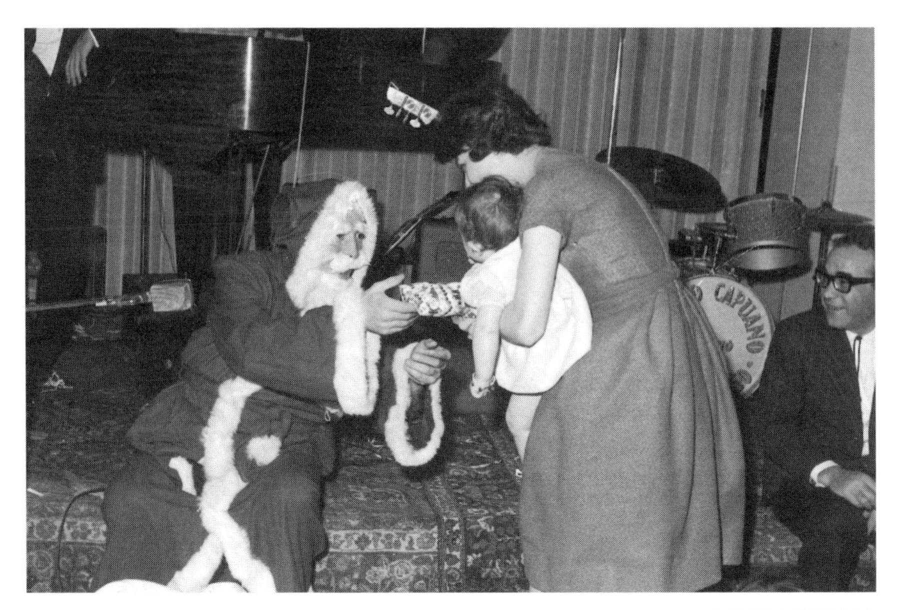

TOP: “Papa Noel” (the author in disguise) in Beirut, 1961. Photo: author’s collection.
BOTTOM: VC.10 introduction to Beirut, with welcoming staff from many parts of the world (author is 2nd from R.). Photo: from BOAC archives.

Our family and three children (Kathryn, Jeannie and Michael) at Frankfurt

Kim Philby was the Middle East Correspondence for the *Observer* newspaper group. He was a brilliant correspondent, who also drank heavily; I was told his daily order from the local shop was one bottle of whisky, one bottle of gin and one bottle of milk (the whisky was for him, the gin for his wife and the milk for a tame baby fox). If visitors came, the order would be doubled. The day before his defection to Russia he was invited as senior Middle East British correspondent onto the newest and largest USA warship to visit this area, so he was able to see all the latest equipment on board just prior to his departure to Russia. He was well known to all the newspaper correspondents, but none of them suspected anything Communistic in his thoughts or actions. The Philbys kept this pet fox cub in their flat, to the dislike of the maid, and they were most upset when they heard that it had had an accident and had fallen off the balcony to its death; well, it was reported as an accident, but they didn't believe that to be true.

Prior to the first World War, Lebanon was known for the beauty of its mountains covered with cedar trees. Unfortunately the Turks cut the trees down during the war to burn on their steam trains, and now there are only about sixteen fully-grown trees left in the whole of Lebanon. Hence the cedar has become a symbol to the country and is included on its national flag. Most of the remaining trees are up in the north of the country, where they are trying to grow more trees, but regrettably the shepherds with their flocks of sheep and goats are given full freedom to roam in Lebanon and they eat all the new green shoots.

Of course, it wasn't passengers who caused the only problems we had to deal with in Beirut; the crews could have their own. Actually, we got on well with the majority of crews, but this did not mean they never caused us any trouble. Many of the pilots and technical crew had been trained in the RAF during the war, and were extremely good at their jobs although one or two still had the urge for a drink or two after a flight.

In Beirut we had a particular bar, the Golden Bar, which was just outside the main crew hotel, The Bristol, and was known to all airline crews and ground staff. Because of this bar the pilots and technical crews could not stay at The Bristol but were sent to another hotel a few miles away. Needless to say some of them always managed to spend an hour or two with the rest of the crew in the Golden Bar during their stopover in Beirut. The cabin crew was also inclined to frequent this bar and quite often stayed far too long; when this happened we would get calls to come and get them out of the bar, not the easiest task but it had to be done. Somehow or other they all turned up for their next flight from Beirut looking perfectly sober and prim & proper.

Mind you, there were some not so good cases. I arrived back from leave on a BOAC flight to find that the Captain was being asked to continue as Captain from Beirut to Karachi instead of night-stopping with the rest of the crew. He was most upset but had no option as it was within his maximum operating hours. The Captain who was due to take the flight to Karachi was completely drunk, only just able to stand up, and his crew had left him at the hotel to sober up; however he decided to take a taxi to the airport, where he was seen by one of the airport officials and escorted up into his office away from all the passengers at the airport. He was adamant he could fly the plane, even though he was in his civilian clothes and wearing his BOAC cap. So the flight went on to Karachi with the same Captain that brought it in and we then managed to get the other Captain back to his hotel and attended to by a doctor. He remained at Beirut for three days getting sober and then was sent home as passenger; he was subsequently grounded and never flew again. It was found that he had major problems at home, and unfortunately he committed suicide some time later.

Whilst in Lebanon we had another addition to the family, a puppy dog. We never intended taking on another dog whilst overseas, and since having Tippy in Gander we had tried not to get involved in the movement of any animal from one country to another, but somehow we did. It all came about because Cliff Clifton, the Senior Liaison Officer at Beirut, had a British wire-haired terrier bitch whose pedigree was a mile long. He and his family, plus the bitch, lived on the floor above us when we had moved house a couple of years on into our Beirut stint. One night we were all out to a party leaving the bitch at home alone, and she must have been in season and attracted a couple of local dogs. Somehow, one of these dogs (we can only guess that it was the larger of the two) got at her and subsequently a few months later she produced a litter of five puppies.

At the time she was due to have the litter, Cliff and family were due to go on leave, and like fools Madge and I agreed to have the bitch and her litter whilst they were away. We had a ground-floor flat with garden so at least we could let them out of the house and naturally, our children got attached to the puppies. Therefore when Cliff and family came back we kept one dog whom we called Pandy; he was the only one of the litter to have his mother's colouring and size, however instead of having the wire-haired terrier-like short curly hair, his hair was long and wavy. So for the rest of Pandy's life he was our dog and he went wherever we went. You will hear more about him later as he made quite a name for himself at some of our postings. The rest of the litter got good homes, and a few months later Cliff was posted to Baghdad in Iraq and he took the bitch and one puppy with him.

Naturally, I did have the odd health problem whilst in Beirut. One particular incident was quite funny eventually, although I didn't think so at the time. One afternoon whilst on duty I suddenly had extreme pain in my lower jaw, which became so unbearable that I decided to contact whichever doctor I could find. With help of the local Duty Officer I made contact with a doctor who invited me to his surgery, and on examining my jaw he decided that I had a blockage in the salivary passage of my lower jaw. He would have to operate to remove this blockage and first he would need to give me an injection to reduce the pain, but he was not approved to administer it, although his father was as he was a dentist.

So we went to his father's surgery a mile or so away. The father was not a young man and his equipment was certainly not modern. His tooth-drilling machine was one of the old pedal-operated types dating back to the last century. Suddenly this whole event became a family affair for the doctor, dentist, his wife and even some of the children, who happened to be at home.

After introductions I was seated in the dentist's chair and prepared for the injection and operation. It was then that I saw the injection unit. If you have seen some very old silent films, you will have seen massive syringes with needles three or four inches long. Well that was the type that was going to be used on me. I had to make a quick decision either to stay or make a hasty retreat, but the pain in my jaw made my mind up for me instantly: I was staying, come what might.

So I had the injection, much to the delight of all the family, who remained close at hand watching the whole procedure. The operation had to wait until my jaw had become numb and then the doctor cut and removed the blockage, a small piece of hard substance like a small stone. Once the pain and the bleeding had stopped I thanked all involved and went back to the airport and my work. The operation was successful and I have had no re-occurrence to date.

In hindsight it has seemed to me like an amusing event. The fascination to my plight shown by the whole Arabic family, and the antiquated equipment used, makes me wonder: was I brave or stupid to agree to the treatment offered?

It was at Beirut that we saw the introduction of the VC.10 pure jet aircraft late in 1962. The four jet engines were situated two on each side of the rear fuselage, resulting in all the noise being made behind the aircraft and therefore making it very quiet for passengers during flight. But overall it was *not* a quiet aircraft and aircraft noise had started to become an issue at some airports, although it was unquestionably the safest modern aircraft of that time. The original model proved not to have a good enough range for the Atlantic non-stop flights, so was used on African, Middle and Far Eastern routes only. Eventually a few years later the larger version, the Super VC.10 (called VC.15 in some books) was built. At this time BOAC were trying to buy British manufactured aircraft, the VC.10/VC.15 being ideal. However, we could not produce enough of them to cover our needs so we had to buy American aircraft as well.

The first ever VC.10 flight was on Friday the 29th June 1962 from Weybridge (the ex-Brooklands race track where the factory was located) to Wisley nearby where the test airfield was located. When it went into service its slogan was "VC Ten-derness." Surprisingly, forty years on they are still flying with the RAF from Brize Norton, some as tankers refuelling fighter planes wherever they are needed and others still carrying troops.

The operational planning for the introduction of this new aircraft was very well thought out. The crew had a special manual in which all known possible potential faults that could be anticipated were listed. Against each was stated whether it could be:

1. Carried as a fault for a certain number of flight sectors or until the aircraft reached base (London).
2. Carried to next turn-around station.
3. Carried, if a Senior Flight Captain and the Engineering Superintendent at main base granted approval.
4. NO-GO. Repair must be made before aircraft makes another take-off.

This was a new way for dealing with technical problems for all types of aircraft and was made possible by the greater use of computers at HQ technical base and on the aircraft itself. It certainly reduced the number of technical delays normally expected with the introduction of a completely new aircraft type.

With this vast reduction of delays during the introduction of the VC.10, the aircraft became the favourite of all the crews and passengers alike, but unfortunately, they could not be manufactured quickly enough to gain American and western world orders, whereas the Boeing and Douglas Aircraft Companies of America were capable of making deliveries within a reasonably short time scale; even BOAC couldn't wait for more VC.10s/15s to be built and so ordered Boeing 707s and then Boeing 747 aircraft, the latter aircraft being very much later on.

During my five years at Beirut, BOAC had three chairmen and each seemed to have different ideas on what was best for BOAC. The first ordered 35 or more VC.10s, the next cancelled half the order and substituted Boeing 707s, but the third changed nothing whilst I was at Beirut. The Manager (Middle East), Ray Bingham, was one of the old timers; he had been a steward on the Imperial Airways Flying Boats prior to becoming an overseas manager, and was in Cairo when I was there as Manager (Egypt) and, although I met him, I did not have much cause to know what he was like. But I do know that after I left Cairo and the Suez war started, he tried to lead all the BOAC staff out of the country via Alexandra but was unsuccessful and they were interned for some months. He then turned up as Manager (Western States of America) when I was at Los Angeles and involved in the non-stop flights to

London. He didn't like the restriction on payload I demanded on the first flights, but he had no option than to accept them.

Now he was my boss again, this time in Lebanon. He suffered from insomnia, sleeping a maximum of two hours in every 24, and travelled throughout his area much of the time. He had a very clever and delightful person as Assistant to Manager (Middle East), Peter Rossette, who came in very useful to me when, just after I arrived in Beirut, I was on duty at 06.00 when a flight diverted from Cairo to Beirut with the Chairman on board. Because of crew flight time limitations it had to night-stop, leaving me with all the passengers plus the Chairman to deal with. With the aid of the MEA Duty Officer all the passengers, including the Chairman and his wife, were sent to the Bristol Hotel. Ray Bingham was off station so I called Peter and he took over looking after the Chairman's needs; in fact he did such a good job of entertaining them that the station was praised officially.

Omah Jundi, our local airport reservations liaison officer, was also involved and did well. However, I can remember another occasion when we had another BOAC guest who was most disgruntled at the treatment he received. He was a famous fashion designer and writer (Cecil Beaton), who had been given a round-the-world flight on which he was expected to write a glowing report for a women's magazine. He arrived at Beirut and was met by Omah Jundi and myself. As I was dealing with the flight departure, I took my leave and left Omah to do his stuff. It would appear from what transpired later that Omah had not been briefed on the importance of this guest and, instead of putting him in a taxi at BOAC expense, he guided him on to the hotel bus service run by MEA. His hotel happened to be the last one visited by the bus, so it was nearly two hours later when he alighted tired, hot & sticky and exceedingly thirsty, and was shown to his room. The next morning all hell broke loose: "Why haven't I been treated properly?" etc. etc. Naturally the writer was making the most of the situation and Ray Bingham wanted everything done to ensure that the rest of his stay was not marred and that he got a good send-off.

In Beirut the available fruit was plentiful and beautiful. One of the fruit merchants we got to know was inundated with orders for large wicker baskets full of fruit to take home, each weighing about 20 Kgs; Ray asked me to be sure and get one on to the aircraft for the writer. This I did, but lo and behold, when Ray Bingham brought him to the airport, he then gave him another basket. I said to Ray: "I've done as you said and already put one on the aircraft for him," to which he responded: "Oh well, let him have the two."

As mentioned earlier, we did give many parties whilst in Beirut and if it was for a special reason and larger than usual, one or two friends would send their maid or waiter to help out with serving the meal or dishing out drinks, plus the washing up. All families seemed to have large apartments that could accommodate 50 or more persons for buffet dinner, in fact on one occasion we had just over 100 seated for dinner, using trestle-type tables on the balcony and in the large hall. Madge used two ovens to cook two turkeys and two hams and I got the job of carving the whole lot! Everyone got a starter, and then meats were served cold but with hot potatoes and salad. Luckily you could hire all the extra glass and china you needed on this sort of occasion.

Spinney's, the largest grocery store in the Middle East, would deliver all the drinks free of charge by the caseful and you only paid for what was consumed; the rest went back the following day at no expense. So you never needed to run out of your guests' needs in the line of drinks.

When these parties first started, the husband was generally welcoming his wife home, and so did the cooking. He would have become quite proficient in cooking, as while the wives were away there were many dinner parties held by the men on a rota basis, and this helped keep up their morale whilst living alone. However, some of the wives were not so pleased to have this task every month by the time I arrived in Beirut; in fact it soon became obvious who were the good cooks.

At one Christmas party, when it came to carving the turkey, it was found that the giblets were still inside the turkey wrapped up in a plastic bag, and the lady of the household said: "It said 'oven-ready' on the packaging, so I put it straight into the oven." At another party I was the unfortunate quest who got the neck of the chicken – certainly no meat on that part. Still you had to take the rough with the smooth on these occasions.

Around this time, different types of animals were now being sent by air all over the world. After the war, the first were monkeys from India to the USA via London. There were full flights of monkeys, but occasionally other types of animals were carried instead. Whilst in Beirut we had a DC-7 of an American Charter Company that arrived with a number of young heifer cows and a young bull. We (BOAC) became involved when the aircraft was unfortunately delayed due to a technical problem and had to spend over 48 hours on the ground awaiting spare parts. The problem for me was: "How do you feed the animals? Must they come off the aircraft? And if so, how do I get them off? Then – more importantly – back on?" Travelling with the animals was a church minister farmer, who told me an interesting story about why these animals were travelling. Apparently there was a religious farming community in Eastern USA who decided to help the Indian farmers improve the breed of cows they had by introducing this breed from the USA. Farmers in this particular area of the USA had given their first calf of the year to be flown to India (Bombay). This was the second year that they had done this and I was shown photographs of some of the newly bred and improved animals now being raised in India.

It was the middle of summer in Beirut, so conditions on board the aircraft were quite nasty for the animals. They had been trucked from the farms to Boston airport, which had taken about 24 hours; they had then been flown from Boston to Shannon in Ireland and then on to Beirut, so they had been on the move for another 24 hours by the time they arrived in Beirut. The religious farmer travelling with the animals had the task of looking after them throughout their journey, so to help him I designed, and had made, troughs to fit the pens in which the animals were stowed. An air-conditioning unit was pumping cold air into the aircraft and so the farmer felt it was all right for the animals to stay on board. We decided that if the aircraft was not serviceable within another six hours, then the animals would have to be offloaded by whatever means we could devise, but fortunately the aircraft was made serviceable and was able to continue to Bombay: what a relief to us all! I later got a message back from the farmer telling me that all the animals arrived safely and in good health.

Beirut was very popular with many Arab nationals, in particular Kuwaitis. The people of Kuwait all became very rich when oil was discovered there, then they came to Lebanon and bought up much of the coastal land and built apartment blocks or hotels, having a great influence on the whole country. They were also used to getting their own way in whatever they wanted to do, and demanded airlines to accept many unusual shipments. One Kuwaiti sheikh found the remains of a Crusader Castle and, having purchased it, had it dismantled and loaded on a truck and brought to the airport; he then wanted to check it in as excess baggage. Of course, the passenger aircraft (a Comet 4) could not carry all this stonework and he was told so. But this was not good enough for the sheikh, who demanded that the flight he was travelling on could not leave until a freighter aircraft had been fully loaded with the Castle stones. So MEA (Middle East Airlines) earmarked one of their DC-3 aircraft, brought it round onto the ramp and had it loaded; the sheikh then boarded his flight and both aircraft left for Kuwait. MEA made a lot of money doing this, because the sheikh actually paid in full for this shipment, but it did disrupt their operations severely.

I also had a difficult time due to a Kuwaiti ruler and his family. It is quite a long story but you need to know the full details to appreciate my predicament. It was at the time that the British Government were holding the final discussions with India, Pakistan and Cyprus over their Commonwealth status. The Government group consisted of 18 persons, including secretaries, and they were all booked in first class. They set out from London on a BEA Comet 4B (another version of the Comet aircraft) and when they checked in, they found that the aircraft only had eight first class seats and that ten of them would have to travel economy class. What an insult to public servants of the British government! This also caused massive eruptions both in BEA and BOAC, as it was then realised that their return to London from Karachi was going to be on BOAC, and while the BOAC VC.10 could be re-configured to include 24 first class seats, this needed early planning and action.

The Government group had been reassured that, for their return trip to London from Karachi, they would all be seated in first class, so at this stage all was well. Then the problems started. Firstly, someone booked the British Ambassador and family from Kuwait, six in total. However, on top of this, a son of the Kuwait ruler turned up in Beirut demanding seats for his family, another group of six. So before the aircraft reached Beirut I was six first class overbooked. London sent me a message saying: "Sorry, do what you can to resolve this problem." But what could I do?

When the flight arrived, I met the Government Group Leader, a titled gentleman, and tried to explain the situation to him. He was adamant that he had explained his view on his group's entitlements many times since he had left London, and there was no way for him to change his position now. He said that if anyone were to be downgraded, this would have to include him and the other most senior members of the party. Furthermore, he was due to see the Prime Minister on his arrival in the UK and would voice his complaint to him at that time.

I was left with no alternative but to see if I could get the British Ambassador of Kuwait and his family to agree to move into economy class. I felt he would understand that I could not downgrade the Ruler of Kuwait's son and family, even though they were the last to make their bookings. Fortunately, he did agree and he and his family moved into economy class for the flight to London.

Of course, other Royal families in the Middle East could also be very demanding; they never came to the check-in counter, the procedure being always completed by an agent employed by the Royal family. So you never knew what the condition of the actual passengers were until they arrived at the aircraft side for departure.

On one occasion, I had the uncle of the Ruler of Saudi Arabia joining with a small group of followers. All was well until his car arrived at the aircraft side after the departure announcement had been made. It was only then that I realised that the uncle was very old and also very sick, and couldn't walk up the steps into the aircraft. He was a big man and it took two of his servants to carry him up the steps. Under normal circumstances, I would have offloaded him, but being in an Arab country that was impossible for diplomatic reasons. So I discussed the matter with the Captain and Purser and they agreed to allow him to stay on board. Fortunately, he survived the flight, was delivered to the hospital in

London, and then sadly died the next day. I could then wipe the sweat from my brow; at least he hadn't died on the aircraft!

Whilst in Beirut I felt we had to visit the Holy Land. It was only an eight-hour car drive away, so Madge and I took our eldest daughter with us to Damascus, Amman and Jerusalem.

A friend who worked for UNESCO in Jordan offered us accommodation in Amman and I then booked a hotel in Jerusalem for a few of the nights. The journey took us by way of Damascus and we spent one night there with some friends. We had a very quick look around and saw the Exhibition Grounds that had been developed a few years earlier. However, the practice of hanging people from street lamp posts encouraged us to move on to Jordan without too much delay. The food provisions were not as good as in Beirut, so we soon made our way out of town and on to Jordan.

Amman was a much more pleasant place to enter. Even the police force acted and dressed similar to the policemen in the UK. We spent one day driving out to see the old Roman city of Jerash, about 40 miles outside Amman; it is a wonderful, well-kept reminder of what sort of places the Romans built, and really worthwhile to visit.

When driving into Jerusalem we passed alongside the Dead Sea and could see people reading the newspaper whilst floating on the water in the sitting position. The sand on the shore leaves your shoes covered with the white salt.

Once in Jerusalem the Travel Agent for BOAC arranged for us to have a local guide to show us all the holy sights nearby such as Hebron and the Garden Tomb. In Hebron we found the Hebron glass manufacturers still making their special green and brown glassware in a similar way to that used two or three thousand years earlier. One very old Arab man was blowing donkey beads; he looked so old that you could imagine he had been there the whole 2,000 years. It was so very primitive that it made it all the more interesting; Jerry Camanarda, the *Times* correspondent, had told us about the place but our local guide had never seen the place before.

By finding the glass factory we were able to select some of the 'imperfect' items that they had made, which were so much more realistic than those bought in the local shops. We bought a set of wine glasses that were all of different shapes, and they caused quite an interesting topic of conversation when used at dinner parties.

Having had our few days in Jerusalem it was then time to go home via Amman and Damascus. Our friend in Amman, being with UNESCO, could get cigarettes cheaply and he offered me 1,000 to take back to Beirut. I accepted the lot without thinking about Customs regulations, and it was only when packing our things in the car that I realised I must hide them during our journey home.

Coming out from Beirut our friend had asked us to bring our own blankets, and fortunately we had recently bought some wonderful blankets in Beirut that had their own clear plastic covers that zipped up and held the blankets when they were not in use. It was within these blankets that I placed the cigarettes and then I placed them on top of the other cases in the car boot.

After doing this we were on our way. We left Jordan with no problem and after an hour or so into Syria the police stopped us at a roadside checkpoint, but the only question they asked was: "Have you any cigarettes?" I had some on the seat next to me, which I showed them, but I did not mention the ones in the boot of the car and they didn't ask me to open the it, so with a wave we were sent on our way. The next stop was the border crossing into Lebanon after passing through Damascus.

Here I had to open the boot and the Customs official, pointing to the two blankets inside their plastic covers, just said: "Take those into the Customs room." I parked the car where he told me and then took the two blankets to the door of the Customs office. Inside, the senior Customs official was arguing with a Lebanese man concerning duty he had to pay. He happened to look up and saw me, so I immediately shouted to him: "I bought these blankets in Beirut," at the same time shaking the blankets, one in each hand, and acting very hurt at being stopped prior to entering Lebanon. Fortunately, that was all I had to do: he waved me away and I returned to my car and drove home.

As you will realise I was now sweating heavily and so thankful that my cheek had enabled me to get past the border and go home. Of course, the friend who gave me the cigarettes never had to report to Customs as he was working for UNESCO, so he could bring anything into or out of the country without fear of being stopped. Neither my wife, my daughter nor I will never forget this incident.

Beirut had been quite an eventful experience for the family and me. Five years in the country had enabled us all to know the Lebanese people and also to get used to Arabic food as well as their customs. They are clever people who travel the world and always make a good living. They will bend the rules as cleverly as any other Arab, and a saying amongst the ex-pats in Beirut was: "The Lebanese will never be the first to recognise Israel, but they will be the first to be second."

So now we were on our way to the next country, Iraq.

CHAPTER 15

BAGHDAD

When it came near the end of my five years at Beirut, I asked HQ if they had another assignment for me; the reply was: "No, not a permanent posting, only temporary assignments." On this basis, I started to pack our things for taking to London and when over halfway through, HQ said they had changed their minds and I was to go to Baghdad, Iraq. This meant a re-think on what to take to Baghdad and what to send home. Half the packed goods had to be unpacked, as we would need them in Baghdad. It made a real mess of my packing arrangements, but somehow I got over it. One good thing was the fact that Pandy could come with us to Baghdad without quarantine, so we found a local kennels who would take care of him while we went to London on leave, having first got HQ agreement that afterwards we could be routed to Baghdad via Beirut to pick up the dog. Once this was confirmed, our baggage for Baghdad was held in Beirut pending our return to pick it up, so we went home for a month and had our leave.

We then set off for Baghdad. We night-stopped in Beirut and collected Pandy, making sure his jabs were up to date, and fixed for our baggage to board the same flight to Baghdad, a MEA flight. All was well until they realised that my tickets had been made out for 120 kg total baggage, whereas we had nearer 800 kg. But it just needed a few words in the right ears and lo and behold, it all went on the flight with us.

Pandy was bigger than I had thought and the kennel I had bought in the UK for him to travel in was far too small; he could get in it and sit down, but could not turn around. Still, we were taking him in the cabin with us, so no problems were envisaged, and he was not put in the kennel until we were boarding the aircraft and walking up the steps. We had been assured that four seats in first class had been retained for us, but as we walked up the front steps, the first look at the cabin revealed that other Arab friends of the staff had also been boarded with the same assurance, and the cabin was completely full; on going through into the economy cabin the only four seats in the aircraft were singles spread throughout the entire cabin. After the cabin crew asked people if they were prepared to move, Madge and the two children finished up seated together, with myself in a middle seat halfway back down the cabin.

So that was our seating problem resolved, but now Pandy needed settling. He didn't like being in the too small kennel, so I let him out and took him back to sit between my legs all the way to Baghdad. I had Arab gentlemen seated either side of me: both seemed to hate dogs and, on top of that, Pandy didn't like Arabs. One passenger was trying to lean out of the window and the other halfway across the aisle for the rest of the flight. Of course, I had a very firm grip on Pandy, but thank goodness the flight was only just over two hours.

Baghdad turned out to be a hot and dusty place, but fortunately we arrived at the end of summer and were moved again just after Easter the following year, so we missed the worst. On arrival, Cliff Clifton, whom I was replacing at Baghdad, met us and, as Pandy had been out of the kennel during the flight, I put him on his lead and walked him off the aircraft. It would appear that Customs thought it was Cliff's dog (don't forget Pandy's mother was in Baghdad) as not once was I questioned about the dog's papers. We just walked through all the formalities with him on the lead and out into the cars that were awaiting our arrival.

The BOAC agent for Iraq owned the house which we were given. The furnishing was old but adequate, and a desert cooler was on the roof, but there were no air conditioners. The houseboy, John, did speak some English, but not as well as the maids we had whilst in Beirut. Shops for food were close at hand but stocks were limited, again not like Beirut. The only thing in favour was that there were only four flights per week, two in the daytime and two in the late evening, so there was no night work as such, a pleasant change from Beirut.

At the airport, my staff included two female passenger assistants (English ladies married to Iraqis), an Iraqi catering officer-*cum*-general handyman and an office boy (runner of messages). Outside of these, there was the Station Engineer (John Eborne – overseas contract), who looked after the technical side of things. Of course, Iraqi Airways were contracted to handle the flights and my staff just had to monitor what they did and issue tickets when required. The cargo side was left to Iraqi airways and I was to advise them if they had a problem. Overall, it didn't look as if it would be a taxing job to run the station.

Our handling agents at Baghdad Airport were Iraqi Airways; they had been formed from the Iraqi Railways, who were still very proud of the train service direct to London. Surprisingly, you could travel to London every day of the week, the train leaving Baghdad every morning at 10.00, and it took a good few days to arrive in London. The rail company had become so proud of their records that they downgraded Iraqi Airways, and the most inefficient staff were transferred from the railway to the airline.

I once had quite an argument with the manager of Iraqi Airways because none of the baggage or cargo trolleys had any brakes. I was informed: "They don't need brakes on the trolleys at the railway station, so why should they have them at the airport?" Of course, the platform at the railway station was very flat and even, and he just couldn't, or wouldn't, recognise the difference between the railway platform and the aircraft ramp. Many aircraft were at risk of being damaged by trolleys freewheeling across the ramp with staff running after them, trying to stop them crashing into aircraft.

On the social side, there were two Clubs available to staff: one, the Alwia Club, was well-established and was a hand-me-down from the old colonial days; the other was the British Club, which had recently been formed, considered necessary because the Alwia Club was no longer exclusively British – local Iraqi businessmen could now become members of the Alwia Club, a thing not heard or thought of in the past.

The Alwia Club had marvellous facilities, with tennis courts, snooker tables, table tennis, swimming pools, a restaurant (excellent cheap food) and the usual British pub-type bar, whereas the British Club was quite small with just a bar, swimming pool, dart boards and snack bar. The pool was boarded over in winter and used as a dance floor at parties, but no other games facilities were provided.

In comparison to all the other stations I had so far been to, Baghdad was the most isolated; the teleprinter lines were forever failing and telephone lines outside of Iraq were limited to four hours per day and routed via operators in Paris, who seemed to take delight in cutting you off. It made life very difficult when you had technical delays and needed information to resolve the problems. On one particular bad delay I spent hours trying to get dispensation for a VC.10 to continue to Beirut for full repair and, even though I managed to keep the line open for an extra twenty minutes over the normal set period, it still wasn't long enough to get the information I needed: we just had to wait for the written confirmation to come through from London. This meant the crew ran out of hours and had to be 'stood down' for rest, so a night stop was necessary. This was when the other problems presented themselves, such as: how do you get entry visas for all the passengers?

This is where our catering officer/handyman handsomely proved his worth. He was well known by the officers in charge of immigration, mainly due to the fact that he supplied them with BOAC bags, postcards, playing cards etc., so we collected all the passengers' passports (some even had Jewish immigration stamps in them), and then he took all of them along to Immigration HQ for processing. Immigration was a part of the Army and fortunately our handyman, armed with more BOAC flight bags and other give-aways, persuaded the Officer-in-Charge to grant visas *gratis* to all the passengers. With this done, the passengers could be taken to a hotel and wined & dined after their long tedious day hanging around at the airport. The handyman had proved once again how generally helpful he was to the station.

During my time at Baghdad, I never received any complaints about the catering on flights. The handyman had ensured that the crews were well cared for during their short stay at the airport, and he went out of his way to look after them. All crews were invited into the Terminal for free coffee and biscuits and set next to each place was a ½ lb block of Iraqi dates. BOAC never paid for this service; the handyman had persuaded the caterers they should provide this service or they could lose their contract. The staff were also well cared for by the handyman, who arranged that we all got a full English breakfast every morning we were on duty. We didn't get the dates, but who cared? Everyone was happy!

With the shortage of good food in Iraq, it was arranged that every so often I could go to Beirut and buy food to bring back. Contract staff gave me their orders and I would do the shopping and return the same day, going out on the BOAC VC.10 and coming back on the MEA Comet 4 the same evening. But it was a tiring trip that didn't always go right; on one occasion, my suitcase was left behind in Beirut and all the fresh meats were not so fresh when they eventually arrived!

Whilst I was in Baghdad the General Manager was fighting to get the position of Station Manager upgraded and at the same time to get me promoted as well. The grade for the Station had not risen for years, due to the previous General Manager's lack of action, and was therefore below the normal grade for this type of airport. He eventually was successful in getting the upgrade for the Station, but not for me, as they found someone else who was already at the new grade to take my place. At first I was disappointed, but in retrospect I was very lucky, as the new man was caught up in the military coup that took place shortly after I had left and he did not have too good a time getting his family safely out of Iraq.

Whilst we were in Baghdad one funny incident occurred that scared Madge one evening when I was working and she was alone at home. She was reading a thrilling book about the Black & Tans in Ireland, and was seated in the lounge with the two children asleep in bed upstairs, when suddenly there was a large bang, similar to a gunshot. The shock of it made her think back to Ireland and the tales she had heard in her youth relating to random Black & Tan shootings, so she ran upstairs and locked herself in with the children, thinking that at any minute someone would be breaking down the doors. But after thirty minutes or so nothing had happened, so she ventured downstairs and, as she entered the lounge, her foot hit some glass. The room had a very large chandelier with numerous candlestick-type bulbs, and the explosion that had given her such a shock was one of these electric light bulbs bursting.

We don't, in this era, give much credit to the influence that Iraq, and in particular Baghdad, had on the development of commercial aviation. But in fact Baghdad had in the early days been a vital staging point on the route to the near and far east and indeed during the whole development of international routes. But now the flying range of modern aircraft has rendered unnecessary so many refuelling (staging) points that had previously been so vital.

The weather in Baghdad was just starting to get really hot when I heard I was to be posted to Frankfurt, Germany. Moving so quickly from Baghdad was a surprise, although not entirely unexpected, and it pleased Madge, as she found the conditions so unstable and unpredictable. One day the President was killed in a helicopter crash and a power battle ensued, whereupon our house boy disappeared in fear of what might happen locally, leaving my son still at school and Madge with no means of getting him home. I had to get the Area Manager's driver to collect him and take him home, so she was not displeased that we were moving once again. It certainly hadn't been that happy a posting for us both.

CHAPTER 16

FRANKFURT

Once again, we had the problem of Pandy, although he could at least enter Germany without quarantine restrictions. However we had to go home to England first, and this would mean us being a few weeks late in arriving in Germany, so we appreciated it when the station engineer, John Eborn, and his wife said they would keep him until we were ready for him in Germany. He seemed happy with them although he proved his dislike for Arabs once again, including their Iraqi cook.

They had a male cook and houseboy, who prepared all the food; however, if he put Pandy's food down on the floor, he just wouldn't eat it, although he would if Mrs Eborn placed the plate on the floor. This didn't happen just once, it was the same every day; the cook would prepare the meal, then he would have to call Mrs Eborn for her to put the plate down for Pandy.

When we eventually arrived in Germany, I sent a message to John Eborn to send Pandy; we were not really ready for a dog as we were still accommodated in a hotel, but felt we could not impose longer on John and his wife. So he took Pandy to the airport with the very large kennel I had obtained for him this time. He was to travel on Lufthansa and naturally I would have to pay the full rate, but the Lufthansa manager suggested to John that a special cardboard kennel was available for dogs this size and would not cost so much, so Pandy was transferred into the smaller cardboard kennel and was loaded into the hold of the aircraft.

The flight was routed via Beirut and on arrival there Pandy decided he was back home, so as soon as the hold door was open he jumped out: he had eaten his way out of the cardboard kennel. Luckily our friends there recognized Pandy and sent me a message that he had been caught and would be travelling the next day, but I never got this message until I had reported to Lufthansa cargo to collect Pandy and had been told: "'No dog on board!" It was therefore a great relief when I knew that he had been caught and was safe. He arrived next day in a wooden kennel provided by Lufthansa and was none the worse for his little excursion in Beirut.

One thing I forgot to mention about my departure from Beirut was what I did with the car. I went to see the General Manager of TMA (Trans Mediterranean Airlines) and asked what special rate he could give me to fly my car home. He offered a price of £50, provided I helped them get clearance of extra flights into UK for carrying fuel into Africa. He gave me the name of their representative in London, an ex-BOAC man, and he got the permission straight away. So when my car arrived at Gatwick Airport I went down and collected it; it was useful for my short break in London.

When we arrived in Frankfurt, I obviously needed a car, so I suggested that BOAC ship it out to me, which they did on BEA. So once again I was driving a right-hand-drive car on the right (or in this case *wrong*) side of the road, but after five years doing the same in Beirut it was no longer a problem for me.

So here we were now, in Germany, and a European posting is quite different to those outside of Europe. The German staff were not particularly helpful, other than for saying which agents you should use to find a house. The agents naturally only spoke German and at that time I unfortunately did not, so I had to do my normal shift and then drive around trying to find the houses suggested by the agents. The Station Manager, Frank Bastard, and his wife Renée told us to find our own place, hopefully not on their doorstep. Incidentally, I never did understand why Frank never changed his surname; I do know, however, that he never signed anything 'F. Bastard'!

Then there was the problem of where to send the children, Kathryn and Michael, to school. By this time Jeannie was already settled in boarding school in England. So, not knowing the system in Germany, I selected a German private school, Anna Schmidt's in the centre of Frankfurt, although it was only later that I found out that children who failed to pass their end-of-year exams on a second attempt were thrown out of the very good German state schools, and their families then had to find a private school that would take their dunces. So, unlike England, these private schools were full of no-goods, lazy idiots and the local dunces, and my choice was therefore a complete failure.

In the meantime we were still living in the hotel along with our dog, not an ideal arrangement, but luckily I then found an excellent ground floor flat in Sachsenhausen, an area near to the River Main and central to Frankfurt: the only problem was it had only two bedrooms and there were five of us during holiday periods. Anyway, we were so fed up with living in the hotel that we decided we could make do as the lounge and dinning rooms were so very large. It also had a garden, which would be 'handy for Pandy,' so we moved in and stayed there for seven eventful years; it proved to be ideal for me, and Madge and the children liked it too.

However no one in the building spoke English and so we had to learn to make ourselves understood by whatever means we could. So I started to take lessons in the evenings; it was difficult to get away from the office but BOAC were at least paying, so it had to be done. The General Manager (Europe) had decided that all overseas staff within Europe had to learn the language of the country to which they were posted. Surprisingly, the German staff became quite helpful when they realised that I was really trying to speak their language.

The year I went to Germany was 1966, World Cup year, with England *versus* Germany in the Final. What a clash within the office! The German staff 'fixed' the operations board to indicate that Germany would win by 2 goals to 1, so without the German staff seeing me I changed the 1 into a 6, showing England as the winner. All hell let loose in the office when this change was noticed, and I felt it best if I went home to watch the match: just me against the rest within the office would have been unbearable. Still, we did win in the end, although the Germans always disputed the result. Once I had some knowledge of German, my work relationships with the locals improved, however we still had the BEA *versus* BOAC combat to contend with.

Pandy and I became well known by the local residents, because I always took him for a walk in the nearby squares. He was such a pretty dog that he attracted people for a chat, good for my attempts to speak German. But he was a bit of a terror and gave Madge many a fright in his attempts to get out of the garden around our flat. He became well known at Frankfurt airport as well; when Madge had to go to England and leave me on my own with Pandy, I used to take him to work with me, where he would lie at my feet under my desk and watch whoever came in to see me.

On one occasion, the secretary to the BEA accountant came in and stood very near to my desk. She had sandals on with her toes uncovered, and Pandy thought they looked tasty and licked them from under the desk. What a shock she had! Luckily, she liked dogs and felt that this was a sign that Pandy liked her, so from then onwards, if I took Pandy to work, she would come every lunch hour to take him for a walk; this would end up in Pandy meeting the crews in Customs whilst she paid them their allowances. He was made a fuss of by everyone, so really I had no problems taking him to work at all.

However, on one occasion he *was* a bit of an embarrassment. We had a King of Nigeria and his Queen due to travel to Kano in Nigeria. He was travelling by road from Bonn and there was a lot of fog on the motorways, so we waited as long as we could, even allowing for a 15-minute delay, but still they didn't arrive, so I closed the flight and went out to ensure it got away. My secretary, Miss Bauer, was left to await the King's eventual arrival and he turned up about 30 minutes later. Forgetting that I had Pandy in the office, she took the King and Queen there to relax whilst we worked out how to get him on another flight to Kano. As soon as they entered the office Pandy really growled at them both; to him they were black, very large individuals and strangers. Miss Bauer finally managed to get Pandy out of the room and the King and Queen were then able to sit down and await my return to the office. Of course, I was able to sort them out with an alternative flight, but it did mean going via London (Heathrow).

At this time we were still in the old terminal at Frankfurt; the lower floor under my office had been built before the war and it was only since the war was over that the second floor had been added, so when you looked out of the windows to the offices you could step down onto the roof of the original building. Pandy jumped out of our window one day and had a run around on the roof; then he misjudged which window he had jumped out of and found the BEA accountant's window open, so the occupant was most surprised to have a dog come suddenly flying in through his window and across his desk. A great laugh for us all!

In Germany dogs were allowed to travel anywhere, so if we were going out for the day, say along the Rhine, Pandy would come with us in the car, on the cruise boats and on the trains back to where the car was parked. Once when we were on leave, some colleagues, Ian and Jan Robinson, offered to have Pandy whilst we were away, and went on one of these boat trips up the Rhine, taking Pandy with them. The boat they were on had many American tourists, and one woman said to Ian: "Say, what sort of dog is he?" As quick as a flash, Ian said: "He's a Lebanese sporting hound." The American woman was thrilled to hear this and called all her friends over saying: "Hey, fellahs, look at this Lebanese sporting hound!" He was the talk of the town that night.

Quite often, we would have to leave Pandy in kennels when we went on leave; he didn't like it, but with the quarantine regulations in the UK we couldn't take him home to England. The kennel owners knew we would pay whatever it cost and so never worried if we were late back off leave. At the end of one of my leaves in 1971, I had a heart attack on the last day and ended up in intensive care and drugged up to the hilt. This delayed my return to Frankfurt by nearly six months, but fortunately I recovered completely and returned to Frankfurt fit to work once again. On the very day I arrived back, the kennels rang to ask if we still wanted Pandy, as he had been with them for seven months by this time. Naturally I said yes. They hadn't wanted to get rid of him but some friends of theirs were interested in having him, hence their call to find out what the situation was. We went to the kennels the next day to pick Pandy up and he recognised us immediately, so you would think we had only been away for a week or so. He was all over us and we took him home very happily.

Being in Frankfurt for such a long time, we made some very good friends, two of which were our doctors, Heinz and Gertrud Leutke. Gertrud spoke very good English and Heinz was a good heart specialist, and they had two children, a girl, Renate, and a boy, Frank. Frank spent many an hour at our house and although he was a lot older than Kathryn and Michael, he would play games with them both for hours. The Leutke's were wealthy and certainly out of our league, however, we got on really well with them, and we have spent many a good evening together both in Germany and England over the years.

As mentioned earlier, my choice of schooling for Kathryn and Michael was not good. It also cost too much as I had to pay for taxis each way for both children; they went together in the morning but came home separately as Kathryn was older than Michael and had a longer school day. When someone other than her normal taxi driver tried to pick up Kathryn, that was it; she would have to go to England to boarding school like Jeannie. She was a year too young for Jeannie's convent school, but under the circumstances and understanding our predicament on schooling in Germany, they agreed to accept her. So off she went, leaving us with just Michael to consider; as he was too young for boarding school in the UK we moved him to the American school in the Taunus Mountains with a taxi ride of 36 km each way each day. The taxi picked up about six children each day, Michael being the first, which meant he was the last home as well. It worked out well, although I was not over-happy with the standard of education. Therefore, as soon as he became eight years old, Michael also went to boarding school in England.

Michael was always an early riser. He would get up and get dressed and be around by the local grocery shop as it opened, at about 4 am. He would collect fresh rolls for our breakfast and be back home before we were even awake, so we didn't hear him go out or come in; otherwise we might have tried to stop him. Apparently he would chat to the grocer and even help him set up the store for his early customers. Considering he was only six years old when he started this practice, it is quite remarkable. When he went to boarding school later, they were most upset at his habit of getting up so early and waking up the rest of the boys, and he was told very firmly that 7 am was the time to get up and not a minute earlier. He told us later that the hours between 5 and 7 am were the longest hours of the day to him.

Almost twenty years later I went back to Frankfurt and went into town on the train. Coming out of the station I started to look for a taxi and, as I approached the first one in the queue, the driver saw me coming and got out of the car to meet me; much to my surprise he said: "Herr Folkard, wie geht es ihnen?" (How are you?); it was the taxi driver who had taken Michael to school every day in the late 1960s. What a coincidence!

Whilst based in Germany I took advantage of the circumstances and bought myself a Mercedes Benz. I obtained the first one through the taxi firm owner who carried my children to school and also covered all the crew movements between airport and hotel and back. It was the newest model and I got the first one to be delivered in Frankfurt. Everyone watched you go by as they hadn't seen this model before; Madge didn't like that at all, but I thought it great. Unfortunately the car was stolen just over a year later from outside our flat; I had come home very late and decided not to disturb the neighbours by opening the garage, so parked the car on the very wide pavement outside the house. The next morning there was no trace of the car, so I had to report the theft to my insurance company and the police. It was never found, but everyone said it could have been stolen to order, something quite common at that time for customers in Greece. I had to wait three months before the insurance company would agree to pay for a replacement, and they insisted it had to be a similar-type car, but even then they only gave me 90% of the new purchase price.

Luckily for me, one of my colleagues was going on leave for six weeks at the time my car went missing, so he loaned his car to me, thereby averting the need for me to hire a car while awaiting the delivery of the replacement Mercedes. I also had four weeks' leave in the UK, which meant I avoided having to hire a car in Germany. To get a quick delivery of my new Mercedes I said that I was moving to Abu Dhabi in the Middle East; I had a friend living there and I used his address. So, being an export order, the waiting time was reduced from 18 months to just 6 weeks. The replacement was an upgrade of my previous model, the Mercedes 230 with six cylinders and a five-speed gearbox but the same colour – cream.

In due course, Madge and I went to Stuttgart to collect the car from the main factory at Sindelfingen. We had the opportunity to look around their museum and were then invited to lunch, which I took as a hint that our car wasn't ready. We were then told over lunch that the gearbox had been delivered one day late and had held up the construction of the car. Although we were offered overnight accommodation in their hotel completely at their expense, I had already told them I had to get back on duty the next day and must return that night to Frankfurt, but in hindsight I should perhaps have taken advantage of the situation and had the night 'on Mercedes,' telephoning the office to regret not being able to return that evening. Needless to say, they drove us to the airport in a brand-new car straight off the production line and with no number plates, and we arrived just in time to get the last flight of the night. But we could not get staff tickets, so had to buy them at the full rate, although I subsequently had the cost refunded by Mercedes Benz. We returned on my next day off to collect the car and it was marvellous to drive and well worth the wait.

I had learnt quite a bit about German cars in the meantime. One most important thing was that, unless you asked for 'safety glass,' the car would be fitted with normal glass, a great hazard in the event of a crash. My previous car had had normal glass and one day, driving at 70 mph, a stone from a passing car had hit the windshield, which had shattered and rained glass in both my and my mother-in-law's laps. Luckily, neither of us was hurt (although she refused to sit in the front seat from then onwards) and a big enough hole allowed me to see where we were going, but it was a cold ride home that day with no windshield. The replacement windshield was safety glass: I insisted on that. Now we are in the EEC I believe German cars are forced to have safety glass fitted the same as in the UK.

My friend from Abu Dhabi then came to Frankfurt to buy a Mercedes for himself to actually take back to Abu Dhabi. Once home he went to the Agent there and claimed a discount from his Agent's commission; surprisingly he was successful, and a few months later we both got a couple of hundred pounds back. Added to this surprise discount, I had saved the long waiting time normally experienced in Germany at that time, and had also got the car at about a quarter of the price of the same car in the UK, so I was very pleased with myself. I drove that car for 16 years, so I certainly got my money's worth.

In Frankfurt the Airport Company, FFAG, were most successful with a temporary Domestic Terminal they built whilst I was in Frankfurt. It was of very simple construction with minimum facilities to passengers but allowed fast check-in and movement of passenger loads. You checked in as you entered the departure gate, so check-in could be as little as ten minutes prior to departure, revolutionary back in the late 1960s. As you boarded the bus to the aircraft, you picked up your lunch, tea or dinner box to carry on to the aircraft. Different colours advised you of their contents, so you still had a choice. This facility was used on the Berlin run operated by BEA and PANAM (Lufthansa were not allowed to operate between West Germany and Berlin until the 1990s).

BOAC/BA also handled the Qantas (Australian) Airline services. They only had about four flights per week, so there was not too much extra for us to monitor. Their flights were strictly monitored from Sydney, and if a delay occurred the crew could not add an extra hour to the rest period for their own convenience; Sydney would immediately send a message correcting the departure time to that given by the minimum rest period legally stated.

One of their flights was a mixed cargo and passenger flight. The Boeing 707 had a large cargo pallet-size door to the front of the aircraft. We could load three pallets in the front and there were about 70 economy seats at the rear of the aircraft. On one of these flights, while I was talking to the flight deck crew a blonde stewardess came into the cockpit to ask what the flight time was to Bahrain, their next destination, to which the first officer said very precisely: "5 hours and 60 minutes." She said "Thank you" and walked off back to the rear of the aircraft while we waited for her to make the announcement to the passengers. Sure enough, she said exactly what she had been told: "Ladies and gentlemen, the flight time to Bahrain will be 5 hours and 60 minutes." The roar of laughter and clapping that came from the passengers had to be heard to be believed, and you can imagine the laughter amongst the flight crew as well.

In Frankfurt I had some confrontations with passengers during delays, even with celebrities such as Des O'Connor. His flight was delayed overnight one evening, so all the passengers were taken to a hotel in the Taunus Mountains and of course a BOAC staff member (Miss Bauer) went with them. The following morning I arranged a coach trip though the mountains, ending up at a 16th century Coach Inn for late lunch. I suggested to Miss Bauer that Des O'Connor and his family might stay and rest at the hotel in the mountains and have their lunch there, but Des decided that he would prefer to take his family on the coach trip with the rest of the passengers, as otherwise they might miss seeing something. But the Taunus Mountain trip was a washout: they were in fog, mist or drizzle the whole time, very disappointing. So they had lost their opportunity to rest up in the hills and strangely enough, I was held to blame. At the airport, we were suffering terrible weather, and the BEA engineers were having great difficulty making the repairs within the normal time scale. Meantime I told the BEA Duty Officer not to bring the passengers to the airport unless the aircraft was fully serviceable, but the next thing I knew was that the passengers were at the airport and screaming for my blood, in particular Des O'Connor.

I tried to explain the situation to him and how I had tried to keep him out of the confusion caused by the delay by suggesting he stayed at the hotel until called: he could have whatever drinks and food he wanted and we would not leave him behind. But he was not able to not accept that he had brought the agitation of the delay on himself and his family, and the argument was becoming quite heated between us when suddenly a thunderbolt hit the airport with a tremendous noise within the terminal, like an 88 mm cannon being fired next to your ear. Fortunately it broke the mood and Des O'Connor walked away immediately he realised how appalling the weather was outside, therefore extending the delay. Other passengers then came up to me in sympathy, realising that I had done all that was practically possible to make the delay as painless as possible to them all. But you never quite got used to being criticized so strongly when you knew you had done everything possible to avoid the consequences of the delay.

I can remember another long delay in which Jon Pertwee (the current Dr Who) was involved. On this occasion it was foggy weather in London which was the problem; he wanted to get back to UK for filming the next morning in Dover. As usual, I was as helpful as possible and managed to find a Lufthansa flight going to Manchester, coupled with a BBC car to drive him to Dover. He was most grateful and wrote to me afterwards explaining what happened after he arrived in Manchester. He eventually got to Dover all right but the weather there was so bad that they could not film for almost a week. Many years later he travelled on BA to Nairobi with his new wife when I was at the bottom of the aircraft steps as he walked off the plane, and he recognised me from halfway up. The Kenyan Duty Officer whom I was training at that time was most impressed in the way he greeted me and the fact that I introduced him to Dr Who.

Whilst in Frankfurt we decided to take a holiday in Hong Kong. Rex Crisp and Wyn were based there and offered to give us accommodation. The flight was via Teheran (Iran) and quite long, but just after departure the Chief Steward came and gave presents to our three children and then surprisingly gave a present to me from the BEA German staff, a packet of wine gums (Maynard's of course!). It was a lunch-time departure from Frankfurt and every lunch-time when I was working I would buy wine gums and go around giving all the staff on duty a few, having the rest myself as I had no time to stop and eat a proper meal. They, the German staff members, decided to do the same for me on my departure on holiday, a wonderful thought and one I much appreciated.

Our return from Hong Kong was arranged via Beirut, giving us the opportunity to see if things had changed much since we left. We arrived very early in the morning and got accommodation at the Beauivarg Hotel. Going up to the seventh floor in the lift it felt as if the building was moving, but we were all so tired we believed it was our fatigue making it feel that way; then the next morning we learnt that there had been an earthquake during the night and many buildings had collapsed, with people injured and many families living out in the open for fear of being crushed within their homes.

Our few days' stay in Beirut was enjoyable although the situation was far from secure politically. Troops were out all over town and little disturbances kept on occurring. An Arab shopkeeper who had been a friend when we lived in Beirut saw us walking around town and took us to his shop, then got one of his friends who had a car to rush us back to our hotel as he felt we were taking too many risks being in this part of town near the University (as in the rest of the world, it is always around Universities that disturbances seem to occur). So, a very exciting and potentially worrying end to our holidays.

Of course, during our stay in Frankfurt, aviation was still developing. Airports had to be ready for the Boeing 747, an extra-large aircraft carrying twice as many passengers as the VC.10 or other conventional aircraft types. BOAC had ordered Boeing 747s but they were not being used on the Frankfurt route. Boeing also brought out the Boeing 757 around this time, and BEA ordered these and introduced them to Frankfurt. These aircraft types were suited to different routes and passenger capacities; the B747 could take up to 500 passengers in full economy in a twin-aisle configuration, whereas the B757 had a maximum of 250/260 seats in a single-aisle arrangement. Since its initial introduction the B747 was developed from the 100 series to the 400 series, the main difference being that the engines were larger and more powerful, allowing a much higher take-off weight and enabling more fuel to be loaded, thereby increasing its range; it also took a much higher payload, so it became more economical to operate. Once again, it meant that some of the intermediate stops could be avoided without having payload drops. Non-stop flights from London to Singapore, Hong Kong and Tokyo were now feasible. Other routes like London to Cape Town were also introduced and also the Atlantic routes like London to Los Angeles became acceptable.

The B757 is a much larger version of the B737 in some ways. The B737 is for short-haul flights such as internal flights within the UK and near-Europe. Lufthansa had quite a few B737 aircraft and they used them fully: from 0600 to 2300 hours they were used as passenger carriers, but between 2300 and 0600 they carried all the internal German post office mail, resulting in the utilization of the fleet being up to 20 hours per day instead of only 12-14 hours.

All three of these Boeing aircraft were very popular with the western world aircrew, being very reliable and easy to handle on the ground, although the B747 needed specialist equipment to handle the baggage, cargo and mail it carried; this equipment was very expense to buy and maintain but as you couldn't do without it the prices for ground handling increased proportionally.

It mustn't be thought that Boeing were the only company building new aircraft. Lockheed were making the Tri-Star, a three-engined aircraft, while Douglas were making the DC-9 twin-jet aircraft for medium to short-haul flights and then the DC-10, another three-engined aircraft with long-range capacity but not quite a large as the B747. In England we had developed the BAC 111 twin-jet aircraft, a relatively small aircraft with 80-90 seats but quite liked by the crew who flew it. The VC.10 and VC.15 had been the main successful aircraft built in the UK, however the Concorde was under construction in UK and France, and this first flew in 1969 and finally became fully certified to carry passengers in December 1975.

Around this time, a consortium of European manufacturers got together to start making Airbus aircraft; France, Germany, Spain and the United Kingdom were all involved and this gave Europe the first chance to compete with Boeing, Douglas and Lockheed in the USA.

When the time arrived for our final move from Germany, we decided to drive home with our main baggage going by air. We had a lot of baggage, and in fact we used four 'Igloo' containers on a Boeing 747; also the roof rack on top of the car made the ferry boat people class us as a caravan instead of a car! Our son Michael travelled in the car with us as he was away from school at that time; he barely had room to sit in the car, the back seat being so full of last-minute items that were left behind when our main baggage had gone to the airport.

The journey home was uneventful, although long. Customs at Dover were not difficult, but we were pleased it was over and now we had to get used to living in the UK for a while. Luckily, we still had a house to live in and the children were still going to boarding school. I had decided that their education must not suffer because of my return to work in the UK, but what a struggle that turned out to be financially.

CHAPTER 17

RETURN TO THE UK

Being back in the UK after so many years overseas, things seemed quite different. Luckily, I was soon given an assignment in BOAC Charter Branch. I had an office in Victoria opposite the Victoria Passenger Terminal in Buckingham Palace Road, and my office was on top of the Victoria Bus Terminal. My title was 'Enforcement Officer' for charter flights controlled by Club Membership numbers, a means used to separate normal commercial passengers from Group Travel groups. This avoided a clash between the scheduled airlines and the charter companies over who could operate special charter flights, which were not advertised on the open market.

The work could be quite boring except for the fact that the Operations Controller would agree flights extra to those offered by the Fleet Managers. As the day of operation approached there would be a great panic to try to find aircraft to operate the service, and quite often we had to give the business to other carriers who had capacity available. On occasions, we paid more to get an aircraft than we had charged the Charter group, so it sounds as if the Operations Controller was irresponsible but this is not the case, as the fleets would always try to keep an aircraft available, up their sleeve as it were, just in case they had an unscheduled technical problem.

By overbooking the aircraft, the Charter Operations Controller always had business available whenever an aircraft was finally found to be available from the fleets. No wastage within the company was permitted; the fleet's spare capacity (which they were trying to hold up their sleeves) was forced away from them, thereby gaining revenue for Charter Branch and BOAC.

When things did go wrong, such as when no aircraft was available, frantic searches would be made to find another airline with capacity to take our load, and this often entailed changes to the flights schedules in addition to the possibility of increased costs for BOAC to absorb. It was then that I got the task of ensuring that the re-arranged operation went well at whichever London airport we were forced to use. I had many a late night sorting out some of these off-scheduled services, and I had to ensure that BOAC's reputation for customer service to passengers was maintained.

I became well known at the London airports, although they couldn't always remember my surname; I was quite often referred to as 'Harry Charters,' and announcements were made such as: "Will Harry Charters kindly report to ticket desk 24 where a charter passenger needs his assistance." My reputation, rightly or wrongly, was that I could solve all charter passenger problems, and in general the airport traffic staff seemed to think I had this gift; anyway, it pleased them all to state: "Agreed by Harry Charters" on any reports they had to complete. As it happens, I never did get any comebacks from the solutions I made or was supposed to have made in respect to these passengers.

There was one particular group, the Divine Light Mission, which made a considerable number of charters for B747-size aircraft. The flights were from either New York or London to India and every one was full. This religious sect had their *guru* in India and they all wanted to see him and be with him. Families would often split up and allow father and children to go whilst the mother stayed behind. They were always very peaceful people, and even when they came back after their week or two in India suffering from dysentery or diarrhoea, they still were easy to handle from the airport's point of view – mind you, the aircraft took some cleaning after each flight.

Because of this complicated control arrangement for scheduled airline charters, we encountered a number of crooked operators making bookings for flights. Sometimes they booked passengers for more than one destination on the same flight, and of course the passengers were unaware of this fact. On one occasion a flight had people saying they had booked to Boston while others said New York and others Montreal or Toronto. This crooked agent booked enough to fill one aircraft and applied to BOAC to provide an aircraft to one of the destinations. They provided all passenger names to BOAC to make it sound legitimate but only stated one destination. Charter Branch then offered an aircraft, issued the tickets and demanded payment under the usual terms (which was never paid), but the agent gave out the date and time of departure to all the booked passengers, who always turned up at the airport, as they had no idea that they were being conned. The agent had previously collected all the money from the passengers and informed them when to arrive at the airport, so they had the charter tickets issued by BOAC, but BOAC had still not received any payment as per schedule. This led to BOAC cancelling the flight altogether, but of course the passengers still turned up, having no knowledge of the crookedness of their agent. At this point, I became involved at the airport when I had to refuse the passengers and try to disperse them from Heathrow, and this particular flight got me on the 6 pm BBC News.

The organisers of the group had ensured that their passengers came to the airport to check in, and they (the agents) even presented themselves as part of the group and argued about having paid their fares, demanding that BOAC took responsibility for their travel. Luckily for me, the plight of this particular flight had already been pointed out to some senior BOAC officials, one of whom, Derek Engeldew, who I knew quite well, had come to the airport knowing that trouble was likely and that I would need help. My instructions were purely to stop any of the passengers being accepted at the check-in, but I had no authority to give any other concessions, and this is where Derek, as Sales Manager UK, could offer passengers the chance to buy normal BOAC tickets to wherever they wanted to go and then agree that they could sign IOUs for the costs. At least this enabled the passengers to travel home, with the problem of collecting the IOUs to be resolved later. I never did find out how many of these were eventually paid, very few I expect, but at least BOAC had managed to extricate itself from a very unsavoury commercial situation.

Derek Engeldew was well known for his sometimes unusual and original sales gimmicks. I knew him from my introduction to training for overseas as he was Training Controller when I started doing my Operations courses. He was helpful to all trainees and was liked by everyone, and his good efforts eventually got him posted to be Sales Manager (Japan).

At this time BOAC were the only airline operating pure jet and turbojet prop aircraft to Japan, VC.10s and Britannias; these were fuelled by kerosene, so Derek decided to make the people in Japan fully aware of this fact and organised petrol distribution points at prominent intersections around Tokyo with a notices saying: "Help yourself, BOAC no longer uses it." This sales gimmick went down well in Japan and Derek got himself good sales figures and eventually further promotion. I should explain that all other airlines were still using high-octane petrol for their flights, with a correspondingly lower safety potential and higher fire risk.

One Charter Club using BOAC extensively was EUPO Air, the owner of which was a large jovial Chinaman, Willy Man, head of the Man family in China, and there were around 6 million 'Mans' within the worldwide family. Naturally his offices were in Soho, and as he had one or two charters each week I made a weekly visit to check the Club membership names against the passengers listed on each of his flights.

Of course regulations are devised to be broken. A Club's membership was limited to around 20,000 people, whereas with this organisation it could be as high as 60,000 at any one time. This meant that the list of Club members was being adjusted each week before I arrived to make my check appear legitimate and, although everyone knew this was the case, no one ever took action against it; it was all made to look *kosher* as it was so highly lucrative to the Club and BOAC.

But these regulations covering charter flights were due to change, and within the airline industry the Government was being pressed to revise the regulations and allow groups of passengers to travel on scheduled flights. Hence, after nearly two years of dealing with this sort of problem, the regulations for charter flights were eased and Charter Groups were permitted to travel on scheduled flights, which resulted in the Charter branch being closed down.

It was now 1972-73 and I needed to get another assignment. Whilst up at Victoria I had now joined a group of old friends, who were now working in the Training Branch as instructors for BOAC. One such was Paddy Dunn, who had changed our life in Gander so many years before, and who by this time was Cargo Training Manager. On the passenger side we had Peter Smallbones. Both were real old-timers who had joined Imperial Airways in their youth, and they were also very good instructors, using their experiences in the UK and abroad to get their subjects home to the staff they were training. They were also very good at 'play-acting' during the lectures, and could act the 'irate passenger at check-in' to perfection.

Peter Smallbones was a proper leg-puller; he embarrassed my daughter Jeannie the first day she started working at Victoria Passenger Terminal with BOAC. I had told him she had started work across the road in the Terminal, and he decided to play a joke on her. During the lunch-hour break, he went over to the Terminal, waited for her to make an announcement for passengers to board the bus for Heathrow, then with all the passengers standing nearby came up to her and said: "Jeannie, did I leave my pyjamas at your place last night?" Jeannie had never seen him before, but did her face go red! Of course, we had a good laugh about this for years after.

Towards the end of my stint in Charter Branch, I sometimes had spare time, most of which I spent in Training Branch helping out, writing new load sheet exercises etc, etc., so when it was confirmed that I was to leave the section I arranged an appointment with the Charter Branch General Manager to see what he had been able to find for my future assignments. But just before I went into his office the General Manager of Training came up to me and said: "Harry, how would you like to join Training Branch to replace Paddy Dunn, as he is retiring"? I was most surprised, as Paddy Dunn hadn't previously mentioned his retirement to me, so I thanked him and said I would let him know after I had seen my present General Manager.

Whilst I was in with the Director of Charters, the General Manager of Traffic called to say that the Commercial Director had asked him if he had any experienced officers looking for overseas assignments. As I knew the Commercial Director very well I was then instructed to go to his office for a discussion. It transpired that the training programme overseas was advancing well, but needed 'on-the spot' tuning of newly-trained Duty Officers at Nairobi Airport. They had trained three local Kenyans and wanted them escorted during their initial months of actually working 'on the job'; this necessitated a two-year assignment, which would allow my family to join me in Nairobi. I told the Director that I had never wanted to return home to UK for work, feeling far more at home working overseas so, although I had had two offers in the same day, I naturally took the overseas assignment.

CHAPTER 18

KENYA

A few weeks later, I was on my way to Nairobi for the two-year assignment, which meant a permanent overseas posting with my family. (Our children Kathryn and Michael stayed in UK boarding schools, while Jeannie, the eldest, came back to our house after work each day). Naturally, they joined us for all their holidays, and when they did, what a wonderful time they had, as Jeannie could drive the car, so took the family around whilst I worked.

It was a happy station with only a few contract staff; the local Kenyans had completed full Duty Officer training, but needed experience with someone like me watching over them. By the time I got to Nairobi only two of the Duty Officers could be left on their own, the other two I split my shifts to monitor.

Flights from Nairobi were mainly transit flights. One went daily on to Johannesburg, returning the same evening to go direct to London; another went to the Seychelles, Mauritius and back, and a third went to N'Dola and Lusaka. All flights were extremely full weight-wise, and even in these more modern times, it was still necessary to either restrict the number of passengers or reduce the cargo uplifted when the sector to be flown was so very long. In Nairobi we had major contracts to uplift fresh vegetables and fruit, so we often had to limit passenger numbers on board. This made it very hard in respect to staff passengers as the cargo, being a commercial load, had priority.

Indeed the method of handling staff passengers could become very unfair in so many ways: staff could become stranded in Nairobi for days on end as other staff would arrive holding higher travel priorities and take the few seats actually available. So I decided to take a stand on this matter, and devised a means whereby staff that had been wait-listed for three days then had their travel priority upgraded over the more senior staff that had just reported for travel. It took a time to enforce this procedure, but I eventually got my way and it worked. Being such a lovely country many staff took advantage of these cheap travel facilities, so it was a pity if return travel problems spoilt their whole holiday. The flight crews were very sympathetic on this matter and often made slight flight plan adjustments to permit the uplift of extra staff when empty seats were available.

Kenya has some of the most wonderful golf courses in the world. They are also at altitude (c. 4,500 ft), so the ball goes further than when you are at sea level. I had bought a half set of clubs to take with me to Nairobi and I put them to good use whilst I was there. It was truly a gentleman's style of golf: you didn't have to carry your clubs as you always had an African caddie who knew the course to suggest which club you should use. However, the games played were no more gentlemanly than anywhere else in the world; there were still the 'bandits' playing in the local competitions, but that didn't worry me too much, as I was such a poor player anyway. I really stood no chance of winning anything, except perhaps the wooden spoon.

Just after I arrived in Nairobi, Dickie Clarkson, one of my bosses from my Gander days, came out for high-level discussions with Kenya Airways and he brought his wife Phil with him. It was suggested that I took Phil golfing whilst he was in meetings and, like a fool, I said I would. The wife of another local manager came along as well, so I was playing against two female golfers, both extremely good players with low handicaps, whereas I was a pure novice. We started at the tenth hole and, as was the custom, the men's tee was well behind the ladies' tee. My first shot was a complete miss of the ball, while my second brought me level with the ladies' tee. For the rest of the game I played in similar fashion: how embarrassing! Still, they were good sports and enjoyed their game against each other. My golf did improve while I was in in Kenya but it never became very good; it's a game you must start at an early age, not at 48 years old . . .

There are a couple of events which particularly stand out in my memory. The first of these occurred when I was driving to the airport one dark and rainy evening, actually following directly behind the engineer who was on duty with me. The main road thorough Nairobi was a black tarmac road and in the rain it looked like polished black marble. When the engineer ahead suddenly swerved in front of me with his brakes full on, I jammed on my brakes and it was only then that I noticed a very large black man dressed in a black suit lying flat out on the road. But the engineer hadn't hit him and it turned out he was just completely drunk and sleeping it off. As we were both in a hurry to get on duty at the airport before the evening flights arrived, I persuaded a driver of another car to park his car with its lights flashing to block the road where this man was laying. I also asked another driver to call for an ambulance; then I left the scene and went on to the airport. As I heard no more about this incident, I have to assume that the black man was all right and that we actually might have saved his life.

The second incident was another of these extremely rare types of occurrences, a 'one-in-a-million' in fact. I took Madge on a trip into the highlands near Nairobi, where the scenery was marvellous; we were returning home when, about 30 miles out from the city, there was a car at the side of the road with the driver trying to change a wheel. As a lady passenger was pacing up and down I felt that they must have been having problems with the wheel change, so I suggested to Madge that I'd stop and see what I could do to help. By this time I had passed the car and had to back up to be near them. I got out of the car and started to walk towards the other car, whereupon the lady passenger looked hard at me and then suddenly exclaimed: "Herr Folkard, wie geht es ihnen? Wir sind aus Frankfurt, Kennedy Allee 54."

It was our former neighbours in Frankfurt, who had lived in the apartment above ours during the last year we were there. How remarkable, there we are, miles out of town on a lonely road when we come across our German neighbours of four years earlier stuck with a wheel change problem just as we drove past. They were in a hired car with an African driver, having a quick look around the countryside during their 24-hour stopover in Kenya. The jack supplied with the car wouldn't lift it enough to enable the wheel to be taken off, so I loaned them mine and then arranged to meet them later that night for a meal and chat about old times.

As you will have gathered, Nairobi was a happy posting for us all; we got on well with the local staff and made the most of our opportunity to see some of the wonders of the world. Living in Nairobi was becoming a little more dangerous, but we were fortunate not to get any trouble directed at ourselves. Conditions did get worse after we left, but our two years there were marvellous.

As with all ex-pats in Kenya, we did have a houseboy and a night watchman. The houseboy was very good, but Madge always kept the cooking to herself whilst he peeled the potatoes etc. After we left, another contract staff member who took over our villa was on his own and found the houseboy to be an excellent chef; in fact he was so good that he got him a job as a chef in the catering unit at the airport used by BA. What had we missed by not using him to his fullest potential?

The night watchman was a very pleasant individual who, we found, liked to play the guitar. He heard Jeannie playing and asked if he could try, and although he tuned the strings wrongly he could still get a reasonable tune out of the instrument. It was Jeannie's first guitar and a very cheap one at that, so when she went back to college she gave it to him, which really pleased him.

During this short stay in Nairobi, David Shepherd visited some of us, selling his paintings of African wild life for which he is now so famous. They cost only a few hundred pounds each then, but we never managed to find the money to buy one. In retrospect, what fools we were, as they fetch up to £30,000 each nowadays. I do have a print copy of one of them hanging at home which was a farewell gift from the contract staff in Nairobi, but wouldn't it be nicer to own an original?!

In the summer of 1975, I received a letter from Rex Crisp, who was now in Muscat, Sultanate of Oman (Middle East, the Arabian Gulf, previously known as the Persian Gulf). He had suggested to Head Office

(BA) that I would be the right person to be his Station Manager in Muscat on secondment to Oman International Services. He wanted to know if I was willing to come to this extremely hot country, which some say is the hottest place on earth. As I knew my term in Nairobi would expire within a few months, I wrote back to him saying yes: yet another chapter in my life was about to start.

CHAPTER 19

DESERT DILEMMA – OMAN AIR 1975-1983

The assignment to Oman was different to any of my previous assignments. I would be working for a local company, OIS (Oman International Services), on secondment from BA, and although BA would still be paying my salary they would charge OIS for my services whatever was considered an appropriate going rate. BA made money through my services, but this gave nothing extra for me.

Rex came to England to interview the applicants, of which I was just one, so perhaps it was good that I had worked with Rex before, as maybe this assisted in giving me the 'nod' over the others. So by September 1975 I found myself landing at Seeb International Airport, Muscat's main airport, at the commencement of what turned out to be an eight-year stint in Oman. Recalling the occasion, I can remember being in the cockpit of a VC.10 watching the approach and landing. The surrounding area did look like real desert but with a massive mountain range inland from the sea. It wasn't the biggest airport I'd ever been working on, but I knew I would be responsible for handling all the different commercial airlines landing there.

It was really hot, with the temperature in the mid-forties Centigrade, quite a contrast from the UK. Rex met me and saw me through the Immigration and Customs formalities; he had already obtained my NOC (No Objection Certificate), which everyone needed prior to arriving in Oman. Rex and Wyn had a large house and I was invited to stay with them for the first week, which gave Rex the opportunity to fully brief me on what was needed to bring the station up to the standard needed for BA, who were shortly to introduce the added service of Flight Operations (Flight Planning) to their passenger and cargo handling requirements.

Rex had formed the Handling Company OIS, having been seconded to them from BA, like myself. When he arrived in Oman the new airport was still being built and was not yet able to accept any aircraft; the current, and very old, airport was at Ruwi, which was in fact nearer to Muscat and was the only other place that aircraft could land. Rex was instrumental in helping to get the new airport open in the early 1970s, with an extremely small terminal, but by the time I arrived the original passenger terminal was in use as the cargo terminal and a much larger terminal had subsequently been built for passengers.

His wife Wyn (a large powerful woman), who not only became his secretary but also took charge of all the cleaners and general services staff, had been a power of strength to him in this task. For example, if a toilet hadn't been cleaned properly, Wyn was quite prepared to do it herself, but heaven help the individual who should have cleaned it in the first place! Both Wyn and Rex had become part of the airport, both respected for their hard work and organisation skills, yet at the same time feared because of the power they had mustered.

It is a major achievement to equip an airport from scratch and to obtain sufficient ground equipment, as well as recruiting and training staff to handle the numbers of flights from a variety of airlines. He had trained drivers to handle the numerous different types of vehicles needed to service aircraft in these modern times, most of whom were local Omanis who had no previous experience on airports or in aviation. Other staff were recruited from airlines in India, Pakistan and Sri Lanka; these had experience in passenger and cargo services, and some even knew 'weight and balance for trim' calculations. This had all been sufficient prior to my arrival, but now I needed to recruit or train staff for the flight operations services needed by BA. Luckily, I did have some BOAC staff on secondment to OIS who were acting as Duty Officers. These had all been fully trained in flight operations and would initially have to do all the flight planning and flight operations work. This gave me time to select and train other local or Asian staff to fulfil this task in the future, as OIS had demanded that local staff be trained to cover all of the business at Muscat.

Before I arrived in Muscat, none of the airlines were operating wide-bodied aircraft through Seeb International Airport; however, this was about to change and my task was to get the station ready for this change. Rex, of course, would make the final decision on the amount of equipment being purchased, but I was expected to say exactly what I felt was needed.

When I arrived in Muscat the number of staff in what was to become my department had reached about 200, and there were another 150 in Engineering and a further 150 in Catering. Over the next eight years, these numbers would almost double. Additionally, we would have our own aircraft, flight deck and cabin crews, bringing the total to over one thousand staff.

With all my children now either at school or college it was only Madge who came to join me at first, when the staff house was made available. This left only our dog to join us from Nairobi; he had been put in good kennels in Nairobi, as he couldn't travel to London without going into quarantine. He was now booked to travel on Sudan Airways from Nairobi to Khartoum and then to Muscat, and he managed it without escaping *en route*; fortunately he accepted Oman without a problem as well. By the time Madge arrived I was starting to get to grips with the problems on the station. The airport buildings were too small for the number of passengers and cargo arriving & departing each day. The construction work in Oman was now top priority; the old ruler had kept Oman back in the eighteenth century but, now that his son was in charge, the developments were designed to bring Oman into the twentieth century almost overnight.

The worst problem at Seeb Airport was in respect to Import Cargo. Hundreds of tons were arriving by air each day on aircraft of all shapes and sizes, some of which were fortunate to be still allowed to fly commercially. On top of this, the construction contractors were leaving their goods at the airport for months, using our space as free storage, so one of my first demands on the Director General of Civil Aviation was to provide a proper cargo area, fully paved, on which this vast amount of cargo could be properly stacked. In the present situation, cargo pallets got moved around and stacked on top of each other and, because the ground was desert sand, much was unevenly stacked and became disturbed and broken or badly damaged. As a result many claims were being submitted to the airlines, who in turn were trying to transfer their claims on to OIS.

Fortunately the Director General of Civil Aviation, who was also Chairman of OIS as well as Chairman of Gulf Air, agreed to two main improvements:

1) To enlarge and pave a new cargo area. This resulted in an area the size of two football pitches becoming available.

2) To initiate a demurrage charge on items not collected within five days of their arrival at Seeb airport.

This latter idea was good, as it meant that the airport would stop being used as a cheap storage place. But the implementation was going to be my major problem; you can easily imagine the opposition to this charge by the construction companies, who now found they had thousands of dollars to pay for the goods we were holding at the airport. But they had been holding the arrival documents for months because, whilst they thought they had free storage, they were in no hurry to collect. The situation was now changed overnight and it would now be cheaper for them to store the goods on their own building sites. So they all went to the DGCA to complain, because they thought it was OIS who was demanding this money without authority from the DGCA; but the DGCA soon told them that it was on their instructions and that OIS were required to collect the payments. So they then came to me to see what I could do to reduce these payments which they had never expected. Although my hands were fairly firmly tied, I was nevertheless able to make medium-size reductions on the largest bills and small deductions on others and, once the initial shock had been accepted, everyone then knew what charges to expect, so naturally shipments were collected within the five free days' storage limit. Initially, consignees who had left as much as 20,000-30,000 kilos of goods for months at the airport found they were going to be charged up to $500 per day, so after 90 days you can realise why they were pleading for reductions to the charges.

However, once these charges were enforced, the rate of collection of all cargo was speeded up and we then found the cargo department could cope far better with the volumes being imported.

Now I must explain about the cargo area. Nearly all cargo at Muscat was stored in the open air. Rain was very rare (although it *did* occur) and therefore the risk of damage to cargo purely due to the weather was minimal. Having said this, in latter years we did start to get frozen and fresh meat shipments from Sydney which required transfer onto Gulf Air flights to Bahrain and elsewhere; if the flights mis-connected, then we did have major problems, such as how to save the cargo when temperatures in the open air could be over 45°C! This led to further cargo development needs, and plans to create a purpose-built warehouse in which frozen and fresh produce could be safely stored prior to collection or transshipment were set in motion. This sort of facility is now in place, but was completed long after I had left Muscat and Oman.

I have maybe given the impression that cargo was the only side of my work that needed massive restructuring and effort, but the passenger side was in just as bad a state; demands for travel into and out of Oman had been so great that the terminal was flooded with passengers far in excess of the capacity for which it had originally been designed. There was a need to improvise in order to keep the flights operating through the station.

Of course, the Dutch firm that had designed the initial airport were constantly being employed to redesign and enlarge the terminal, and I became much involved in monitoring and advising on this matter.

It isn't possible to enlarge a terminal overnight, and with the airport in full operation, development and enlargement plans needed very careful consideration. The airport could not close for a few months, but has to maintain its 24-hour service, so any development had to be introduced piecemeal so as to avoid excessive delays to the current passengers and airlines.

There were also certain restrictions implied locally by the local authorities. Oman was a Police State, and the Inspector General controlled Police, Customs and Immigration, a mighty powerful man. If he said that transit and joining passengers could not be mixed together within the terminal buildings, then all planning had to reflect this fact. It meant you had to plan to have a departure lounge and a transit lounge with no direct connection between the two. I felt that this segregation would cease sometime in the future and made this view known. Naturally, the present authorities shot me down, but I was pleased I had made my thoughts known to the designers. They in turn could see the logic of my thoughts and so, over lunch one day, we looked in detail at the plans. The designer had the transit passengers going to the first floor lounge whilst the joining passengers stayed on the ground floor. Between the two lounges they had planned a narrow staircase purely for the use of staff needing to get from one lounge to the other. Based on my theory, this was widened into a three-metre-wide stairwell, wide enough for passenger use should this permission subsequently be granted.

Surprisingly, when the terminal development was completed, which was after my departure from Oman, the separated lounges idea for transit and joining passengers was found to be operationally impractical and the idea was dropped within a month of the enlarged terminal becoming operational. So all passengers had the use of both lounges and the enlarged stairwell became fully operational, which meant that the space used for the separate shops at each level could be halved or extra shops introduced. It was also a staff saving to OAS – OIS was renamed Oman Aviation Services a year or so before I left, when it became an airline as well as a handling agent – as there was now only one departure gate; two would have been required were the passengers to be separated.

Staff level requirements were always growing, from which I realised that I would have to be constantly on recruitment trips to obtain the required staff. I now had to plan visits to Bombay, Calcutta, Delhi, Colombo and Karachi, to name a few of the places for recruitment. Naturally the airlines at these places dreaded people like me coming to tempt their trained personnel away. The Middle East Airports of Dubai, Abu Dhabi, Bahrain etc. were paradises for the Asian working population, as they could earn vast amounts of money in comparison to their pay at home, meaning that they could send regular payments home to their families. Mind you, there is the black side to this high money-earning ability: they could not afford to get the sack, and if they did, many were unable to return home; the families had got so used to receiving monthly payments that they would blame the person for allowing himself to be sacked and they would beat him mercilessly if he showed up at home.

As there were so many of us conducting these recruitment trips the supply of suitably trained people was becoming more and more difficult to find, so the competition was harder each time. The whole of the Middle Eastern area was constantly enlarging its airports due to the increased demands of the travelling population, and constant replacements or additional numbers of staff were required. The Airlines in India, Pakistan and Sri Lanka did a remarkable job finding new staff and then training them, only for us to pinch. Mind you, the sources from which they found these men seemed to be unlimited, the population of this continent being so vast.

When going on one of these recruitment trips you always had to prepare well in advance of your intended travel date. Firstly, you let the staff on your own station know which country/town you were visiting. This allowed them to ensure that their friends knew of your visit, and by this means you could be sure that there would be plenty of trained or partly-trained people to interview. The more advance information you gave, the better the response would be to your recruitment drive, and it was even better when you could give them the exact time and place where you would be carrying out the interviews.

On my first few recruitment trips both to India/Bombay and to Sri Lanka/Colombo I was overwhelmed with applicants. Although I was looking for as few as five or six staff, I would find as many as thirty to forty people waiting to be seen, and I always saw them all, even though the Indian personnel officer would have preferred to refuse some without seeing them. My reason for this action was that I soon learnt that you could not always believe the qualifications you were being offered, as they could easily be bought in these countries. Therefore, it was better to interview the potential staff member and make your own mind up as to whether he would be suitable for your needs back in Oman.

On one of these early trips to Bombay, I interviewed a white Indian with ginger hair. When I finally realised he was a pure breed Indian I couldn't believe my eyes, as initially I had felt he must have come from Europe and got stuck in India looking for work. I did offer him a job, which he accepted, and he wasn't too bad at his work, so from then on I had a more open mind when going looking for staff in Asian countries.

Of all the recruitment trips I did, I always preferred the Colombo trips. I found the Sri Lanka staff very pleasant to talk to and very keen to succeed, and they were generally well educated although, as I mentioned earlier, you could never accept that they had passed all the exams their educational certificates indicated. The staff were also keen to come to Muscat to work, having been well briefed by their friends already there. Whenever I landed in Colombo I would find myself surrounded by two or three local staff wanting to be interviewed there and then while I was still seated on the plane; they were worried in case I hadn't received their CV, or that I would be too busy to see them the next day. If I hadn't had their CV, they would give it to me straight away and I in turn would always assure them that I would see them the next day. Naturally they were worried about losing their present jobs in Colombo, which is why they wanted to see me whilst out of sight of their present managers in the airport terminal.

Interviewing for staff in the Middle East required some adjustment. The applicants could be ruthless in their methods of trying to persuade you that they were the best on offer and that they knew everything you needed them to do. They would have Certificates of Education a mile long, all very plausibly printed and stamped, so someone in these places must have been making a fortune printing all these bogus certificates. To counteract these attempts to fool me, I wrote a written test paper in English and arithmetic which each applicant had to complete before his face-to-face interview. Armed with the results of these tests, I could then start the interview and make notes on just how good he or she actually was.

It was rare that a female was interviewed outside of Muscat, as at that time we had no female accommodation available in Muscat. But if recruiting local staff, then we had plenty of females to see. Surprisingly, while I sit here writing, I am looking at a farewell gift that one of the young Omani ladies gave me; it is a wooden desk stand with a small wooden aeroplane (a biplane with wooden propeller) at one end and a business card holder at the other. It has been on my desk ever since and I am very proud of it. The girl was just seventeen years old when I gave her her first job, and she was also the first Omani female employed in the company.

All Managers at the Middle East airports had tales to tell of how they fared on their recruitment trips, and we always let each other know of any pitfalls suffered. One such tale was concerning the Engineering Manager at one of the largest Middle East airports. He had been to recruit about twenty staff and had had nearly one hundred applicants, each of whom had sat his written test before being interviewed. He selected the best twenty and came back quite happily to his station, after which all went well for over a year. Then one day one of these recruits had an accident whilst driving on the aircraft ramp, so he was given the appropriate Accident Report forms to complete and was sat at a desk outside the manager's office. After an hour he was still just looking at the forms and hadn't written a word, so the manager questioned him, only to be told: "Sir, I cannot read or write."

"How did you pass the written test on recruitment?"

"Sir, my cousin took that test for me!"

You can imagine the manager's surprise; he was well experienced and just couldn't believe how this man had fooled him. It just goes to show how careful you had to be when recruiting in Asia. In general, I think I was fortunate not to be caught out by the staff I engaged. Maybe they didn't all turn out as well as I thought they would, but at least they could all read and write.

On one of the Colombo recruitment trips my taxi back to the airport ran out of fuel. The driver, a very jolly young man, had gleaned from me previously that I had been recruiting staff, so had therefore been out of his way to acquaint me with all his abilities. He said he had previously worked at Colombo airport in catering, but when I asked why he wasn't still at the airport, he admitted he had been fired because he was late to work; nevertheless he felt that, irrespective of his lack of reliability, he was still the sort of person to whom I should give the opportunity to work abroad. So when we ran out of petrol only a mile or so from the hotel, you can imagine how impressed I was and I certainly told him so. Fortunately, he did go out of his way to find another taxi for me quickly and I arrived at the airport just in time to get my flight back to Muscat.

On all my trips to India, Pakistan or Sri Lanka, I always ate in the hotel restaurants. I didn't take a chance on the variety of eating places in the cities of Bombay, Karachi, Delhi, Calcutta or Colombo. Mind you, I did have to eat a meal in the Indian Airlines canteen in Bombay airport on one occasion, but this was not on a recruitment trip; it happened when I took Said Hilal, one of my most senior Omani ramp supervisors, to Bombay for instruction on the in-hold loading systems of their Airbus A300 aircraft. They were introducing services through Muscat and I wanted to be sure that we were all fully aware of the changes of procedures necessary for their particular flights. When the instruction session ended we were both invited for lunch and, as their guests, it would have been an insult to refuse, so off I went to join them. The canteen had very primitive facilities and there was little evidence of hygiene anywhere in the area. It was the usual 'chicken grab' type of meal, hot curry and no cutlery (except for me). For Said Hilal this was completely normal, but I was pleased when the meal was over and we could get back to the hotel. It was here I learnt just how quickly Said Hilal could drink. I left him at the bar whilst I went up to my room to clean up, and it was fortunate that he only drank beer, not spirits, as when I came down I was amazed at the size of the bill he had rung up in such a short time. He naturally expected me to pay for his drinks, as he assumed that the manager was always paid allowances to treat staff when off station. I suppose I should have known what he would do if he was given the chance. Having had, for him, a reasonable drink, he then went off to visit some of his friends in Bombay, leaving me to do whatever I could find of interest in Bombay (not much when on your own).

On one of my trips to India, I decided to go to Trivandium in the southwest corner of India. To get a direct flight there rather than going via Bombay, I had first to go to Dubai and join an Air India Boeing 707 service. The flight was economy class only with a total seat capacity of 162, and there were 161 Indian nationals and myself joining in Dubai. Every Indian had his own twin-speaker portable music centre with him, and once we were airborne they all began playing their favourite cassettes, so as each one was different you can imagine the resulting noise within the aircraft cabin, which continued for the rest of the journey, some four to five hours.

The airport at Trivandium was quite small, and had only one runway with a hill in the middle; it also got very hot there and the terminal buildings had no air conditioning. The immigration authorities collected all the passports as the passengers disembarked and made them take seats, then calling them by name in alphabetical order. Luckily for me they made an exception and called me first because of my nationality; I was much relieved, as I didn't fancy sitting an hour or more waiting to be let into the country.

On this occasion, the Personnel Manager, Colin Brennan, was in Trivandium at the same time. He had been looking for staff in Bombay with the Catering Manager prior to visiting Trivandium on the same sort of mission. They had flown down from Bombay a few days earlier and the Catering Manager Alan Bishop had already flown back to Oman. Colin met me at the airport and off we went to get hotel rooms. In Trivandium there is a beautiful hotel built into the cliff face with every room having its own balcony overlooking a marvellous moon-shaped golden sandy bay and the sea. It was government-owned and because of this would only take 50% bookings in advance. Previously the manager had been caught out when a government minister had arrived demanding rooms for his group at a time when the hotel was completely full, and the rumpus this had caused meant he never again sold all his rooms in advance. So this odd situation of rooms being *available* but *not obtainable* until 8 or 9 pm each day became the norm and, although this was his way of avoiding any further serious altercations with the government, it certainly didn't help people like Colin and myself.

This was the situation now confronting us in Trivandium. We decided that, rather than sit around on the chance of a room becoming available, Colin and I should make the trip up the cliff face to the next best hotel in town. This was situated overlooking the same bay but from much higher up, and further away from the beach, not the short walk that the other hotel offered. At this hotel an elderly uniformed Indian, who was the perfect image of the 'Indian man servant' of the 1800s and 1900s when British people settled and colonized that area of Asia, greeted us very pleasantly and became our manservant for the whole of our stay in the hotel. Firstly, he took us to reception to sign in, then showed us to our rooms. He then told us where to go to see the beautiful sunset and at the same time brought us two ice-cold beers to drink prior to dinner. When we went in for dinner, we found him once again being our waiter and advising us on what to choose. After dinner we found that he had turned the bed covers down ready for us, and he also awoke us the next day with a nice cup of tea. Naturally he also served us at breakfast, carried our cases to reception, called a taxi and generally did everything he could think of to try and make our stay as comfortable as possible. He made only one mistake: he left one of our packages out of the taxi when we departed, but we found this out on arrival at the airport, and luckily the Indian personnel officer of OAS, who came from this part of India, was travelling later than us, so he collected the package and brought it to Muscat the next day.

TOP: A Fokker F.27 introduced into Muscat for Oman Aviation.
Photo: author's collection.
BOTTOM: Concorde and the Red Arrows fly over Kensington during the "50 years of Heathrow" celebrations; the author was an invited guest.
Photo: author's collection.

TOP: The world's largest aircraft, the Antonov 225 *Mryia*.
Photo: Nick Challoner.
BOTTOM: The world's largest commercial aircraft, the Antonov 124.
Photo: Aeroflot.

Colin and I were going to Colombo, a very short flight from Trivandium, to conduct additional recruitment, however our flight was delayed by nearly six hours. We eventually got a meal provided by Indian Airlines, but under the very primitive conditions within the airport. With no normal cutlery available, the restaurant staff located a kitchen spoon each for Colin and I. Everyone else just used their hands, the normal practice in their own homes. I must say the meal was very tasty and we got on well with the passengers seated at our table, even though they didn't speak much English

In Colombo we felt as if we were back in civilisation once again, although I must say the Trivandium trip will always hold pleasing memories for me. The rest of our travel and business arrangements on this occasion went well and our return to Muscat was welcome.

Working for an Arab company in any Arab country can have its worrying and trying moments for any non-Arab person. There are still many tribal laws and courts of law that are alien to us as Europeans. To most senior Arabs, the fact that you are being paid to run their affairs and businesses means that you must always produce the right results, no matter how unlikely.

As manager of the handling company you were held personally responsible for any article given to your company for delivery abroad. On one occasion, a piece of diplomatic mail from Oman to the Ambassador in Yemen went missing. The demand came from the Foreign Minister's office for the person in charge – i.e. me – to go to Yemen and find the bag. Fortunately, I was unable to get a visa quickly and I managed to persuade the authorities that an Arabic-speaking Omani would have more chance of finding the bag than I would. On this occasion, the person I sent came back having successfully found the item; it was in the Omani Embassy residence in Sa'ana Yemen, having been dropped in the corner of the room used to prepare outbound shipments instead of with the inbound shipments. Apologies for proving they were in the wrong were never received.

A similar event happened within the first few months of my arrival in Muscat. A diplomatic bag sent via Doha to Baghdad went missing. We were certain it had been shipped correctly on the flight from Muscat to Doha, so we felt the bag must be there. Doha said it wasn't and didn't seem to be concerned about locating the missing item. I arrived in the office one morning, to be summoned to the Director General of Civil Aviation's office to account for this missing item.

He listened for a few minutes and then said: "You must go yourself and find this item."

I responded by saying: "I will arrange for one of my staff to go."

"No, you must go yourself, *now*."

He was the boss and that was that; so I had to go as instructed. Within the hour I was on a plane flying to Doha, having previously sent a signal to them to expect my arrival.

What I was expected to do at this strange airport, knowing no one and having to rely on the manager there to help me, I just don't know! The manager supported his staff's assertion that the mailbag was not on station and he didn't like the idea that I doubted this. Therefore on arrival I was told quite plainly: "You are wasting your time and mine."

However, I did locate an Indian cargo agent there who was keen to move to Muscat, and we searched all the airport cargo and mail premises for some hours. Fortunately, we did eventually find the missing bag of diplomatic mail and I decided to bring it back to Muscat with me, but the next flight back was not until 4 am the next day and without a visa to Qatar I was forced to await departure in the departure lounge, not that pleasant a place.

The next day I arrived back in Muscat around 7 am and, instead of being allowed to go home to rest, I was dragged into a meeting with the Direct General of Civil Aviation to be asked: "How big an area do you need for your new cargo unit?"

As I had to decide there and then, I made sure it was going to be big enough, and when I said how much I felt I needed, the American Manager of the airport services company (PANAM) commented: "That's the size of two football pitches!"

But I stuck firmly to my decision and eventually this was the size I was granted. My decision was proved right in the end and everyone was thankful of that fact. Once completed it was soon filled with cargo.

For the whole time I was in Oman, I worked a seven-day week, although I stayed at home on Fridays "on call" – it was that sort of job. I found it better to be available to make decisions immediately rather than wait until the next day to unravel situations.

Irrespective of this, I really did enjoy myself in Muscat. Having inherited a developing airport in need of massive increases in staff and equipment in addition to enlargement of the structural facilities, it was a case for most of the time I was there of trying to catch up with the increased demands of that era in air travel.

Wide-bodied aircraft were being introduced by the major airlines. Gulf Air were first with their Tri-Stars, followed by Air India with Airbus A300s and eventually Boeing B747s. KLM and UTA brought the DC-10 and BA the Boeing 747. With BA came the demand for operational flight planning, which was eventually achieved successfully.

Wide-bodied aircraft not only carried more passengers (240-350, as compared with other types with only 100-180), but they also had greater cargo capacity. They also introduced the use of 'containers' within the holds, in which you stacked the baggage and cargo pieces, and these containers required mechanical lifting equipment such as FMC container and pallet high-loaders. To move them around the airport needed container and pallet dollies as transporters towed by a small tractor. To store them off the ground you also needed special racks for the empty ones awaiting use. These racks saved them being thrown to the ground and subsequently damaged.

All these requirements brought many questions such as: How many dollies were necessary? How many FMCs were required to handle more than one aircraft at a time? Would changes need to be made to the baggage arrival and departure facilities, entailing redesigning and then building?

Therefore, it wasn't just the fact that the aircraft were bigger and carried more passengers that caused the re-planning of airports throughout the world. In some cases, runways had to be extended to allow for higher take-off weights of these new giant aircraft. This actually occurred at Muscat to improve the payload possibilities for BA's Boeing 747 operations to London & Singapore direct from Muscat.

Prior to the first wide-bodied aircraft arriving at Muscat, we organised 'paper exercises' to show how the various pieces of equipment would be positioned around the aircraft. There was little space to spare when positioning the catering high-loader and the FMC high-loader to the hold doors. The refuellers also needed to be precisely positioned to refuel the aircraft whilst not interfering with loading and unloading. Through these paper exercises, all our staff, plus any other interested parties involved in servicing a transit or turn-round, became personally concerned; they all grew to appreciate the need for correct equipment parking. It also showed how easily a flight could be delayed if they didn't position their equipment correctly as soon as the aircraft parked on the ramp. If the refuelling truck parked incorrectly, then the catering and loading equipment couldn't get to the aircraft.

This procedure proved really worthwhile; as an example, when the first Gulf Air Tri-Star service landed late from Bahrain, we were able to do a 35-minute transit, which allowed the flight to depart on schedule. (We were normally allowed 60 minutes for each transit.)

Prior to this we had a training flight arranged with Gulf Air. When this aircraft came on the ramp, I had all the staff involved lined up with the Duty Officer out front to salute its arrival; as there were over 50 staff, it was quite impressive.

Rex had been very forward-thinking in his approach to staff training on station. He had employed Mohd Seif and Said Hilal, who were excellent equipment operators, and they had in turn instructed other Omanis in the art. As my office overlooked the ramp I could watch many of the activities going on, and I could proudly boast that, when a aircraft stopped on the ramp, the forward steps would be in position within 30 seconds and that, if the crew opened the door, passengers could be disembarking within one minute. It was wonderful to watch the precision with which the steps were aligned and positioned, and this applied to the rest of the traffic equipment services (provided by my department) used on these wide-bodied flights. A real pride of service had been fostered in all the traffic staff and they did everything possible to ensure that our good reputation became widely talked about throughout the Gulf area.

With the wide-bodied aircraft, it became necessary to be stricter on granting arrival and departure slots to the airlines. The increase in passengers joining and disembarking from these larger aircraft would stretch the facilities for both OIS and Immigration & Customs. If I allowed congestion within the terminal through pure weight of passenger numbers, then flights would be delayed unacceptably. As these wide-bodied flights required so much extra equipment on the ramp for each flight and we had only a limited number of units to provide, the sensible separation of flights was essential. I held co-ordination meetings with Customs, Immigration, Catering and Engineering to decide exactly what timings were acceptable and, if there were too great a clash, we would request the airline to plan its flight at a different time. As expected, this caused many an argument between the airline managers and myself, each expecting the other airline to change its schedule, but after much discussion agreement would be obtained and the schedules established for another season. From then onwards, we only had real problems when an airline sent a aircraft larger than that approved.

This problem is worldwide, and every airport has its 'slots' Committee to resolve the slot issues. At London Heathrow, Gatwick and Stansted, a private company now resolves the issues; it has full power to ban an airline's schedule if it considers that the airport's capacity may be overloaded at any time.

Whilst I had my work, Madge got used to shopping and living in the heat of Oman. She even tried to make something out of the garden area adjacent to our villa, which was not easy as it was really only desert. Still, somehow or other she made some progress and we did eventually get a few flowers to grow.

The Arabs of Oman were quite different to those in Lebanon. In many ways, they were not so educated and, in fact, they still had primitive ideas. They could be either very hard or very easy to negotiate with, and you never knew which way they would react. Sometimes you could suddenly find you had a sit-down strike over a simple matter and needed the local Government Labour Minister to intervene. However, when you expected to have to seek the Minister's help, they would accept your instructions without a qualm.

During my stay in Muscat, we only had one aircraft accident, but before saying anything more on this, I must give you the details related to this particular aircraft and its crew. The aircraft was a DC-6, a very old aircraft that was owned and operated by an American pilot; in fact, he had three of these aircraft when I first arrived in Muscat. The DGCA hired him because he was very cheap and was undercutting all other potential bidders. They, the DGCA, were only interested at that time in anything for economy and were not looking towards the finer principles of air safety in their operations. They required to carry workers and equipment between Muscat and Salalah airports, and if this was the cheapest means it served their purpose. The pilot was also doing similar business in the UAE with the same aircraft and his maintenance schedules seemed to be almost non-existent.

My friend John Webb had the same function as mine in Dubai, and we spoke together concerning our fears about the operational safety of this service. The American was refusing any technical assistance from both sets of engineers, yet was still trying to use our ground equipment without payment. Because of his attitude and lack of a professional approach towards the necessity of maintaining his aircraft, we both put pressure on our respective DGCAs to refuse to accept his flights on safety grounds, saying that "they would in time, result in accidents and loss of life." This concern was eventually accepted and they decided not to give him any more licences to operate within the two countries.

With this decision he was eventually banned from Oman and the UAE, but it was not the last we saw of him. A few years later, we had a request from Cyprus Airways for a freighter service to land at Muscat, which was naturally approved. The flight arrived at around midnight and only then did we realise that it was the same aircraft and captain that we had banned from operating within Oman. The cargo was offloaded and the aircraft then took off empty except for its three crew members and the captain, who was once again reminded of his ban on using Oman airspace.

After take-off the plane turned left instead of right and flew straight into the mountains. Of course, everyone on board perished and we had to have a full enquiry into the incident. When we examined the crew records we found that only the pilot was fully qualified to fly the plane, while the rest had limited documents and no real flying qualifications. The fact that we had previously banned this aircraft and it's owner/operator from using Seeb airport meant that we were saved from too much criticism; however, it does go to show how important it is to watch out for these rogue operators.

I did see a similar type of operation with another American pilot/owner of a DC-7C aircraft; this was operating within India and was hired by the Indian Government to bring the Indian Army horses and equipment to Muscat for the Sultan's birthday celebrations. The first time it arrived the rear main exit door was just about level with the truck collecting the horses, so they could be led off the aircraft by their grooms. The next time it arrived the rear main exit was about three feet higher than the same truck, so the unloading of horses was much more difficult. We spoke to the Captain to find out just how he had arranged the attitude in flight to be so different, and he laughed and said: "Yes, I got the trim wrong on the first trip. We were very tail-heavy and I had to fly holding the control column pressed forward to stop us from climbing. On this second trip I had the trim set better, so the aircraft flew much better too." This pilot was prepared to operate his aircraft in almost any attitude, something never acceptable to pilots of scheduled airlines. During the war, this sort of pilot would have taken on very risky operations, which sometimes had the backing of Commanding Officers as a necessary risk under wartime circumstances. In peacetime, however this was not necessary or acceptable. Fortunately, there was no accident on this occasion.

It was just as well that there were very few pilot-owners around in the Middle East; our main operators were professional companies who generally kept within the aviation law, and they certainly made sure that their aircraft were given appropriate maintenance and repair. Mind you, if a 'buck' could be won, I am sure they would have turned a 'Nelson's eye' to obscure regulations.

OIS was a monopolistic handling company, and all commercial flights landing at Seeb International airport had to be serviced by them. Many small commercial delivery companies would object to paying our fees as they felt they could do all the necessary actions without any assistance. However, as a Government-appointed firm we were expected to earn the maximum finance for our shareholders.

We provided all the in-flight catering for services operating through Muscat, and we had the only commercially available aircraft engineering establishment for servicing flights landing on the airport. The Sultan's Air Force and Royal Flight facilities were also there, but they would not service any other aircraft than their own. Even then, when they had a large amount of movements to service they would hire equipment from us to do the job.

When the Queen made her visit to Oman she arrived on the Royal Yacht Britannia and flew direct to London on a BA VC.10. The aircraft had to be parked in the Sultan's Royal Flight ramp, but OAS was still responsible for everything except security.

By this time one of my Omani duty officers had been fully trained to do the flight plan to London. It was quite an honour to him to do this and he felt quite proud to have been given the task. It was a long flight even for the VC.10 and so very careful flight planning was necessary. Naturally I was monitoring his progress and just before the Captain arrived for his briefing, I asked him if he had any fuel spare for the flight, and he said he had just over 1,000 kg extra available, so this pleased us both.

I told the Captain this but left the Omani duty officer to finish the briefing. Surprisingly I then found out that the payload had increased by about 1,000 kgs. How did this happen? I soon found out. The Queen, when in the departure lounge, had been given some Omani dates with the stones replaced by almonds. The Sultan had heard her say that she thought they tasted wonderful and hence 1,000 kg of these dates were located and loaded on the aircraft: the Sultan had given her a last minute gift. With Royal flights you must always be prepared for the unexpected and cope with the consequences.

The training of Omanis was one of my major tasks whilst in Oman. The country wanted their citizens to replace the ex-pats brought in initially. They were sent on courses to British Airways at London and other airlines to learn the industry. Some were very bright and picked up the knowledge quickly, but as soon as they learned a bit they then expected to be promoted and given massive pay rises. This was not always possible and it was necessary to restrict their promotions and pay until they got practical experience of using the knowledge they had grasped. It was difficult keeping them keen and eager to do the job without giving them the pay raises they were demanding.

Of course, they are now all receiving the benefit of their studies and hard work. They are now managing Oman Air, doing the jobs others and I taught them. I went back to see how they were doing about five years ago and they all showed me all the respect and honour that I could have expected.

I was very thrilled to see the developments that I had initiated fully completed. The cargo buildings were in full operational order. Frozen meats and fresh vegetables could now be stored safely to await their collection or for on-shipment to their final destination. The passenger terminal had also been enlarged even further than the plans I had been involved with and passenger numbers had risen accordingly. Business was good for Oman Air.

Going back to when I was in charge, I had instructed my staff on how to approach small private aircraft landing at Muscat. When a small private plane landed I told them to immediately attend to its positioning on the ramp, ask the captain what service he needed, ascertain where he was going next, whether he needed refuelling etc. etc. Then, irrespective of the Captain's response, OIS had to submit to him the minimum invoice for our services. Naturally, most objected to paying anything but, under the terms of our airport contract, every flight had to be serviced by OIS, and for this there was a payment due. Once I told my staff to tell a complaining captain: "You have landed at Seeb airport and we are required to provide whatever services are necessary. We have offered you all the services available on the airport and by making these available to you, you are therefore obliged to pay." Some would still argue and they were sent to my office, where I gave them a fuller explanation: there were no 'freebies.'

Of course, we did get called to the local court on occasions. On one occasion Mac, our engineering manager, had to go to Salalah to get a rental payment out of a firm renting space within our staff accommodation. The hearing was held at the local Sherifa Court, which just had a judge and no jury; it was full of Arabs and Mac was seated in the biggest high chair in the courtroom. Abdul Rasoul, our "Mister Fix-it," went with him and sat himself down on a stool alongside. The judge was in his chair on a raised platform and there were people coming and going and speaking to him all the time. Then the judge began to sing, which Max thought this must be part of the special procedures involved, but then he stopped and said something in Arabic that Max could not understand but which did seem to be directed at him. So he turned to Abdul and asked him what had been said. Abdul told him: "The judge was singing to pass away the time whilst he awaited the defendant's arrival in court and he wanted to know if you had enjoyed this singing." Dutifully Max said yes as he couldn't very well say otherwise.

Salalah was the second major airport under my jurisdiction. It was being enlarged and developed the same as Muscat (Seeb), and there were regular meetings called which I had to attend. The development was a joint effort to cover military as well as civil aviation needs, so I could always get a flight down on one of the Air Force BAC.111 flights or occasionally on the Sultan's personal VC.10.

Salalah was not as large as Seeb and the terminal facilities had to cope with only around 500 passengers at any one time, but it still had to have VIP facilities large enough to cope with the Sultan and his VIP guests. The meetings were always held at the Dutch designer's offices, which were off airport. On one occasion, we had a tremendous storm during our meeting, and within an hour the whole area became flooded. The roads back to the airport were almost washed away and became impassable, so we were stuck in these offices. Fortunately, the military were at the meeting and they had helicopters (Pumas), which they called to rescue the whole group. It was my first time airborne in this way.

As a foreigner in Oman you were allowed to have alcoholic drink if you applied for a licence, and subject to your position the amount was then limited. My licence was signed in Arabic, with the signature looking like a happy smiling face; the Arab having the licensing job must have had a good sense of humour.

Drinking and driving was prohibited, naturally. If there was any alcohol in your blood you lost your licence and could even be sent to jail. Needless to say we all attended parties, drank a fair share of alcoholic drink and then drove home, but in those days the traffic wasn't too heavy and we got away with it; it would not be possible there nowadays.

Surprisingly, many Arabs drank heavily; they could go to hotels or clubs and be sold alcoholic drinks, in fact, they would join clubs just to be able to get a drink. Money seemed to be no object. At the Sailing Club, there were a couple of very heavy drinkers, both local Arabs. The Club committee decided that they should get rid of them once and for all, so they changed the Club rules to state that anyone who wanted to be a member had to own a sailing boat, and this, they thought, would rid them of these two individuals. But no such luck! They each went out and bought a boat, brought it to the Club area and then proceeded to carry on drinking as usual; it made their drinking a bit more expensive, but who cared? They certainly didn't!

In the Arab world, you have to understand that you never take "No" for an answer. If someone says "No," then you have either asked in the wrong way or asked the wrong question, so you have to think again and re-submit your request in a different way. The true Arab gets around this sort of situation by the use of his eyes; when he has been harassed by another Arab he will somehow or other fix his eyes in such a way that it would appear as if he is looking straight though the person in front of him. How they do this I do not know, but I have seen it actually happen.

What else can I say about Oman, its people and my time there? It is a lovable country, very beautiful in parts; for example, it is the largest greengage growing area in the Middle East. But in other ways it can still be one of the hardest places to live in. It is developing rapidly and is even letting its womenfolk become educated and employed; but it has benefited by being late in developing, as it has seen the failures of construction planning in other parts of the Middle East and in my opinion has made every effort to avoid these pitfalls.

The biggest money earner for the Government is PDO (Petroleum Development Oman) and they have their own flight operations department and aircraft leased from Gulf Air. The airport manager for PDO operations was another BA secondment and naturally we got along fine together. PDO had their own compound down on the coast a few miles nearer to Muscat than Seeb Airport; they were the oil barons of Oman and so had marvellous facilities for their staff: swimming pools, a golf club, and clubhouses for meals or dancing. The staff accommodation was also very good, so a posting to PDO was well thought of by BA.

The F.27s they used had special flanges on either side of the nose wheels to enable them to use the inland desert landing strips. I managed to go on one or two of these flights into the interior and it was truly amazing what had developed over the years. You could see the oil pumps continuously working along the pipeline right up to Muscat and then into the sea to loading platforms a mile or so offshore.

Whilst I was there, PDO decided to use solar energy to drive these oil pumps; prior to this they had had to send a refuelling truck along the pipeline to supply the pump engines with oil, very difficult terrain and quite dangerous on occasions. By changing to solar energy all they had to do was to wash the solar panels every month, a simple task for a man using a Land Rover or similar four-wheel-drive small vehicle. The pumps then kept on working indefinitely.

As mentioned earlier, OIS became OAS (Oman Aviation Services), and this then changed to Oman Aviation. As I was their Manager (Ground Services) I had a great involvement in forming this new airline, and now we had our own aircraft, flight, and cabin crews, so we were to start operating to many remote places in Oman. The aircraft type selected was the F.27 Fokker Friendship, a high-winged type with two Rolls Royce turboprops capable of carrying 40 passengers. All Arab states wanted their own airline and Oman was no exception.

I had to go to some of these new places to arrange appropriate ground handling for our flights. One such place was Musuldum, way up in the northernmost corner of Oman on the west side of the straits at the entrance to the Arabian Gulf (previously known as the Persian Gulf). The airport there had been developed as an air force base for jet fighters and, as there was very little flat land in amongst the mountains, there was a massive mountain at one end of the runway and the other end a gap between mountains through which you had to approach for landings and take-offs. On the approach there were high cliffs either side towering way above the approach height, so close that there was no way you could land if the approach was in cloud. This also meant you had to fly through this gap on departure, so prior to take-off the crew would ask you to find out which was your nearest escape door in the event of a crash.

On my second trip to this place, we were in our newest F.27, which had only flown about 100 hours. We had the usual emergency briefing before take-off and commenced our take-off run, but when we had been airborne for only about three minutes our port engine caught fire; an emergency was called and the engine was feathered while the engine fire extinguisher doused the flames. This meant that we had to carry out a 180-degree turn between the cliffs in order to land back at Musuldum. Everyone was watching very closely as the pilot made this turn on only the starboard engine, but fortunately everything went well and we landed safely. Of course, that aircraft had to wait for an engineering crew and a new engine, which would take a few days, but as all of us on board were staff we needed to get back on station at Seeb as quickly as possible. Fortunately one of our Skyvan aircraft had just landed and so we all decided to go back on it but, as it had no seats – other than for the crew – we had to either sit on the floor or stand all the way to Seeb airport. As an aside, the twin-engine Skyvans were built by Shorts in Belfast and were normally used to carry freight, but by standing behind the captain you could look over his shoulder to see where you were going. It is the first and only time that I have flown standing up!

Oman Air now has a massive HQ, a new passenger terminal, and enlarged cargo buildings with all the facilities I had submitted in my plans for improvement. The road systems have grown, and the highway between airport and town is now a six-lane dual carriageway with large grass verges bordered with palm and other trees on either side of the road. No more Irish bridges (where the road goes down *into* the riverbed (*wadi*) rather than over it), an idea first suggested to the Sultan early on in his rule, when he was after maximum security for his travels. A security advisor told him that rebels could be hidden under normal bridges and attack him as he went by, thus the 'Irish' bridge idea was born. All the Embassies have moved to a designated area and their buildings have had to conform to an appropriate styling. It all looks very beautiful and far more accessible.

There are a number of very new hotels, which are being recognised as some of the most beautiful in the world. Relatively speaking they are not too expensive; however, they are fairly dear, although the settings surrounding them are fantastic and beautiful and really worth seeing.

Mind you, they haven't always had success in their building projects. They designed and built a Conference Centre in which to hold Arab Nation conferences, then the Sultan took one look at it and called it a failure and unacceptable for the purpose. But the building still stands and has been converted into another hotel, which is very useful as it is very near Seeb airport.

Whilst in Oman I decided to retire from British Airways and join OAS. I didn't move from Muscat as I joined OAS as a directly-engaged staff member, and I was doing the same job, but this time being paid directly by OAS and not BA, a situation that lasted for another three years. But BA didn't like the fact that the Ground Services Manager was no longer one of their staff, as they believed it took a lot of the control away from them, so in 1983 I was replaced with another BA man, who stayed a couple of years more before handing over totally to the Omanis I had originally started to train.

Therefore, it was now back to England for full retirement. I had no other plans at this time.

CHAPTER 20

RETIREMENT TO GATWICK

All your working life you think about how nice it is going to be when you retire. The burden of rising at the crack of dawn will be removed and you will have time to do all the things that you have put aside over the years. To keep fit you plan to join a golf Club and play a round of golf at least every other day, attend a gym, and in general use your spare time to ensure you keep healthy and fit.

Then the time comes and you think: "Do I really want to give up work? Am I sure time won't drag while I fiddle around the house? Will golf become a bore?" These were some of the things going through my mind during my journey home from Oman.

I had thought about retirement whilst in Oman, and had got the idea that England would be too cold after so many years in the sun and heat. In fact, during my last two years in Oman I had visited Spain and found a builder who had agreed to build a villa for me. The price was right and so everything seemed to be in order. Six months later, I went on holiday to Spain, hoping to be able to move into my own villa, but I wasn't so lucky: the villa was built but not on the plot of land I expected. The layout didn't fit the plot it was on and although there was a garage, there was no way you could get a car into it.

The builder was most apologetic and agreed to sell that villa and use all the money I had paid him to build another villa on a better plot of land. He took us around until we found a plot I liked and he agreed to build a villa to the plans I gave him, which had been prepared by an architect in Alicante. He adjusted the general plan to my instructions: I knew what layout I wanted and the size of each room was therefore changed according to my wishes. I even decided the type of roof, size of patio etc. . . .

Six months later, I returned once again and found that he had made a start on the villa, but the progress was very slow. We had a few words with the builder but of course, I had to return to Oman thinking that I would eventually get my place in the sun. Then within a few weeks of my return to Oman I received a message saying that the builder had disappeared without trace, and that all the money I had paid him was lost.

I was fortunate to be able to get special leave and return to Spain in an attempt to redeem something out of what was left. I went to see my Spanish bank manager and, when he heard what had happened, he surprised me by going out of his way to find me another builder and negotiate a fair price for completing the villa. Although I was a number of thousands of pounds out of pocket, at least it looked as if I would get my villa in due course.

At this stage, I was wondering whether my venture into property in the sun was really worthwhile. However, having invested so much money, I felt it was better to invest a little more to get what I wanted rather than to lose everything that I had so far spent.

Happily, there has been a successful conclusion to this saga, and I do now own a wonderful villa in the sun. So, twenty years on, it would appear I took the right decision to proceed, as the villa is now worth at least five times what I paid in total.

But on my arrival home, I soon realised I was still far too young (58) not to work; I also found that my BOAC/BA pension was far too small to live on. So after a few months I had to make some effort to obtain more funds. The first thing I did was to sell the car I had brought back from Oman, a Volvo 244 which, although over two years old, still looked like new; in fact, it looked too new when I brought it in through Customs at Heathrow airport, and that's another story which is worthwhile relating.

Whilst in Oman I had bought this Volvo with the intention of bringing it home when I left the country. Naturally, I had not expected to move until the car was at least two years old and could therefore be imported into Britain without paying duty. When the time came to move, the chief engineer at Volvo said he would get the car properly cleaned before shipment, so I took him up on his offer and put the car in for a clean at the Volvo workshops. When finished I collected it and drove it the few miles to the airport, and that night it was airlifted to Heathrow airport on the BA non-stop flight (yes, the Boeing 747 holds are big enough to load cars of this size). I arrived back in the UK a few days later and went to the airport to collect the car after clearing the documents through the Customs Long Room. The clearance took much longer than expected and I was getting worried about what was wrong when eventually two customs officers approached me and said: "We are not certain you have shown the correct year in respect to this car."

I replied: "I can assure you I have had that car well over two years."

Their reply was: "It doesn't look as if it has been used all that much."

It was then that I told them of the special cleaning it had been given by Volvo in Muscat.

They started to laugh. "Now we know why it looks so new. We were certain you were trying to fiddle the regulations so as to get a brand-new car imported less the normal duty charges and having clocked up some mileage in the hope of fooling Customs." Now they believed my story the car was finally cleared for my collection.

I never intended selling the car so soon after arriving home, but I soon realised that my funds were far too small to run two cars, the old Mercedes and the Volvo. For sentimental reasons I kept the old

Mercedes, but the Volvo was a beautiful car and easier to sell, and additionally I did make a small profit.

The second thing I did was to sell our beautiful house in Weybridge, which I have regretted ever since; it was so well situated and so spacious, and it was quite a 'come-down' to go into a luxury ground floor maisonette close by. I put a lot of work in on the maisonette before we moved in and this did compensate in some ways for giving up the house; I completely rewired and refitted the kitchen and bathroom and redecorated the rest of the rooms. The maisonette was comfortable and spacious, but it was not the same as having a large detached house of some historic interest

My former house had originally been owned by Lord Locke-King and used as his garage. He was the owner of the Brooklands racetrack, where all pre-war motor car and motorcycle races had been held; the highly banked and curved track had made racing in the early days a most exciting event to see. Then when Lord Locke-King died, his wife, Dame Locke-King, took up residence in a large house adjacent to the garage, and then when she in turn died, the aircraft manufacturing company Vickers-Armstrong bought the racetrack, her home and the garage, the latter being on two floors, the upper floor being originally the residence for the mechanics and drivers. Vickers later sold the garage to a member of the Chairman's family, who lived there until he sold it to me a number of years later.

I was off sick from Frankfurt at the time after my heart attack, so I spent my time drawing up the plans for converting the property into a five-bedroom detached house with separate double garage. There was about a third of an acre of land with the house, and when the local council approved the plans I found a builder willing to complete the conversion. Although I made money when I sold it, I would, in hindsight, have been far better off if I hadn't: the value today is five to six times higher than what I sold it for.

In actual fact we did not stay long in the maisonette as we decided to move nearer to our daughter Jeannie over in Billericay, Essex. There we found an extended semi overlooking the grounds of a large school. We made money on the sale of the maisonette, so the double moves were beneficial. But even after these moves I was still not financially settled, and had to find some other way of getting an income once again, so I joined a litigation company (debt collectors but not the door-to-door variety), but I'm afraid my sales techniques were not good enough for me to make a reasonable living, so I gave that up after a few months.

I then became a Christmas postman in Billericay. Although I was over-age, the manager asked me after a month or so if I was willing to work full-time? However, before I could agree, an old colleague, Ian Robinson, who had been working with me in Germany many years earlier, contacted me and suggested that I could perhaps head a new company applying to become the third Ground Handling Agency at Gatwick airport.

This was something out of the blue, totally unexpected and really worth considering, so I went to see Ian the next Saturday afternoon at a small flying school in Kent where he was giving flying lessons part-time while he worked for British Airport Authorities (BAA) HQ at Gatwick. We had lunch in a local pub where Ian explained the whole project. I took notes and agreed to see the Chairman and Operations Director for lunch on the following Monday; meanwhile my mind was racing around thinking about what I needed to have with me to show I was up to the task being set. That Saturday night and all day Sunday I worked on a plan of attack on this major assignment; I certainly burned the midnight oil that weekend and typed out the structure of the staffing needs for such a project.

On the Monday, I returned to Gatwick Airport and joined Ian Robinson there before meeting the Chairman and Director for lunch. The Chairman, Peter Charolambus, and Director, David Allen, were easy to get along with, and during the meal the subject of the airport job was raised. They had previously obtained some knowledge of my past experience in aviation from Ian and, knowing that Ian had also briefed me on what was expected, they were excitedly impressed when I produced the company structure required to fulfil the task; I think Ian was also impressed with what I had produced in such a short time.

So I was enlisted to head the project at Gatwick Airport, and a further meeting was arranged with another of the directors to settle the remuneration that would be offered for me to start. Later that week I had another fine luncheon with this other director to set up the deal. I had in the meantime spoken to an old friend, my bank manager, and got advice on how much to ask for, but of course I had not worked in England for over ten years, so did not have any up-to-date knowledge on salary scales. But surprisingly there were no problems and a deal was struck there and then, and the weekly salary I would have got as a postman would now become my daily take-home pay in future, on top of which I would also be able to claim expenses.

With Ian already at Gatwick, he was able to introduce me to many of the BAA Managers involved in appointing the third agency at the airport. Of course, I soon found out who was likely to become the third Agency, Servisair, who were already established at Stansted Airport and who had allowed Gatwick Handling to set up as the second handling company at that airport. The BAA had offered them first choice at Gatwick if they allowed Gatwick Handling into Stansted. It was then that they (BAA) realised that under Government and EU regulations they had to throw the appointment open to all comers and could not directly appoint

Servisair at Gatwick; they had to arrange for competitive tenders between all companies wishing to apply. The Civil Aviation Authority's commitment was to give the airlines a multi-choice of handlers at all airports, including those operated by the BAA. Mind you, Servisair still had to come up with reasonable charges for their services to the airlines, so there was still a slight chance that someone else could eventually outbid them.

The next few months were hectic, as the company offices were near Heathrow airport and, on top of that, I had to spend much time at Gatwick. So living in Essex meant I spent plenty of time in the car driving around the M25 which, despite the traffic, made it possible to carry out my responsibilities.

Partners in this adventure included an Arab Company of whom I had heard whilst I was in Oman, who were trying to get into the BAA airports in and around London by any means. Although they were catering experts who had outlets all over the world, their prime business was in hospital catering supply, and had, in recent years, expanded into airline catering in Dubai and Abu Dhabi. To get their foot into any of the London airports in any capacity would then allow them to eventually bring in their own catering expertise. Although they did not achieve their aim with my project, they did get into London Heathrow as caterers for Swissair a few years later.

Peter and David had other outlets already established in the import and export of fresh food products, coupled with their own fleet of large transporters that travelled the length and breath of England as well as Europe. Knowing that I had been much involved with cargo in aviation, they also used me to resolve some of their warehousing space problems with these other concerns. This was useful to me, as it would keep my income going in the event of the Gatwick airport project failing, which looked likely due to Servisair's firm position with the BAA.

Whilst on this project at Gatwick airport, I also came across an old friend, Rod Hoare, whom I had previously known when he first went overseas as a BOAC trainee on assignment. At the time we were both still in BOAC and he had joined me in Beirut, Lebanon. This was over twenty years previously, and in the meantime he had left BOAC/BA for a few years and had now come back as Operations Director for British Caledonian Airlines at Gatwick. This airline eventually became part of BA, but that was much later on.

This was a fortunate encounter for me. Whilst having a general conversation with Rod, I mentioned the fact that I could see Servisair getting the agency at Gatwick and that my assignment at the airport would then end. He then advised me that Aeroflot were looking for someone to monitor the handling of their flights through Gatwick. Caledonian Airlines were the handling agents for these flights but

Aeroflot needed an independent monitor to ensure they got the best possible handling service. He agreed to introduce me to the general manager of Aeroflot for UK and Ireland, and from this I got an interview in Piccadilly a few weeks later.

As expected Servisair were appointed the third handling company at Gatwick airport, although I still maintain we submitted as good an offer as they did, but the dice was loaded against us. By this time, I had become part of Peter Charolambus's main company, still on a consultancy basis. He had become involved in an American computer company, Zenith Data Systems, and this company was expanding at such a massive rate that they could never quite keep up with the expansion of warehousing space they required. I got the task of finding means to store their goods and also to set up the distribution network they required. It was quite a task, and was eventually spoilt by Peter, who became greedy and counteracted all my economies by overcharging Zenith on the freight forwarding rates. I had negotiated with various transport firms and obtained very competitive rates for distributing the massive amounts of goods they had. However, Peter added a massive surcharge to my prices, which all came to light a year or so later, fortunately, for me, long after I had left the consultancy.

I took up Rod Hoare's offer and had the interview with Mr Merzoyan, the Aeroflot General Manager, who was surprised to note that I was the same age as himself (not far off retirement); however, he and his assistant Vitali Sereda (the Commercial Manager) accepted my offer and I became their representative at Gatwick Airport on the 27th June 1987.

CHAPTER 21

AEROFLOT (THE DOUBLE-HEADED EAGLE)

Aeroflot used Gatwick for charter flights only every Saturday and Sunday, so this meant I could still keep my weekday work going with Zenith Data Systems and Peter's Pan Express company. For the next nine to twelve months I never had a day off, working seven days a week and enjoying every minute of it.

The Aeroflot work was putting the kerosene oil smell back in my blood. My daughter would always say: "Dad, you smell of airports and kerosene again." After working at airports for 40 years this was, to her, the normal aroma of aviation personnel!

The weekends were quite hectic. There would be between five and six flights arriving each day and they would all arrive within a two-hour period, so I used to contact the control tower ramp controller to endeavour to get him to plan the parking of Aeroflot aircraft near to one another. If they managed this, then my task was made easier, but naturally this did not always happen and then I had real problems.

The task Aeroflot set me was to meet every flight, pay the crew the small sterling allowance to which they were entitled, submit their flight plan to ATC and give them the weather briefing, having already obtained the clearance. Additionally, I was expected to resolve any problems at check-in and generally look after the arriving and departing passengers, really quite a tall order considering the number of flights arriving and departing so close together.

Getting the aircraft parked near to one another was essential to ensure I could fulfil all my tasks. If they were spread out all over Gatwick, a large airport with over 150 parking stands and considerable distances between stands, then I would have difficulty finding out which flights had landed and where they had been parked. At Gatwick, not all aircraft obtained jetty-served stands. Some have to be parked on open stands, which could be miles apart, so one of my first tasks was to obtain a driving permit and airport driving licence and have my car insured to cover accidents up to £40 million.

I could collect the weather folders in advance from the Met. office, and I could also submit their flight clearance to ATC. Mind you, this is where my operational training in BOAC played its part. So few details were received from Russia that I had to calculate the timings myself and quote them in the Flight Plan.

Once a flight was on the ground I needed to get the crew names on a special form and they had to sign for the allowance I duly had to pay them. The cash allowance for each flight was always the same, £3.96 for each crew member. They would then ask: "Can we have it in dollars?", so to cover this request I always went in advance to the bank on the airport and changed money from sterling to dollars, asking for small denominations. Then I could pay them the $6 or $7 they were each due. Needless to say, sometimes they wanted to have sterling, so this meant I always had to have some £3.96 packets with me as well.

To cover these allowance payments I was given an advance of around £1,000, from which I paid the crew, and then, with the allowance sheets they had signed, I could replenish my funds from the Town Office. This meant that if a sheet was lost I would be out of pocket by the amount I had paid out, but this never actually happened.

Included with the weather charts I would add the information concerning *en route* navigation aids, or NOTAMs (Notices Operational To Airmen).

Having greeted one flight I would then rush to the next to do a similar job, and then the next, but I had to remember to get back to each flight prior to the doors closing in order to get their allowance sheets. Whilst this was going on, I still had to keep in touch with the check-in desks and resolve the numerous problems that nearly always occurred. Each flight would normally be full both in and out and of course there were quite often standby passengers, who had to be accepted strictly to Head Office instructions if a seat became available. If arriving passengers' baggage failed to arrive, then I had to become involved and ensure correct tracer action was initiated.

Additionally, crews would like to do some shopping. They needed to take advantage of the shops on the airport to get goods that were not available in Russia. They would crowd into my small car (a Vauxhall Nova) and I would drop them off as near to the shops as possible on my way to meeting the next flight or to see another flight depart.

On departure, the crew would sometimes ask me to be on the headset for the push-back and engine start-up procedures. Although I didn't speak Russian, the crews preferred to have me on the headset rather than one of the Caledonian ground staff; I think it was because I was Aeroflot staff and this made them feel more sure of themselves.

I would only be about four hours at the airport on each day, but it was 'rush, rush, rush' all the time: keeping tabs on each flight in respect to check-in, ground services (whether the buses were available to meet the flight), if there were enough of them, and if a delay occurred, who caused it? Did the refuellers arrive on time, and did they load the fuel correctly and fast enough? Had they the additive mixer available for the Tu.154B-type aircraft? (The Tu.154B was the older type of Tu.154 and they needed to put an additive into the fuel on each occasion.) The mixer unit was kept at Gatwick and the refueller had to ensure he towed it to the aircraft on time, otherwise we would have a refuelling delay. All this sort of monitoring had to be done on a regular basis.

It was the sort of job where you had to know who was doing what and be on friendly terms wherever possible so that you could get the maximum assistance at all times. As a result I became well known at Gatwick. Aeroflot was different to other airlines; in some ways they were a 'mystery' airline to many people and were therefore held at arms' length if at all possible. The Russians are dogmatic as far as principles are concerned and do not suffer fools at all. I believe I also became known as "Harry the Hat" as I was given a large Russian military-style hat to make me stand out from the crowd. The hat had gold braid ('scrambled egg') along its peak, and a very high front that made you look extremely tall. They wanted the Russian passengers to be able to recognise me at the airport and be reassured that I was the one who would be able to resolve whatever their problems might be.

It was an extremely busy, happy and amusing two years of very hard work, during which time I made many, many friends and still have contact with a lot of them. Many incidents occurred which caused me stress, but in the end, I felt it was worth it all.

Quite often I felt it was like being a pioneer in aviation when working with the Russians. In so many ways they were ahead of the Western world in aviation matters; as an example they were the first to put a man in space. Some of the aircraft designed in the late 1960s or early 1970s used principles that were incorporated only in advanced western aircraft like the Concorde. The Tu.154 for example, a three-engined aircraft, had the ability to move fuel around its various wing tanks to enable the aircraft trim to be adjusted during all aspects of flight. The Concorde could only fly supersonically because of using this principle to adjust its trim *en route*.

This meant that the Russian crews always had the ability to adjust the aircraft trim during flight, a very useful feature when, as sometimes happened, an unintentional error in loading the aircraft had occurred on the ground, and it is the reason that these older-type Tu.154 aircraft were in service for so many years in Russia. From April 2002 they have been forbidden at Western airports because of their noise levels on landing and take-off although their airworthiness has never been in question; it is just that without a complete refit of engines they are just too noisy for airports in the Western world under Chapter 111 regulations.

The Russian crews had complete faith in their aircraft and, because they had flown them for so many years, knew the extreme capacity to which the aircraft could operate. As with most BOAC pilots on VC.10 or VC.15 aircraft, they were always willing to accept loading up to an absolute maximum because they knew the aircraft could accept a far higher load factor than that published or generally permitted.

My feeling of being a pioneer in aviation was brought about by the old-fashioned look of the Russian aircraft. They had made giant steps in improving the technical ability of their aircraft, but because they made no attempt to make them look flashy or shiny like the Americans they always looked drab and old-fashioned; yet they were really positive, sturdy and reliable planes that would never let you down, and certainly kept to schedule daily – you could almost set your watch by them.

Their Il.86 aircraft had also been in service for thirty years with an outstanding record of air safety. At the time of writing (2002) only one of them has crashed and that was this year on a positioning flight from Moscow to St. Petersburg. No other large commercial aircraft type in the world has equalled this record. One other Il.86 has been destroyed previously, however that was while it was on the ground and under repair at New Delhi airport in India; the engineers were changing an engine on the ramp when another aircraft hit it whilst attempting to take off on a test flight after repair.

So the aircraft being used at Gatwick for these charter flights were well tried and tested and definitely safe. However, the era for Aeroflot passenger charter flights was to cease as the regulations changed to permit charter passengers to be booked as groups on the scheduled flights. All Aeroflot scheduled flights were to operate into and out of Heathrow; only the St. Petersburg flights would continue to use Gatwick airport on scheduled flights when charter operations ceased. This meant I needed to subsequently focus my attention more on Heathrow, Aeroflot's main active airport. The last charter flight left Gatwick on 28 May 1990, which was almost exactly 3 years after I had met my first Aeroflot flight at Gatwick.

Whilst with Aeroflot at Gatwick, I was still working Monday to Friday for Peter at Pan Express or through him with Zenith Data Systems, and this arrangement lasted, surprisingly, for another eight months; it was to me a very lucrative period and, although quite stressful, I wanted it to last as long as possible, although it meant leaving home every morning by 6.30 am and arriving home just before 8.00 pm, depending on the traffic delays suffered on the M25.

When this work ceased, I had time to look towards Aeroflot at Heathrow for more activity. They had very few staff, treated their passengers like unwanted sheep, and needed to be modernised and introduced to the Western approach as far as passenger and cargo handling was concerned. I therefore attempted to get involved at the airport and the eventual outcome was that I was transferred to Heathrow on (at first) a consultancy basis.

Yuri was the current Station Manager at Heathrow, an extremely large and pleasant man. He had been at the airport for almost three years and had never had a day off other then a three-week leave break in

Moscow; he wasn't all that pleased to see me at the airport, which didn't make my introduction any easier, but he was just so busy with his normal duties that it was difficult for him to find time to consider any changes. It must be remembered that he was Station Engineer as well as Station Manager; the overseas staffing principle within Aeroflot was to have a Station Engineer and then make him cover the Station Manager's duties as well. He was therefore an engineer first and foremost and covered those duties as a priority, and then if he had the time or inclination he would then consider the passenger and cargo problems. The end result was that cargo and passengers would be offloaded somewhat unceremoniously without any real attempt at resolving any on-load possibilities.

For these reasons, the reputation of the passenger service within Aeroflot was severely criticized in London and, indeed, worldwide. When coerced into organising a customer service function, the Russians only acted on behalf of Russian citizens, whom they knew had some power which could force them into action. Foreign passengers didn't have any say at all, and it was this customer service aspect that I wanted to improve, especially at London.

Not long after I went to Heathrow there was a change in management for Aeroflot in London; Vitali Sereda took over as General Manager (UK and Ireland) on the retirement of Merzoyan, and Mark Balabolin came in as Station Engineer & Station Manager. Vitali had got to know me quite well and knew how keen I was to get customer service improved. Mark soon got to know me and supported my ideas for improvements at Heathrow, so we became very good friends and started to work as a team.

After the initial shock, the rest of the Aeroflot staff then started to accept me on the station, and this meant I was gradually able to influence the actual approach shown to passengers and to cargo. It was not easy in respect to cargo, as there were always shortages of pallets or containers onto which to load it. Containerised aircraft have little space for loose cargo or baggage without containers or pallets, so often you are forced to leave it behind.

Sometimes there was not even enough equipment on station to cover all the passengers' baggage, which naturally had priority over cargo and mail, and it took years before these shortages were eliminated altogether; in fact we had to wait until a few years after the Airbus A310 was introduced before modern containers were purchased to supplement and eventually replace the Russian-made, and extremely heavy, containers; these were not approved for use on the Airbus 310, and so we had to keep separate supplies of them.

Of course the Western world, who looked at Aeroflot as their direct competitor, was unaware that Aeroflot was really only an internal (domestic) airline with a relatively small international division. The facts were that Aeroflot carried millions of passengers throughout Russia.

Within Russia, with its vast distances and ten hours of time change from west to east (twice that of the USA from west to east coast), it even operated to 'Moscow time' on all internal (domestic) routes, taking no notice of the Western world's Greenwich Mean Time (GMT). Russian towns, railway stations and airports had to have two clocks, one quoting the local time and the other Moscow time. Train, bus and plane timetables were issued with Moscow and local timings shown.

Under Communism, the company (Aeroflot) was extremely large; it had 96,000 aircrew and a total staff of nearly 500,000 men and women. And its fleet of aircraft numbered 16,000, ten times more than any Western equivalent, so it was really a vast enterprise, although operated mainly on a domestic basis. Under Communism, anything related to flying within Russia was the responsibility of Aeroflot with its military and civilian divisions; therefore air traffic controllers were Aeroflot staff, partly civilian and partly military. The airport management, maintenance and facilitation staff had a similar split. The actual airline workers were not classed as military, but the military could be classified as Aeroflot when required or deemed necessary. The large numbers quoted previously refer to what might be termed the civilian section of Aeroflot (the non military Department of Aviation).

Within the first year of my service at Heathrow, the Civil Aviation Management in Moscow decided it was time to separate all the military operations. Aeroflot asked me to find out how the British Government had set up the distinct divisions of:

1. Civil Aviation Authorities
2. British Airport Authorities
3. Airlines (British Airways, British Midland etc)

In reply I obtained copies of the relevant Government White Papers issued on this matter and forwarded them to Moscow. That same principle has now been used in Russia to separate the aviation industry functions. As a result, Aeroflot staff levels have dropped by a massive amount, as they no longer include air traffic control or airport management and airport maintenance staff.

Additionally, in latter years Communism no longer rules, and Aeroflot has been allowed to be partly privatised. In doing so the airline wing of the old Aeroflot was broken up into numerous small airlines. At one time, there were over 400 airlines within Russia, but this has since been reduced to well under 100. The present-day Aeroflot has internal (domestic) and international competition within Russia, and no longer has a monopoly status. The new Director General of Civil Aviation has had her work cut out getting the technical and management aspects of these numerous airlines checked and verified; many were so poorly organised and maintained that she had to remove their licences to operate on safety grounds.

Aeroflot is still the largest of the groups and has more state backing than any of the others. It still operates to about 125 countries worldwide, although this is a reduction by some 20 or more to those previously served. Under the old Communist government, the Russian Ambassador in any country could demand an Aeroflot scheduled service to his country of residence, even if there were no commercial reasons for the flight. That has since been changed: Aeroflot will now only answer the Ambassador's request if it is commercially sound to fly to that particular station or on that route.

During the Communism era, Aeroflot's international wing only used the most experienced flight technical crews and their overseas staffs were selected from the best ground personnel available. All personnel going overseas had to be fully vetted to ensure they were good Communists. Once selected they were given special training, operationally and technically; however the cabin crew were not considered quite so important and they could still fly on both internal and international flights, with those speaking some English flying mainly on the Western world routes.

Cabin crew always found it hard to differentiate between the level of service expected within the Western world and that when carrying Western passengers on Eastern routes. The aircraft used on international services were the same as those used on internal flights, although three or four reserve aircraft were assigned to every overseas flight. In this way, if the first one became unserviceable, then the next one – or the next one – would be used, with the result that overseas flights always seemed to be on time, a very good plug for Communism. Of course, the domestic flights could be often delayed if the original aircraft had been transferred to an overseas service.

Ever since Communism was introduced, the Russians have always tried to advertise it as the best solution for the people living under its control; for example, everyone should get fair shares, and no one should be without the bare necessities of life. In general they achieved this, although some certainly got more than others.

Russians working outside the country were required to ensure that they spoke about their homeland with much affection, so in this respect Aeroflot had to show how efficient they were. No one would ever admit that the system was not working, and every effort was made to ensure that the Western world was given a glossy picture of the efficiency and power behind the administration; of course this helped to keep the "Iron Curtain" in place.

The major airports within Russia were operationally very sound but had very limited terminal facilities. The large Il.86, a 350-'economy'-seater aircraft developed to use "open ramp" airport layouts, had three very large stairwells with fold-down stairs a metre and one half wide for loading or off-loading passengers; this was ideal when carrying domestic passengers, where no immigration or customs procedures applied. Passengers could also carry their own bags onto the aircraft and place them directly into the lower deck baggage racks fitted at the top of the stair-well. Therefore the airport authorities only built larger terminal buildings where it was absolutely essential. Hence it is only within the last five or so years that terminal building projects have been introduced. The runway and taxiway facilities for aircraft movement exceed those provided in the Western world, and this is sometimes quite a shock to Western pilots when they find the runway twice as wide as they are used to.

With this attitude, it can easily be realised how little comfort is available for passengers on the ground at Russian airports. The modernisation of terminal buildings is proceeding, but it will take some time to be completed. Arguments over airport terminal construction that the West has settled over the last 20-30 years have still to be resolved within Russia. General attitudes of the immigration and customs staff will need to change in order to get a smoother control over passenger movements within airports. For instance, customs and immigration officers are still demanding individual rooms rather than open-plan offices, and it has been so hard to get this matter settled that the whole matter of terminal construction has been extensively delayed; this has hampered some development attempts at airports around Moscow for years.

Travel facilitation in Russia is in its infancy. Russia under Communist rule offered air travel to everyone and at a minimum price, but more often than not you only got on the flights if your status was high enough or if there happened to be a seat available. As a local person you could not book a firm seat, so Russian passengers were used to queuing and having to argue over seating; on the other hand, 'firm' seats were always available to foreigners on domestic flights. Air travel for Russians within Russia was very cheap; even coming to the UK, a Russian passenger would only pay about £25 return as against the normal fare of over £400 for other passengers. Within Russia the rail and air fares were the same, but now that Communism no longer rules, the Russian people have had to accept the changes and pay the same as everyone else. You can understand what a vast change this has made to travel facilities within the country, and why not all Russians are pleased about the demise of Communism.

But I am jumping ahead of myself. When I first became involved at Heathrow in 1987, Russia was still under Communist rule, with the barriers this imposed. Naturally, all Russian staff were Communists, so you had to remind yourself of this when dealing with them. Things that I felt to be unacceptable were classed as normal and acceptable to them.

Even the Polish staff, who had been employed locally, felt obliged to accept this situation as they had, of course, originally been Communists themselves. These staff members were: Kasia (who was Polish and married, with two children and a Polish husband), Gabi (also Polish but with one son and married to an Australian) and Jack Paton (Spanish with an English wife and a small boy of 4 and a girl of 9). Jack retired when he reached 65 and returned to Valencia in Spain, where he had two properties, but unfortunately he only lived for about six more months, just enough time to get his family settled in their new schools and home.

Originally they (the airport staff) could not see me being of any use to Aeroflot London, as they felt I was too old but, surprisingly, they admitted they were wrong some four or five years later. Then it was accepted that I was their new Local Manager and from then onwards it was possible to introduce gradually the much-needed changes in customer service.

Firstly, I persuaded them that passengers who had been offloaded did have the rights to complain and should not be shut out of the office and ignored: some attempt had to be made to resolve their problems.

Secondly, that it was necessary to have a proper baggage tracing unit, dealing with missing baggage and making settlement of claims.

Thirdly, they needed to be able to demand and receive an adequate supply of container and pallet handling equipment from Moscow. This was needed to cover the large loads of cargo, post office mail and passengers' baggage delivered for each flight. Rejection of commercial cargo, mail or baggage was detrimental to Aeroflot. Loose loading of items on containerised aircraft should never be allowed to occur.

All of this brought about my reasoning for why we needed extra staffing at Heathrow in order to be compatible with other Western airlines. We needed to recruit extra staff and in doing so, develop and improve all the ground service facilities to our passengers, cargo, mail and crews, making them more compatible with those given by Western airlines at Heathrow and other airports worldwide.

Naturally, these changes could not be, and were not, achieved overnight. Firstly, I had to persuade Mark Balabolin of the need for these changes, then he in turn had to get Vitali Sereda's agreement, and in turn they had to get the agreement of Head Office in Moscow: this was not the easiest of things to do, as central Communist control was still very much in command.

But, much to their credit, they did get the agreement of Moscow and gradually we increased our airport staff from three up to seven plus myself. In addition, Moscow agreed that on a station the size of Heathrow, one engineer who had to assume the additional responsibilities of station manager needed another engineer to assist him. So in as well as the seven staff we now had a station manager, a

Russian engineer and myself. The other new staff I selected were: Anita and Ruth (both recently qualified Russian-speaking graduates from Universities in the UK), Gavin (a well-spoken young man with a little airline experience and very presentable) and Patricia (a very experienced ticketing agent who had worked at Heathrow for a number of years). This group, coupled with the original Aeroflot staff, formed our new team at Heathrow and they stayed together for about three years. Mark, although a qualified aircraft engineer, was also trained to be Station Manager and, with his general managerial capabilities and the new engineer on Station to support him, the two functions could now be properly covered without forcing the Russians to work every day of the week. Aircraft were coming in at all times of both day and night and all needed to be attended to and serviced properly.

I expect that it was due to the cold war situation between West and East that the Aeroflot flight crews always carried guns. So on night-stopping services the guns were collected by the police, locked up overnight and then returned to the crew just before departure the next day. The crew did not have visas but an advance list was, of course, registered with UK Immigration; the arriving crew lists then had to be presented to Immigration and Customs to get final clearance to stay overnight. Naturally, Special Branch got these lists and had ample time to vet them and confirm they were permitted to land (and, later, leave the airport). But the situation is far more relaxed nowadays.

Not all Russian crews were fluent in English, although the percentage that could speak English far outweighed the number who could speak Russian. Because of this language problem, Moscow insisted that a Russian met the flight on every occasion. In these early days, there waw no way in which I could take the place of a Russian, although later the crews knew me so well that I was accepted if a Russian was for some reason not available.

What eventually persuaded Moscow that we needed extra staff was the fact that the passenger loads to and from Heathrow had greatly increased. The inclusion of charter flight passengers, coupled with the large numbers of Indian and Pakistan passengers using Aeroflot services, meant the flights were always completely full – in fact, most flights were well overbooked. The lack of proper reservation control in Moscow played a part, especially as the fares to some destinations were cheaper than those of most other IATA airlines. There was only one stop between London and Delhi, Bombay, Karachi & Dacca; additionally, we were also offering cheaper flights to Bangkok and Tokyo, and this attracted many 'back-packer' passengers, in particular to Bangkok.

At Heathrow, Aeroflot had a reciprocal service handling agreement with British Airways, which meant that British Airways flights had Aeroflot Staff to handle them in Russia. In the same way, we had British

Airways staff handling our flights at Heathrow. This agreement was signed when Aeroflot first began services to Heathrow in 1952. BEA had started flights to Moscow at the same time and it was considered by both airlines to be a marvellous advantage, but Aeroflot didn't modernise in Moscow as quickly as BEA/BA did in the UK and so the agreement became very one-sided in Aeroflot's favour.

The handling service given by BA to Aeroflot could be good but, as the passenger loads increased, then the demands presented by Aeroflot, coupled with the old-fashioned conditions available at that time in Terminal 2, meant the service remained poor. The Terminal facilities needed many improvements before any improved handling service could be implemented. Of course, we complained bitterly to BA, but to no avail. (Mind you, BA complained bitterly in Moscow about Aeroflot's handling, but once again to no avail!)

Once we had the increased staff numbers, we were then able to put more pressure on the British Airways Contract Handling Department and in this way get a marked improvement for our services. However, no matter what we found wrong with the BA service, we were not allowed to change our handling agents; this was forbidden by Moscow, who desired to keep a reciprocal agreement which was so useful to them.

The next few years were difficult but happy for me. I had originally been a consultant to Aeroflot and had been paid on the invoices I submitted monthly. I was paid a daily rate for the number of days I worked, which suited me as I could claim income relief as a self-employed person, which included the cost of running my car.

However, when I became 65 years old, Vitali Sereda said to me: "Moscow do not like the idea of paying you as a consultant any longer; they want you to join Aeroflot as a full-time staff member"

This really surprised me, but when I asked: "Do they know my age?", I was told: "That doesn't matter."

It didn't matter to me either; I only needed to know how much I was going to be paid. It was then that Vitali explained: "The salary is (so much)" and then added: "For that you will have to work *every weekend* and for *six days* each week."

The amount offered was truly enough, so it left me little or no reason to reject the offer. But even the pay for six days a week including every weekend was less than I had been getting for working as a consultant for both Aeroflot and Pan Express simultaneously. I therefore accepted the offer and became a full-time staff member of Aeroflot UK. This was June 1990 and a new beginning for me at just 65 years of age; for quite a few years I was only to have Mondays off, but Madge and I settled to this arrangement quite happily.

With this settled, I became fully immersed in Aeroflot matters. I was given the title of Assistant Station Manager and as such represented the company at AOC (Airline Operators Committee) and BARUK (Board of Airline Representatives United Kingdom) meetings; this latter was much to my surprise as it was normally attended by the airline's most senior General Managers.

Mark Balabolin turned out to be the most perfect manager you could wish for. He had no favourites, treated everyone correctly and supported me fully. We all became part of a team, pulled together well and did our best for Aeroflot generally. It was a happy atmosphere to work in and I like to think that I fully played my part in these developments. All the staff that have subsequently left Aeroflot do talk proudly about their period with us in Terminal 2 Heathrow as part of the Aeroflot team.

Inherited with my title at Heathrow was the added responsibility for all other airports used by Aeroflot within the United Kingdom. This meant my going to Manchester at a later stage to resolve the handling agreement mix-up between British Airways (Manchester) and Gatwick Handling (Manchester).

At Manchester, as with all other airports used by BA, British Airways were contracted to handle any Aeroflot flight that happened to land (a reciprocal agreement once again). However, when Mr Sereda went to Manchester to set up handling of the new scheduled services being introduced, he decided to appoint Gatwick Handling (Manchester) to cover these scheduled services, and this unfortunately conflicted with the agreement signed in 1952 for the reciprocal handling contract between Russia and the United Kingdom. In the old contract it stated that BA would handle all Aeroflot flights landing at any other airports operated by BA within the UK; therefore, we now had one handling agent for scheduled flights to Manchester and another to handle diverted flights, and as you can imagine this caused some confusion in Manchester on occasions. A flight would land and each handling company would wait to see whether the other handling company was meeting the flight. I eventually got it agreed in Manchester that all flights would be handled by Gatwick Handling (Manchester).

I also got involved at another airport when we had an Antonov 124 going into Prestwick, in Scotland, and I was sent to arrange the crew accommodation and flight handling. The An.124 is the largest commercial aircraft flying today; it had also made the longest flight in history when it flew on a circular route over Russia for 25 hours 30 minutes and covered 12,324 miles on 6th-7th May 1987. It had initially been permitted to carry 180 tonnes of cargo, although this had subsequently to be reduced to 110 tonnes to comply with Western regulations. You could get at least 10 double-decker buses inside its fuselage, which gives some idea of the space available within the aircraft. Above the cargo bay, there is also an additional passenger/crew sleeping area, which can seat up to 50 people. It is a very impressive aircraft indeed with its built-in gantries, each of which can lift 5 tonnes, so you can combine the four gantries, lift 20-tonne items, and carry them the whole length of the fuselage, which is truly very impressive. Antonov have since made a bigger version now called the Antonov 225 (*Mriya)* and in Russia this is being used for carrying the space Ship *Butan* on top of the fuselage in the same fashion that the Americans move the space shuttle; the quoted payload for this aircraft is a massive 250 tonnes.

Anyway, the occasion for this An.124 going to Prestwick was to pick up some very large pipeline valves that had been made in Scotland. They were to replace those damaged in a recent oil pipeline fire which had occurred in Siberia. Each unit weighed about 5 tonnes but the gantries build within the aircraft could lift and carry two at a time the whole length of its fuselage. This meant that loading was very fast, and after loading over 80 tonnes the aircraft still looked empty!

This same aircraft came to Gatwick Airport at a later date and the whole of Gatwick Airport staff came out to meet it. On board were three helicopters plus their crews, a total of 50 people, bound for the Helicopter Trade Fair at Redhill aerodrome, and Customs had a terrible time trying to sort out crew from passengers as none of them were wearing uniforms. On top of this there were all the Gatwick ground staff who had got on board and by this time seemed to be everywhere on the aircraft. An aircraft of this size causes quite a stir, which is why so many people crowded out onto the ramp area; I reckon that anyone who had an airport pass turned up on the ramp.

Afterwards I was summoned before the Customs Surveyor to account for why I hadn't requested barriers and a police presence to hold back the crowds. I got a good ticking off, but he seemed to appreciate that I couldn't be expected to know just how much interest the aircraft was going to create. It hadn't been a problem up in Prestwick, but that is not such a busy airport as Gatwick.

After unloading, the helicopters were serviced and then flown to Redhill, where they stayed for four days. Meanwhile the Antonov 124 returned to Moscow, but then came back again later to collect the helicopters. The Antonov does cause ATC some problems: it needs to stand at the end of the runway prior to take-off with all four engines at full power for at least four minutes before releasing the brakes. In this way, the engines have built up full take-off power before the aircraft starts its takeoff run, similar to the procedures used in the early days of jet travel with the Comet 1 aircraft. This take-off delay is peculiar to this aircraft type only, so it tends to upset the normal take-off procedures at airports and has to be specially allowed for in the ATC 'separation' calculations. Even with this sort of restriction, it is still a remarkable aircraft: no other presently flying has a greater capacity.

TOP: The Aeroflot team at Heathrow: Gabi, Mark Balabolin and myself.
Photo: MJP Photography, Isleworth.
BOTTOM: Kasia and myself at Heathrow. Photos: author's collection.

Jeremy Spake in his Heathrow office. Photo: the author.

The author presents footballing equipment sponsored by Aeroflot to the Holy Cross School team at South Ockendon. Photo: Thurrock Gazette.

TOP: A presentation to H.M. The Queen at Heathrow Terminal 2, 1999. Photo: Heathrow Airport Ltd.
BOTTOM: The author's retirement from Aeroflot in December 1999. Photo: author's collection.

The next airport I became really involved with was Stansted in Essex. I was asked to meet Vitali Sereda in Piccadilly and to accompany him to see Sir John Egan, Chief Executive of BAA (British Airport Authorities) at their Head Office in the Victoria area of London. It was only when the discussions started that I learnt that Aeroflot were being granted permission to operate six flights per week to and from the USA through Stansted Airport, Essex and that these flights were due to commence in two months' time.

It was a very interesting meeting and made me even better known within the BAA generally: it also meant that my feet would not touch the ground for the next eight weeks. I had to arrange for an Aeroflot office at Stansted, plus all the equipment necessary to run a airline operations office. This meant arranging for such things as, telephones, SITA (Societé Internationale de Telecommunications Aeronautique) telex lines and furniture for a suite of offices. I understood that a Russian would be based there as Station Manager, so I didn't spare any expense in furnishing the place on his behalf, whoever it would be. On top of this there would have to be local staff to work the Station, only one to start with but possibly more once it was in full swing. Then we needed a Ground Handling Agent and there were two at the Station, Servisair and GHI (Gatwick Handling, Stansted). I knew the managers of both; the first, Alan Brough, was in Bahrain whilst I was in Muscat and the other (Denis Cockram) was ex-BA Gatwick, who then joined GHI Gatwick and was their first station manager at Manchester; he had subsequently been transferred to Stansted as station manager.

I choose GHI Stansted as they did not have too many airlines to handle and had far more space available in their cargo warehouse. This choice turned out for the best, because although the American flights never did begin operations, it was decided to route the freighter flights via Stansted instead of Heathrow (no slots were available at Heathrow for freighters) and, for good measure, two of the three St. Petersburg flights were moved from Gatwick.

My first recruit for Stansted was John Stevens. He had no experience in scheduled airline work but had managed a small private airport having many small business and private aircraft operations. So I stood the risk on him coping with our type of operation, and he didn't do too badly during the year he was with us. He was much involved with aircraft in general and was a part-time librarian at Duxford's Aviation Museum. He also had his own computer library on aircraft built worldwide over the previous 70 years. He left eventually because he won his case at the work tribunal with his previous employers and they persuaded him to go back to running the small airport. His house was within the airport's grounds, so it really was the best place for him to reside and work.

His replacement was Simon Hepper. He had quite a lot of experience but had been made redundant by DanAir. It turned out to be a good option for him as he was able to move his family back up from Devon and get back into aviation. He seized the opportunity later on to set up his own business at Stansted and managed to become a representative, not only for Aeroflot, but also for CSA, the Czechoslovakian airline. He no longer represents Aeroflot but still has other involvements with airlines at Stansted and also Belfast in Northern Ireland (he had been in Belfast with DanAir prior to being made redundant).

Naturally, there had to be changes in management within Aeroflot London. Vitali Sereda's time in London was coming to an end, and his new commercial manager, Victor Ilyukhin, was due to take over, but Vitali seemed to be in no hurry to leave London until he was assured of what was available for him in Moscow. Fortunately for me, Victor and I had hit it off from the beginning; he had been Station Manager at Heathrow many years before and he knew a number of the BA staff that were still working for the contract handling section. Then he had moved to Rome and made quite a name for himself there, rising high enough to become General Manager in UK. Aeroflot did develop well under his guidance and a good working relationship remained between Town Office and the Airport.

The efforts the Russian staff would make to ensure they were not embarrassed by having Russian officials offloaded in London could be quite extreme. They naturally always got me to try to resolve the problem any way I could. On one occasion, there was a delegation of senior police visiting the UK as guests of the British Police authorities. They were entertained too well and one of the police officials became so drunk that he could not stand steady on his feet, but there was no way that his wife, another policewoman of similar rank, who was part of the group and a very large woman too, was going to leave her husband behind, so with help of a few colleagues they tried to pour him on board. Surprisingly, the cabin crew had no qualms about letting him on board and so every effort was made, but he was so far beyond helping himself that eventually we ended up trying to sit him on a baggage trolley and wheeling him along the ramp finger (jetty) and into the plane.

I was in the thick of these efforts to get him on board, but eventually I had to say: "I'm sorry, he cannot travel; we will get the airport police to give him a night in the cells and let him travel on the next flight, which is tomorrow." By rights, he should have bought another ticket, as his ticket was only valid for that day's flight, but I knew the Russians would permit him to use it because of the circumstances. His wife refused to travel without him, so we took her off as well and Boris arranged accommodation for her at the Embassy. For any other national they would have refused to board a passenger in this alcoholic state.

Some changes were forced on us by the BAA; we had to move from our office, which at the time was in Terminal 2, when the airside development took place. They were enlarging the immigration offices into our office area and so we had no choice. The other offices on offer were much nicer and in the new block which had been built on the west end of the Terminal; but unfortunately I had just spent £35,000 refurbishing the old offices with new wiring and new office furniture. However, because we were being forced to move out, BAA were prepared to cover the costs of partitioning the new office in a similar manner, so all the new furniture could still be used and moved with us.

The new offices had large windows and gave us a good view of the south-western part of the airport, so we were not displeased with this move, although we didn't say this to the BAA. We had a special section which gave our passengers access to the office but without getting into our working area. They could discuss their problems across a counter, which kept us at least at arms' length.

Shortly after this move to these offices, I was asked to become Chairman of the Terminal 2 AOC, which caused me much extra work but meant that Aeroflot had a much higher profile within the terminal. It was at the busiest time for the terminal development: there were two years of enlargement and modernisation of the airside of the terminal, followed by another two years of landside improvements.

Being AOC Chairman I was greatly involved in the enlargement programme. I stayed as Chairman for the first three years, but then handed over to another Station Manager. The Queen had opened Terminal 2 back in the 1960s and she kindly consented to open the new airside improvements. As the current AOC Chairman, I was introduced to the Queen on this occasion and she well recalled having been in the same area so many years earlier.

I enjoyed the challenge of the AOC and, although it caused me many hours of extra work, I am very proud of what was achieved in co-operation between the airlines and the BAA development planners. Terminal 2 is now as modern as any other Terminal at Heathrow Airport.

With the landside improvements, we finally had the opportunity to have our own ticket issuing desk in the main check-in area. The ticketing staff did not relish having to go down there to work, as it meant they had a lot more direct contact with the passengers and their friends; they were used to being within the office away from that area, and not so often confronted with passengers who wanted to let off steam. Passengers and their friends can be most unpleasant to staff when they feel they haven't been served quite appropriately; this especially happens when they realise they are not getting away without paying for their enormous amounts of excess baggage, and staff have to become very hard-skinned not to break down and cry as the result of the abuse given to them on such occasions. It doesn't seem to matter what nationality or religion the passengers are, they can still be absolutely beastly.

During Victor Ilyukhin's term in London we had a visit by President Yeltzin; his flight went into Brize Norton (the RAF base) and guess who had to go to ensure the arrangements there were OK? Me, of course! It was a two-day effort, and of course John Major, the Prime Minister, greeted the President. I didn't manage to shake their hands but I was very close to them both. I had to do my usual task by getting BA to supply about 100 men's & women's first class toiletry bags, which were very much appreciated by the Russians within the President's entourage.

We had had a previous visit by the President but that was into Heathrow London Airport. Here visits by dignitaries of many nations were organised. The only problem we had on this occasion was the weather (fog), as we had not accounted for the strength of resolve within Russian Aeroflot crews to ensure that their President landed at the place where he was expected. Despite the weather the flight landed on time and we had to send a "Follow Me" car out to bring him the aircraft safely to the Royal Flight stand.

About this time a new travel agency was formed and Victor Ilyukhin was directly involved. Unfortunately, it seemed that Mark Balabolin had voiced his opinion about it too forcefully, and consequently got his marching orders back to Moscow. We were all most upset, but knew it was better if we didn't get involved in the UK arrangements for Russian staff. Mark was badly missed by the airport staff; his relationship with us all had meant we were a very efficient team and we were sorry to see the leader removed from the team.

The new man to replace Mark, Boris Ermine, was not an engineer and had no previous experience at airport management. He had understood that he was coming to London to work in the Town Office and was not expecting to be involved with the operational and other airport-type work.

Boris was a very smooth character, a bit of a linguist, who had been assigned to JAL (Japan Air Lines) in Moscow to cover their protocol aspects. He learnt Japanese and I am sure he did a very good job for JAL; however, Heathrow Station Manager was a totally different function and it was going to take him some time to get to know his new vocation and his required involvement.

His arrival suited Victor Ilyukhin and we found that our ticketing arrangements were changing, which upset the ticket issue staff, but with the Station Manager supporting the changes the situation could not be resisted at a local level. Things were eventually sorted, but not until we had another General Manager, Zurab Sohokia, a fairly young and very high flying ex-management trainee, and destined to become Manager USA at some future date. He replaced Victor as General Manager but, as with Vitali Sereda, Victor did not want to go back to Moscow and in the end decided to retire from Aeroflot and to remain in London.

Zurab Sohokia had some disputes with Victor Ilyukhin over his UK business link-up with Aeroflot. It all happened behind closed doors, so we local staff were not party to any of it. Zurab was a young man and quite good-looking; the girls in the office felt he was the 'bee's knees' and he did have some calming effect on the station, but knowing he was earmarked for Manager USA after a couple of years in London, he was not going to rock the boat too much whilst he was here, and as expected he did go on to New York.

Whilst he was in London I had recruited a new staff member, Jeremy Spake. He had originally been trained by BA and had subsequently worked for CSA in Terminal 2 Heathrow. He was a knowledgeable person with a Russian mother and so spoke pretty good Russian. He made quite a difference in the office, which had been dominated by females in the ticketing and customer service functions. Fortunately, he was good at his work, did work extremely hard and eventually was accepted by the rest of the staff, although he did try to become very dominant within the office and so some arguments with the management occurred; however, the office functions and friendships remained intact.

One day a letter was forwarded to the airport from Town Office asking for our comments, and, as always, it came to me. The letter was from the BBC, who were planning to do a series called *Airport* and asking if Aeroflot would participate with them. My comments were that that would be fine provided they didn't interfere with our operations. So Zurab Sahokia decided that this gave the green light to go ahead and agreed to join the programme. This saw the making of a TV star in Jeremy Spake, who was extrovert enough to come over wonderfully well in the programme. He has subsequently left Aeroflot and has made quite a good career for himself in TV, radio and after-dinner speaking. He even has his own fan club with members as far away as Norway.

The BBC series was very successful and was not bad in respect to Aeroflot, in fact it gave us quite a lot of good publicity although some of the BAA management thought it was not too good for the Airport. It would seem that the BAA complaints were mainly directed against Jeremy Spake personally for the weekly column he wrote for the Airport newspaper. All these sorts of projects inevitably puts some strain on staff relationships and, on some occasions, duties were switched in order to get Jeremy where the BBC wanted to film him. However, careful handling generally resolved any upset before it had any effect on the relationships within the team.

Jeremy had many good points in his favour but his success with the BBC made him feel he could do and say what he pleased to all the managers, including myself. However, he was efficient and an excellent reservations and ticketing agent: his training with BA had ensured this fact.

During the filming of the second series we had yet another change of General Manager, and as the new man did not want any further programmes, the series ended as far as Aeroflot was concerned, much against the BBC's and Jeremy's wishes.

The Russian managers emphasised that, no matter how good you were with your work, it didn't give you the right to imply that they were inefficient. With the series finished, Jeremy showed his displeasure and was very outspoken, and this did lead to some friction; he therefore submitted his resignation, which was accepted.

This change of management did make quite a difference within Aeroflot airport staff. The new General Manager, Boris Krivchenko, had been at Shannon in Ireland for about 20 years, where Aeroflot had the largest operation of any airline with some 56 flights per week. Naturally, he had had much support from Shannon's Irish airport management, who were aiming to foster the continuation of this lucrative Aeroflot business, but of course he didn't get quite so much attention at Heathrow, as Aeroflot were not one of the big airlines there. Unfortunately, his efforts got him on the wrong side of the local staff, as to them it seemed that he was trying to economize at their expense by changing the contract terms. For 20 years or more, because we always had minimum numbers, the staff only manned the office three hours before a flight and a maximum of two to three hours after the flight had gone. The new GM (Boris Krivchenko) wanted the office manned from at least 09.00 to 18.00 daily, but with no extra staff; to do this meant that our practice of having one person covering ticketing and check-in and another seeing to the transit/turn-round procedures at the departure gate must cease. With only one person on duty, only selected procedures could be covered by our own staff; our Agents would be expected to attend to functions with a minimum of monitoring.

In theory, this should have been possible, but the changes necessary were not easy to implement at Heathrow without a lot of alteration to the then current organisation; he naturally got fairly strong opposition from the local staff, purely because of the extra hours they were going to have to work, as they would definitely have to work the full contracted hours, 40 per week. This in turn necessitated changes in the number of weekends off they presently enjoyed, something that was bitterly opposed by the married staff.

As you can imagine much debate ensued, and the last six months or so of my time with Aeroflot was far from harmonious because of these changes. Whether this was a reflection of the procedures Boris had had in place in Shannon I'm not certain, but they certainly caused problems at Heathrow. Work in Shannon on the passenger side was very limited in comparison to that at Heathrow. We had large loads of joining passengers, potentially causing a multitude of problems, whereas Shannon only really dealt with transit passengers who were confined to the transit lounge.

I have so far failed to mention that between Zurab Sahokia and Boris Krivchenko we had another general manager, Yury Mnatsakanov. He was slightly older than most GMs and very pleasant-natured, and actually decided that I was working too many long hours, so he agreed to reduce my contract so that I worked a five-day 40-hour week; this I did but of course he reduced my salary slightly as well.

Unfortunately, he didn't last too long as he was promoted to Senior Commercial Director in Moscow. However, whilst he was in London he asked me to accompany him to the schedule negotiations with British Airways, which were aimed at equal division of the revenue earned between Moscow/London/Moscow. To make it work required Aeroflot to operate a late flight every night from London (departure 22.30) and BA to do the same out of Moscow. In this way neither airline had to have night-stopping crew. Agreement was not eventually reached, but the seed was sown in Yury's mind and he started to introduce late flights from London on four nights a week. But neither the Russian airport staff nor the local airport staff were too pleased with these late flights, as they necessitated working until 23.30 on the nights on which they operated. These late flights were only possible because we now had a total of ten Boeing 737/400 type aircraft, brand new and of course operating well within the Chapter 111 noise regulations.

Whilst Mnatsakanov was in the UK as General Manager, he insisted on only having Western world aircraft such as the Airbus 310, Boeing B777, B767, or B737 flying into London; this meant that the service given on board (in flight) was greatly improved as all mod cons were on board these aircraft types, just the same as on BA or any other Western world airline. It took a while before Moscow took full notice of this demand, but in the end they followed his instructions. These Western-built aircraft will eventually be replaced by Russian-built aircraft which are under development at this time.

The initial attempt in Russia to build a modern aircraft was only partly successful with the Il.96. Technically it was very advanced as far as the cockpit, engines and flight controls were concerned, but the manufacturers never modernised the passenger cabins. It has the same seats and galleys as are used in the Il.86 built 30 years earlier. The Il.96 was introduced on the Atlantic route to New York, as it had the range to fly Moscow-New York non stop, but what about in-flight entertainment on such a long flight? As no such equipment had been built into the seats, all they could do was to at the last minute was to fit a film projector at the rear of the aircraft with a screen at the front, with the normal loudspeakers on the aircraft being used to provide the sound track. This meant that when the film was on, you *all* had to see it and listen to it, whether you wanted to or not. As you might expect, a Russian film didn't necessarily go down well with its American passengers, a step backwards as far as modern travel was concerned, indeed very primitive! In fact I was extremely disappointed when I inspected an Il.96 at Heathrow. It is hard to believe the short-sightedness of the manufacturers in failing to read the market requirements for a modern aircraft.

But there are now other modern Russian aircraft coming on line. Aeroflot is getting them shortly, but other Russian carriers are already using the Tu.204 and Tu.214 for short- to medium-range flights and the Tu.334 will soon be introduced on the medium- to long-range sectors. The Il.96M has been going through a long programme of development using American Pratt & Witney engines and Collins electronics; with these components the payload has increased to that of a Boeing B747/400 series and the Americans are getting rather worried as commercially they cost much less to produce than the B747. In fact, they are trying to stop completely the engines being sent from USA to Russia, so it is possible that the whole procedure may be stopped in the near future.

Our joining passengers were well pleased with this step to modernise Aeroflot services and we didn't find any difficulty filling the seats with passengers. Even the evening services started to get improved loads; it could save a lot of money for passengers with a destination inside Russia and needing a connection in Moscow, as they left London at 22.30 and arrived at Moscow at 05.30 (Moscow time). This meant they were able to make connection with all morning flights from Moscow onwards into Russia, and therefore saved the cost of an hotel ($140) plus the taxi fares into and out of Moscow from the airport, which could be as much as another $200. With this sort of savings, many passengers now prefer to take the night flight to Moscow and continue on to their final destination without stopover in Moscow.

As these late flights are operated by American-type aircraft, there is now no need for a Russian engineer to meet the flight. The engineering 'turn round' maintenance is contracted out to either Lufthansa for the B737 or Delta Airlines for the B767. A Russian still has to meet the flight, but no other Aeroflot staff are necessary.

Reflecting on my thirteen and a half years with Aeroflot, I can truly say that I made a difference to the procedures, efficiency and customer service afforded the travelling Aeroflot passengers. My name became known in Moscow and St. Petersburg, although some of the Russians would have preferred to have got rid of me as I definitely made them see the need to be more efficient.

During 1999 I came to the conclusion I should retire again! I was well into my 75th year and we needed to move nearer to my eldest daughter Jeannie. My wife Madge could not drive, so in the event of anything happening to me, I needed to know that Madge would be close to Jeannie and her family.

Having made the decision, the announcement was finally made, and at Heathrow a farewell party was organised within Terminal 2. I received many wonderful gifts from the many airlines because of my AOC work. Even Heathrow Airport Limited (HAL) gave me the official picture of Heathrow airport, with a photo of me with my Russian hat on. It was signed: *Presented To Harry On His Retirement,* and I am extremely proud of this picture.

So here I am, sixteen years after returning from the overseas life in Oman, retiring once again. Was I now going to be able to do all those things I had put off over my working lifetime in aviation?

CHAPTER 22

PERMANENT RETIREMENT

There were no long journeys home on this retirement, so no real chance of having much thought about whether this, my third attempt at retirement, was to be the last one. Somehow I think it will be. Why should I find it necessary to continue wanting to work? It is time to think about resting.

This is the logical approach that I should be adopting at this time, but it is still not firm in my mind. I still feel that I can and should do more, but what? So for the last two years I have been doing all manner of things to pass the time, in an effort to get used to retirement and whatever that means.

Needless to say, I have been to the airport on a number of occasions, always looking into the Aeroflot office and usually having lunch with some of the BAA Planning Managers. I even attended the IATA London Airports Conference, just to see what there was new to consider.

Vitali Sereda is now back in London as General Manager once again. He was happy here previously and it suits his children if he is in London. His son is working here and his daughter is attending University for a couple of years. For me it was nice to see him once again and, much to my surprise, he asked me to help out in resolving some slot times at Heathrow. And he paid me well for doing so, which meant we were both satisfied.

Another thing I did was to join a wonderful golf & country Club here in Billericay; they have a superb gymnasium and I try to attend at least twice a week. Golf is good, but unfortunately I haven't made as much use of the facilities as I should have, but with this next summer (2004) now not too far away I promise myself that I will make a greater effort.

I've had a bit of a problem with my health; my angina was playing up and I needed to have a triple heart bypass in June 2002. But that was nearly two years ago now and I am now feeling quite fit once again and able to do most things, making me quite happy with life.

While recuperating from this health problem, I have tried to review what I have done in my lifetime. Were the decisions I made at all the crucial turning points correct? Should I have done things differently? What did I miss out on? After thinking in this way for a while, you realise that you don't get second chances; once a decision is made, it is all over and you are left with what you have and nothing else. So even if I could say: "It would have been better if I did it *this* way," there is really no point in 'crying over spilt milk.'

What I have said to myself on many occasions is: “I have had a marvellous life, enjoyed almost all of it and feel God has been really good to me. He gave me a wonderful wife and three kids who have given me so much happiness, so no complaints at all. This means that all I have to do from now onwards is enjoy the rest of the time that I am given, and “Thanks be to God.”

This manuscript has been scrutinised, edited and cleared for publication in May 2004. If you are reading it, then I have been successful! Thumbs up and all that. I hope you enjoyed the read.